WHEN COURAGE PREVAILED

Dear Carol

With appreciation & gratitude

Esther Gitman

Jan. 27, 2011

WHEN COURAGE PREVAILED

The Rescue and Survival of Jews in the Independent State of Croatia 1941–1945

ESTHER GITMAN

PARAGON HOUSE

First Edition 2011

Published in the United States by
Paragon House
1925 Oakcrest Ave, Suite 7
St. Paul, MN 55113
www.paragonhouse.com

Library of Congress Cataloging-in-Publication Data

Gitman, Esther.
When courage prevailed : the rescue and survival of Jews in the independent state of Croatia, 1941–1945 / by Esther Gitman.
   p. cm.
Includes bibliographical references and index.
Summary: "A historical study of the treatment of Jews in Yugoslavia after Nazi ideology was adopted, with an emphasis on the ways Jews survived and were rescued by those who put their own lives in peril"--Provided by publisher.
   ISBN 978-1-55778-894-8 (pbk. : alk. paper) 1. Holocaust, Jewish (1939-1945)--Yugoslavia. 2.
Jews--Yugoslavia--History--20th century. 3. Jews--Persecutions--Yugoslavia.
4. World War, 1939-1945--Jews--Rescue--Yugoslavia. 5.
Yugoslavia--History--Axis occupation, 1941–1945. 6. Yugoslavia--Ethnic relations. I. Title.
   DS135.Y8G58 2011
   940.53'183509497--dc22
                  2010035984

The paper used in this publication meets the minimum requirements of American National Standard for Information Sciences—Permanence of Paper for Printed Library Materials, ANSI standard Z39.48-1992.

Manufactured in the United States of America
10 9 8 7 6 5 4 3 2 1

For current information about all releases from Paragon House, visit the website at http://www.ParagonHouse.com

To my beloved grandchildren,
Gabrielle, Gilad, Elisheva, Odelia, Yarden, and Orlee,
with a hope that they will live in a kinder and gentler world.

Contents

Acknowledgements

Many individuals and organizations have generously supported this work. I cannot thank all, but I owe special gratitude to Professors Dalia Ofer, Carol Rittner, and John Roth. I would also like to acknowledge my mentors Professors Jane Gerber and Elisheva Carlebach from the Graduate Center of the City University of New York.

I owe a special gratitude to the United States Holocaust Memorial Museum and the Center for Advanced Holocaust Studies for awarding me the Barbara and Richard Rosenberg Fellowship in the 2006–2007 academic years for my postdoctoral research. Similarly, I am grateful to the Fulbright Committee for granting me a fellowship to Zagreb for 2002–2003. As a Fulbright student I received sustained assistance from the Croatian Ministry of Science and Technology.

While in Zagreb, I was greatly assisted by Dr. Ivo Goldstein, a professor of history at the University of Zagreb, who agreed to be my mentor. Dr. Jure Krišto, a member of the Croatian Institute for History, also provided invaluable assistance in areas pertaining to the Catholic Church. The Director of the Croatian State Archive, Dr. Josip Kolanović, together with the head of the research department, Ljubica Pleše, responded very generously to my requests for documents. My unending appreciation goes to my friend and librarian Ljerka Raić, who spared no effort in accompanying me on my interviews with survivors and rescuers. Also, I would like to thank Dr. Amy Hackett for editing the manuscript.

My unending appreciation is extended to the survivors and rescuers whom I had the privilege to interview and whose stories are described in this book. They shared with me their painful and joyous memories of what they faced with immense courage and an unyielding determination.

Finally, I want to thank my husband, Dr. Israel Gitman, who throughout our lives together has encouraged me to undertake tasks that I dreamed about but thought were beyond my reach; whenever in doubt, he always was there to lend a helping hand and a reassurance that I was on the right track.

Abbreviations

AIFM	Archives of the Italian Foreign Ministry
AFŽ	*Antifašistièki front žena* (Antifascist Women Front)
AJC	American Jewish Committee
BiH	*Bosna i Hercegovina* (Bosnia-Herzegovina)
DELASEM	*Delegazione Assistenza Emigranti e Profughi Ebrei* (Assistance to Jews)
GESTAPO	*Geheime Staatspolizei–Tajna državna policlja* (Gestapo, Gestapo Police)
GUZ	Glavni urudžbeni zapisnik (Main Registration File)
HDA	*Hrvatski državni arhiv, Zagreb* (Croatian State Archive)
HICEM	Hebrew Immigrant Colonization Emigration
HIAS	Hebrew Sheltering and Immigrant
IHP	*Institut za hrvatsku povljest* (Institute for Croatian History)
IRC	International Red Cross
JA	*Jugoslavenska armija* (Yugoslav Army)
JDC/ JOINT	American Jewish Joint Distribution Committee
JIM	*Jevrejski istorijskl muzej, Beograd* (Jewish Historical Museum, Belgrade.)
MUP	*Ministarstvo o unutarnjih (unutrasnjih) poslova* (Ministry of Internal Affairs)
NAZ	*Nadbiskupski arhiv Zagreb* (Archive of the Archbishopric of Zagreb)
NDH	*Nezavisna Država Hrvatska* (The Independent Sttate of Croatia)
NOB	*Narodno-oslobodilačka borba* (People's Liberation War)
ORT	Organization for Rehabilitation and Training

OSS   Office of Strategic Services

OZNA   *Odjeljenje za zaštitu naroda* (Division for People's Protection)

RSHA   *Reichssicherheitshauptamt* (Reich's Main Security Office)

RUR   *Ravnateljstvo ustaskog redarstva* (Headquarter of Ustaše Police)

SD   *Sicherheitsdienst—Slušba sigurnosti* (German police)

UNRRA   United National Relief and Rehabilitation Administration

UNS   *Ustaška nadzorna služba* (Usthashe Supervisory Police)

Waffen SS   *Schutz-Staffel—Zaštitne snage* (A multi-ethnic and multi-national military force)

WRB   War Refugee Board

ZAVNOH   *Zemaljsko antifasisticko vijeće narodnog oslobođenja Hrvatske* (Anti-Fascist Bord Peoples' Liberation of Croatia)

ZKRZ   *Zemaljska komislja za utvrdivanje zločina okupatora* (National Commission)

ZBJEG   The masses of refugees that followed the Partisans, from 1943 to 1945

ŽOZ   *Židovska opčina Zagreb* (Jewish Community Zagreb)

Guide to Croatian and Bosnian Pronunciations

The Croatian and Bosnian consonants for which the pronunciation differs from English usage are shown below.

c	*ts,* as in "tsar"
ć	*ch,* (soft) as the "t" in "future"
č	*ch,* (hard) as the "tch" in "teacher"
dj	*j,* (soft) as the "g" in "organization"
dž,	*j,* (hard) as the "j" in "jug"
j	*y,* as in "yugoslavia"
lj	*li,* as in "medallion"
nj	*ny,* as in "canyon"
š	*sh,* as in "shoulder"
ž	*zh* as in "Zhivago"

Croatian and Serbian are phonetic languages, pronounced as they are written. Standard Croatian is written in the Latin alphabet with special diacritical marks. For the Croatian words, proper spelling was used, even for words such as Ustashe (Ustaše) plural and Ustasha (Ustaša) for singular. However, for the plural of the word Chetnik (Četnik) the correct word is (Četnici). In the case of Četnik (Četniks), I chose to add the English convention of adding a final "s".

Introduction

We must dare to think "unthinkable" thoughts. We must learn to explore all the options and possibilities that confront us in a complex and rapidly changing world. We must learn to welcome and not to fear the voices of dissent. We must dare to think about "unthinkable things" because when things become unthinkable, thinking stops and action becomes mindless. (Senator William Fulbright, March 27, 1964)

When Courage Prevailed tells the story of the rescue of Jews in the Independent State of Croatia during World War II. Compared to the primary battlefields of that conflict, historians have paid relatively little attention to the Nazi occupation of Yugoslavia, not least because of the linguistic challenges and the peninsula's notorious ethnic and political fragmentation. Not surprisingly then, the Holocaust in those territories, first called The Kingdom of the Serbs, Croats, and Slovenes after World War I, has also received relatively little attention. The historiography of the Holocaust itself began as primarily a study of the Nazis, including their ideology and the atrocities carried out in their name. Only later did that such studies expand to take in the perspectives of the victims.

In choosing to focus on the rescue of Jews and those who chose to help them survive, this book examines a subject that—despite the popularity of Steven Spielberg's *Schindler's List*—remains little examined. This book argues that we cannot really comprehend the Holocaust without considering the fact that some Jews did escape the Final Solution, even after the outbreak of war made any escape incomparably more difficult. Moreover, by examining the dynamics of rescue in a complex geographic area that is less trodden by historians, we can perhaps more clearly identify some of the comparative factors that either encouraged rescue or made it virtually impossible.

The Independent State of Croatia—officially the *Nezavisna Država Hrvatska* (NDH)—comprised the territories of Croatia[1] and Bosnia-Herzegovina (BiH).[2] It was created out of the dismembered Kingdom of Yugoslavia on April 10, 1941, by the Axis partners, Nazi Germany and Fascist Italy, joined by minor partners Hungary and Bulgaria. The Axis installed the Ustaše, Croatian insurgents, headed by Ante Pavelić, to rule this new entity. Pavelić had been living in exile, most recently in Italy, for over a decade. During his exile, he engaged in various conspiratorial activities, including the assassinations in 1935 of King Alexander Karadjordjević of Yugoslavia and French Foreign Minister Barthou in Marseille.[3]

From its inception, the collaborationist NDH regime aimed to create a pure Croatian state in the ethnic quagmire that was the Balkan Peninsula. To fulfill this ambitious objective, the Ustaše planned to expel one third of the Serbs from Croatian territory, convert the second third to Catholicism, and exterminate the rest. They also intended to annihilate the Jews and the Roma, as well as Croatian dissidents, who by their conduct allegedly had damaged the honor and the vital interests of the Croatian people. Accordingly, the NDH regime enacted racial legislation patterned on the Nazi model and instituted a reign of terror enforced by the Ustaše police, the SS, the Gestapo, and the auxiliary force of the *Volksdeutsche,* (Croatian citizens of German ancestry). Ordinary citizens who were found assisting Jews and other undesirable non-Croatian elements stood accused of treason (*veleizdaja*).

This book's thesis is that, despite the government's warning of severe punishment, thousands of NDH citizens risked their lives and those of their family members by choosing to assist in the rescue of Jews. Archival material, supported by my interviews of survivors and rescuers, tells the stories of how these individual rescuers came to their aid, as did various national and international humanitarian organizations, individual clergy and nuns, officials in the Ustaše government, Italian troops and citizens, and the Partisans fighting the Nazi occupation. The reasons for, and means of, assistance differed: some offered shelter, obtained forged exit visas, or provided food, while others accepted belongings for safekeeping, or transported Jews across enemy lines disguised in Muslim garb or even Ustaše uniforms. And still others sheltered small children whose parents had joined the Partisans or had been taken to concentration camps.

It is essential to clarify that the Croatian people neither elected nor selected Pavelić and his Ustaše; this regime was chosen and imposed on them by the Axis powers.[4] Thus it is not surprising that a large number of Croats were not blinded by the Ustaše's authority. They despised foreign occupation, as well as the Nazis' racial ideology and the Italians' irredentist claims on Croatian territory. As a result, NDH's young and old from various ethnic and religious groups extended assistance to their persecuted fellow citizens. Some even dared to defy the occupation forces directly by joining the Partisans, in numbers that eventually grew to at least 150,000.[5]

WHAT CONSTITUTES "RESCUE"

Nazi Germany, Fascist Italy, and the Ustaše, including both its Croat and Muslim adherents, strove to create the perception that the rescue of a Jew was an act of subversion that placed the rescuer in equivalent legal peril to the Jew. Accepting the general framework of Nazi ideology regarding the Jewish Question and the Final Solution, the Ustaše implemented racial laws and disseminated antisemitic propaganda. However, Pavelić made one significant change to the Nazi definition of "Jew." Rather than relying on the criteria of three Jewish grandparents, he empowered himself as head of state to recognize new categories specific to Croatia: "Honorary Aryan" and "Aryan Rights." The Nazis, naturally, objected to the change, primarily because it introduced arbitrary and subjective criteria that invited corrupt practices.[6] Nonetheless, this idiosyncratic definition facilitated the rescue and survival of some of Croatia's Jews. At this point, however, it is imperative to recognize that a change occurred between the Nazi racial ideology and that of the Ustaše. Nazi ideology is characterized by the fact that it placed the Jews outside the limit of humanity. "It did not view the Jews as a low variant of the human race, but rather as mere organic matter."[7] Thus, the Holocaust in NDH, while it should be viewed as an abomination, has a frame of reference that is different from the one which characterized the National Socialist antisemitism, and thus we can speak of rescue of Jews.

Because the term "rescue" has many and various usages, it is necessary to provide a definition relevant to the situation of NDH Jews during World War II. This is no easy task, in part because the issue of the rescue of Jews by non-Jews is still emotionally charged; indeed for decades survivors chose not to discuss it. This has recently begun to change, as rescuers began telling their stories. Some of the survivors I interviewed admitted that, in the face of atrocities that claimed 75 percent of the Jewish population, their own rescue felt like a betrayal of those who had perished. Acknowledging the help of good people, non-Jews from all ethnic groups, was also difficult. These survivors could sometimes be encouraged to end their self-imposed silence by posing indirect questions, such as: Must a rescue effort result in the ultimate survival of an individual? This question was relevant because often an individual was rescued, only to succumb to typhus or some other calamity before any possibility of liberation. Other such questions included: Must rescue refer only to a deliberate act undertaken by non-Jews, rather than to any act that resulted in a rescue? Should monetary exchange be an issue for defining rescue? Must the rescuer encounter risk? The responses to these questions by survivors and rescuers and the material on the subject collated by Yad Vashem in Jerusalem helped to clarify the definition of rescue that was utilized in this book:

> Rescue is a deliberate act taken by non-Jews in an effort to save Jews, which involves a risk. [8]

Risk implies a possibility of loss, be it of money, status, or, potentially, life. As explained, assisting Jews in Croatia under the Ustaše regime was considered treason, punishable by death. Even in cases where a government official requested a Jew's release from a concentration camp and obtained approval by the NDH minister of the interior, the act entailed a potential risk if the official fell out of favor. Thus, even a high-ranking Ustaše could incur risk by aiding Jews, as was the case with Minister of Health Dr. Ivo Petrić. [9] It follows that rescue as defined here requires more than random or unintentional activities that result in the saving of a life. Accordingly, this book uses terms such as "reprieve" or "assistance" for cases where Jews were saved but without risk to the other person involved, whom I call a "sympathizer" or "helper," not a "rescuer."

This book also deems an act to have been a rescue even when monetary reward was received. The reason is that, in most cases, the amount of money received by the rescuer was not substantial enough to outweigh the personal risk. Furthermore, local Jewish groups that entrusted individuals with rescue missions often insisted upon payment in order to make the rescue a binding and a repeated transaction. In addition, many Jews wished to provide payment in return for services rendered and risks taken on their behalf.[10]

Only rarely was one person or entity responsible for a survivor's rescue, and in some instances there were as many as twenty different rescuers. In such cases, who then was the "rescuer"—the first person, the last one, or all of them? For example, in 1941 the Ustaše captured Albert Maestro from Sarajevo and sent him to the Jasenovac concentration camp, from which, with the help of several individuals, he managed to escape. In 1945, he was invited to testify before the National Commission for the Ascertainment of Crimes Committed against the Jews by the Occupiers and their Collaborators (hereafter National Commission). Maestro described in great detail the atrocities committed in Jasenovac, as well as naming the perpetrators and exposing their crimes. Still, despite the hardships he experienced in the camp, Maestro did not forget to thank the Croatian peasants of the Jasenovac region:

> [T]he civilian population of the villages Jasenovac and Krapje at every opportunity helped us with food and, by so doing, they ran the risk of being deported to the death camps…. The peasants at every opportunity inconspicuously dropped pieces of bread and dried meat and they consoled us with nice thoughts and kind words. In the name of the few of us that managed to survive Jasenovac and in the name of many of those that are no longer with us, I thank them because they prolonged our lives until the opportunity for escape presented itself and, with their help, we managed to survive.[11]

Initially, it seemed to me that Maestro might have exaggerated the help he received from the peasants, although it was intriguing to think that a few morsels of bread and encouraging words could have saved his life and the lives of other Jews. But after reviewing many such cases, I came to understand that there were nearly always many rescuers along the way, each of whom did his or her share at a specific moment in time. The Croatian peasants, along with many others, formed a link in a long chain of rescuers that Maestro encountered over four arduous years. Similarly, Joseph Indig-Ithai's account of his five-year experience, with the children known as the Children of Villa Emma, makes clear that the rescue of these children would have been impossible without ongoing help from Croatian, Slovenian, and Italian non-Jews:

> We had the good fortune, however, to come across other Righteous Gentiles as we were buffeted by our destiny. There were many more that sympathized with us and gave us help on our long journey. It was important for our children to see that not only Nazis existed in this world, but also good people who had not lost the faith and courage to be humane. [12]

In those days, every show of humanity and scrap of food went a long way and may have made the difference between life and death.[13]

But, in the face of the enormous tragedy that befell the Jews of the NDH, many who returned home first mourned their losses; understandably, telling the story of their rescue was not a high priority. For example, Ljerka Auferber, originally from Osijek, described her effort to flee her Ustaše pursuers. When they were just about to grab her, a manager from her father's former business picked her up in his car and drove without stopping for six hours until they reached Ilidza, a small village near Sarajevo, where he had many relatives.[14] The manager's family members and neighbors cared for Ljerka until, after long deliberations, they placed her in the home of a young couple of her own age. For one year, this couple fed and catered to all her needs, even to the extent of surrendering their bedroom. Yet, after the war, Ljerka was so absorbed in settling her own life that she never thanked the couple for saving her, nor did she register their names as "Righteous Gentiles" with Yad Vashem. Now that they are dead, she regrets her silence and feels compelled to tell her story.

Incidents of "forgetfulness" were both a way of coping with reality and a way of pretending that nothing had happened. Ljerka strongly believed that survivors had a need to catch up on their lives; the war had stolen four years from them, and they were not inclined to dwell on the past. Also, there was a great urge among survivors to expose the atrocities of World War II—so the whole world would know and remember what happened. Thus, speaking of rescue seemed counterproductive to the two main objectives they set for themselves. Furthermore, historians in Croatia and in other parts of Yugoslavia were busy writing thousands of books, articles, and monographs, focusing on the machinery of murder. They paid scant attention to other subjects, most specifically to rescue, other than the rescue by the Italians and the Partisans, although it was in fact an integral part of the Holocaust.

One also rarely encounters stories that describe the danger, hardship, and courage required of those who had chosen to rescue Jews or others who were pursued by the occupiers and their collaborators. It was only when I interviewed Milislav Ercegović of Dubrovnik that I became aware of the pain and suffering experienced not only by the rescuer but also by the rescuer's family. [15] In 2003, when Ercegović celebrated his eighty-fifth birthday, a long time had passed since his father, Miho, and brother, Velimir, engaged in the rescue of Jewish refugees. Yet he vividly recalled every detail of how they both were preoccupied day and night with refugees fleeing from the NDH to Dubrovnik on the Dalmatian coast. Whenever Emanuel Tolentino, the secretary of the Jewish Community of Dubrovnik, needed to find safe accommodations for refugees he turned to his Catholic friend Miho Ercegović for advice and assistance. With tears covering his old face, Ercegović told me about the underground activities that went on in his father's store:

> You know, my father kept seven Jewish refugees hidden in his bookstore and he found shelter and accommodation for scores of others. For his seditious activities, he was imprisoned several times and was

sentenced to serve time in a prison in Sarajevo. Rescue of Jews was an all-consuming passion of his, but he failed to take note of the fear and anxiety experienced by his own five children and his wife. He failed to consider what would have happened to us if he was put to death.[16]

A similar episode was related by Jaška Kalogera, who saved several Jewish families and eventually was caught and sentenced to the Jasenovac concentration camp, where he was incarcerated for one year.[17]

Slavko Goldstein, the coauthor of the book *Holocaust in Zagreb*, told me the story of his rescue. Slavko was only thirteen when the Ustaše sent both his parents to a detention center in Zagreb. His younger brother was sent to his grandparents in Tuzla, Bosnia. Thus Slavko was alone in Osijek until the family's Catholic maid gave him shelter in her village, Banski Kovačevać. All 300 villagers knew about his whereabouts, but despite frequent searches, they kept quiet and did not report him to the Ustaše. Although the villagers had not themselves given the boy shelter, they were nevertheless *benevolent bystanders;* without playing an active role they took sides.[18] A similar story was told by Teodora Basch, who was born in Zagreb on January 31, 1938. When the Nazis invaded Yugoslavia, Teodora was visiting her maternal grandparents in Ludberg, a town that became part of NDH. In the meantime, in June 1941, her parents and infant brother Zdravko were arrested. Luckily, their housekeeper managed to rescue her baby brother, Zdravko, from prison and she brought him to Ludberg. Shortly thereafter, Theodora's grandfather, Rabbi Josef Leopold, and his wife were arrested and deported. From that time on Teodora's aunt, her mother's sister Giza, and her Catholic husband, Ljudevit Vrančić, took over the care for the children. Toward the end of the war, her aunt Giza was arrested and deported to Auschwitz. Her Catholic uncle took care of Teodora and her brother. The town residents knew that the two children were the rabbi's grandchildren, yet they chose to be silent.[19] Slavko, Teodora, and Zdravko were three among many other children to be rescued by a whole village or town.

Hundreds of NDH citizens experienced hardship and suffering when they chose to save Jews. By so doing they mounted an attack on the totalitarian regimes of the occupiers and the Ustaše collaborators.

Some of these rescuers Yad Vashem recognized with the "Righteous among the Nations" award for their courage and rescue activities, but many hundreds still await recognition.

HISTORIOGRAPHY OF RESCUE IN THE NDH

The vast expanse of Holocaust literature contains little on Croatia. Though considerable documentation exists, historians largely ignored the subject of rescue of Jews by Croatian officials, Catholic clergy, humanitarian organizations, and by ordinary citizens from all ethnic and religious groups. Between 1941 and 1945, out of the 39,500 pre-war Jewish population of Croatia and Bosnia-Herzegovina, the Ustaše murdered 15,000 Jews in home-grown concentration camps and assisted in sending over 8,000 others to Nazi camps in Germany and Eastern Europe; more died fighting the Ustaše or the Četniks, or succumbed to various diseases. These figures have led scholars to assume that the Croats were universally murderous. From this perspective, any rescues that might have occurred must have been marginal phenomena. Furthermore, until the mid-1990s the archives in the countries of the former Yugoslavia remained closed and only selected historians who followed the Titoist line enjoyed access. Thus most historians (Yugoslavian and foreign) have focused on the multifaceted civil war that, along with the world war, devastated Yugoslavia during those years, on the Jewish Holocaust, and on elucidating atrocities. Rescue as a subject of research hardly figured in the agenda.

Previous scholarship on rescue remains so scant that it can be summarized in a few lines. In 1955, Leon Poliakov and Jacques Sabille wrote *Jews under the Italian Occupation*, the first book on the subject; the authors focused on the Italian Army and Foreign Ministry representatives in Croatia. This was followed nearly two decades later by Daniel Carpi's article, "The Rescue of Jews in the Italian Zone of Occupied Croatia." In 1980, the Yugoslav historian Jaša Romano dedicated his book, *The Jews of Yugoslavia, 1941–1945: Victims of Genocide and Freedom Fighters*, to the rescue of Jews by the Partisans. Jonathan Steinberg's 1990 work,

All or Nothing: The Axis and the Holocaust, touches on the region, but does not address rescue systematically and ends in 1943. In 2005, H. James Burgwyn's book, *Empire on the Adriatic: Mussolini's Conquest of Yugoslavia, 1941–1943,* largely overlooked the rescue of Jews in Croatia.

Historians who have written about rescues either by Italians or by Partisans seem to have assumed that Jews could easily move about in the Ustaše- and German-controlled territories, and that their rescue began once they reached either the Italian zone of occupation or Partisan-controlled territories. In fact, it was virtually impossible for Jews to move about, and those who did so depended on non-Jews for visas, travel permits, hiding places, and much more. Survival was complicated by Yugoslavia's dismemberment by Germany and its satellites and puppets. Every would-be survivor had to be both brave and resourceful, and each would owe a debt of gratitude to non-Jews. And when the Italian soldiers abandoned their occupation zone after Italy's capitulation in September 1943, the Jews remained defenseless until the Partisans took over. Often, friends and neighbors appealed to the Ministry of the Interior for the release of individual Jews. Employers and employees beseeched the Ministry of Finance to obtain the release of Jewish workers, employers, and managers from concentration camps. Many of these efforts entailed great risk. My documentation reveals the practical and the ethical motives animating rescue.

To paint a more complete picture, I have searched contemporary newspapers, legal publications, archival documents, intelligence records, and survivor testimonies gathered by Yugoslavia's postwar National Commission, memoirs, and rare secondary literature in Serbo-Croatian. Due to the declassification of U.S. intelligence and State Department records under the Nazi War Crimes Disclosure Act of 1998, many one-sided perspectives are slowly being replaced by more nuanced versions. My personal interviews are particularly valuable, allowing me to weave individual stories into a structural analysis that identifies seven categories of rescue to explain how a quarter of Croatia's Jews—9,500 people—survived the Holocaust. I conducted most of the archival research for this book in 2002 and 2003, primarily in Zagreb, which houses a wealth of documents. Some missing pieces of information were added during my visits to other cities in Croatia, including Osijek, Vukovar, and Dubrovnik. In addition, I used archives in Sarajevo, the capital of Bosnia-Herzegovina, at the Yad Vashem Holocaust Museum in Jerusalem and the United States Memorial Holocaust Museum (USHMM) in Washington D.C. My interviews with rescuers and survivors, conducted primarily in Croatia, Bosnia, and Israel, provide valuable insights, some otherwise unavailable, about the individual experiences of those who lived through this period.

This book is organized in six chapters that discuss specific and distinct categories of rescuers: Jews in the Interwar Period; Rescue by Ordinary Citizens; Rescue by NDH Officials; Rescue by the Archbishop of Zagreb; Rescue by Humanitarian Organizations; Rescue by Italian Soldiers, Diplomats, and Ordinary Citizens; and Rescue by the Partisans.

CHAPTER 1: JEWS IN THE INTERWAR PERIOD

This chapter summarizes the unification of the South Slavs into the Kingdom of Serbs, Croats, and Slovenes on December 1, 1918, renamed the Kingdom of Yugoslavia in 1929. For the first time, with the insistence of the kingdom, 115 separate Jewish Communities united and in 1929 the Federation of Jewish Religious Communities was established. As a whole, during these years Yugoslavia's Jews prospered. Their "golden age" ended abruptly with the establishment of the Ustaše-ruled NDH and its antisemitic agenda. This chapter discusses the Axis-facilitated assumption of power by Pavelić and his insurgents as well as the roots of collaboration and atrocities during World War II in Yugoslavia's religious and national composition and the incomplete process of unification.

CHAPTER 2: RESCUE BY ORDINARY CITIZENS

Ordinary citizens, despite threats of punishment, offered shelter, forged exit visas, supplied food, tipped off Jews about round-ups, and transported them across enemy lines wearing Muslim garb and even Ustaše uniforms. Petition letters (which seem to be unique to Croatia) demonstrate widespread involvement in rescue efforts: After Alexander Šandor Loyi was sent to the Jasenovac concentration camp, seventy-six residents of Donja Lomnica begged the minister of the interior to free him.

CHAPTER 3: RESCUE BY NDH OFFICIALS

The Ustaše regime itself shielded selected categories of Jews, such as "Honorary Aryans," a special honor it bestowed upon Jews who had made extensive contribution to Croatia. The government also extended "Aryan rights" to a few thousand businessmen and professionals who did not enjoy de jure recognition as "Aryans." Many Jewish physicians and their immediate families—650 people in all—were saved by a plan approved by Ante Pavelić and his ministers to combat endemic syphilis among the Muslim population in Bosnia.

CHAPTER 4: RESCUE BY THE ARCHBISHOP OF ZAGREB

Dr. Alojzije Stepinac, Archbishop of Zagreb, rescued fifty-eight Jews being expelled from a home for the elderly by transferring them to archbishopric property; he also rendered aid to the Jewish Community of Zagreb, to Jews in mixed marriages, to Jewish orphans, and to scores of other individual Jews. Despite German threats, in a July 7, 1943, sermon he declared: "If God gave this right [to be considered an equal human being] to all mankind there is no government on earth that can take it away."

CHAPTER 5: RESCUE BY ITALIAN SOLDIERS, DIPLOMATS, AND ORDINARY CITIZENS

Italian personnel stationed in Slovenia and Croatia were generally indifferent to the Ustaše's genocidal plans. They often issued travel papers to Jews, even forged passports, and after 1942 refused to extradite them to the Ustaše. While humanitarian rescue was not uncommon,

Italian officers often made coldly calculated decisions to save the honor of the Italian Army by resisting German demands to hand over Jews. Altogether some 7,500 Yugoslavian Jews, mostly from Croatia and Bosnia-Herzegovina, were thus saved between 1941 and Italy's departure in 1943.

CHAPTER 6: RESCUE BY THE PARTISANS

The Partisans took over in the territories deserted by Italian troops after their country's capitulation in September 1943. They assumed responsibility for 5,000 Jews, many of whom joined their cause as combat troops or auxiliary. They also tried to help other Jews escape to Italy. This chapter also describes the rescue efforts of Allied military. After May 1944, the care for Jewish survivors was entrusted to the Displaced Persons Organization (under the Intergovernmental Committee on Refugees), the JOINT, the Quakers, and the Friends' Ambulance Unit; these survivors were able to begin returning to their homes in May 1945.

The stories of rescue in this book do not ignore the roles that such factors as liquid assets and sheer luck played in Holocaust survival. Nonetheless, I hope that readers will take from them an appreciation that people of conscience can effectively resist racist and fascist regimes if they harness their energies to do what is just and humane.

Map of Yugoslavia and Neighbors

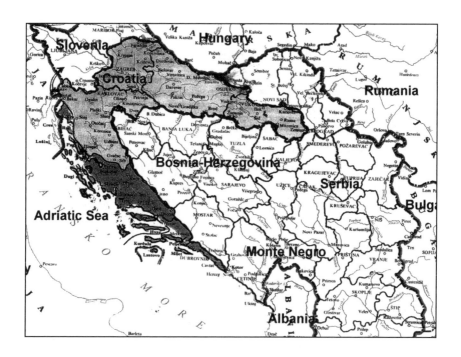

1

The Unification of the Serbs, Croats, and Slovenes, 1918–1941

Yugoslavia's situation was particularly problematic in that some of its constituent territories, in particular Croatia, had a long history under the Austro-Hungarian umbrella, while other states had been part of the Ottoman Empire. Bosnia-Herzegovina was first Ottoman, then Austro-Hungarian, and Serbia gained independence from the Ottomans in 1878. The territories that came together as Yugoslavia would be marked by their disparate cultural and political legacies for decades to come. The tensions between these legacies played out with particular consequence in the uneasy relationship between Yugoslavia's two largest ethnic groups: Serbs and Croats. To further complicate matters, Serbs, Croats, Bosnians, and assorted other ethnic groups—each itself a potential nationality—lived to a greater or lesser extent in proximity to or even amongst one another. Much of this is, of course, familiar from recent history.

In October 1918, in expectation of the demise of the Austro-Hungarian Empire, ethnic Croats, Slovenes, and Serbs living in Croatian territory met in Zagreb to form a provisional National Council. Their primary concern, given the looming power vacuum, was encroachment by their stronger neighbors, in particular Italy, Bulgaria, and Hungary. Under these circumstances, the delegates revived the concept of Yugoslavism as a foundation for national unification.[1] While the idea of unification was not new, the concept was not clearly defined. The Great

Powers as well as the Serbian delegates maintained that a new Yugoslavia required a strong military leader and a centralized government. Most Croats looked to a federal republic on the U.S. model, with many rights retained by the states. On October 19, 1918, the Croatian Diet—the territorial parliament from the Austro-Hungarian imperial structure—declared that it would consider the decisions of the National Council as binding in matters of unification. On October 28, the Croatian Diet severed its ties with the Austro-Hungarian Empire. The following day, Croatia-Slavonia, as well as Rijeka (Fiume) and Dalmatia, on the Adriatic coast, proclaimed their independence.[2]

Once freed from the bonds of the Austro-Hungarian Empire, the National Council, on October 31, 1918, informed the Allied powers of its decision to create a permanent and officially recognized state of Croats, Serbs, and Slovenes. The Allies, weary after a succession of Balkan wars, agreed to the Council's proposal, which held out a promise of numerical and territorial strength. However, they wanted the new state to be organized under the banner of the Serbian monarch Aleksander Karadjordjević, who not only was considered to be a strong military and political leader but had been part of the victorious alliance.[3] Nonetheless, the Great Powers, in this period before the peace conference, left it to the South Slavs themselves to determine how to proceed with unifying the Croatian territories represented by the National Council with the Kingdom of Serbia and Montenegro.[4] Within a month, on December 1, 1918, the Kingdom of the Serbs, Croats, and Slovenes was formed in Belgrade. By the time the victorious powers met in Versailles in January 1919, the new kingdom already had a provisional government and parliament.

By insisting on unification under the leadership of the Serbian monarch, the Allied powers ignored potential conflicts due to cultural and religious differences among its ethnic groups. Although the notion of Yugoslavia as a nation-state literally invoked the existence of a South Slav people, each of the leading candidates for dominance within the proposed new state aimed to retain its religious liberties, national integrity, and sovereignty. For example, the Serbs practiced Serbian Orthodoxy, whereas the Croats and Slovenes were Roman Catholics. The Serbs identified themselves as a Balkan people, while the Croats and Slovenes occupied the borderland between the Balkan Peninsula and Central Europe. Both the Vatican and the Hapsburg emperors valued the Croats for holding the line against Ottoman efforts to expand their empire into Central Europe.[5]

When World War I began, Croatia had achieved a level of self-rule, but was firmly part of the Austro-Hungarian Empire, and its culture was oriented toward Vienna and Budapest. After centuries of control by and revolts against both the Ottoman and Hapsburg empires, Serbia was recognized as an independent kingdom, although Austrian troops continued to occupy Bosnia and other areas to which Serbia laid claim. Thus, the cultural and political experiences of the Croats and the Serbs were vastly different. Their languages, although largely alike, presented dialectical variations. Moreover, they used two different alphabets: Cyrillic for the Serbs; Latin for the Croats and Slovenes. The linguistic differences were further exacerbated by the existence of a separate Slovenian language and by a "Serbo-Croatian" language, neither Serbian nor Croat, which incorporated many Turkish words and was used in Bosnia-Herzegovina.[6] In addition, the Balkan Peninsula contained a sizable number of ethnic and religious minorities including Germans, Hungarians, Albanians, Slovaks, Romanians and Jews.

When World War I ended, four multinational empires lay in ruins. Despite its efforts to draw coherent national borders for the successor states, the Versailles Peace Conference faced a harsh reality: Without massive and forced population transfers, the possibilities for creating ethnically homogeneous nation-states in Central, Eastern and Southeastern Europe were few. In an effort to compensate for this problem, the concluding treaties compelled the Kingdom of the Serbs, Croats, and Slovenes, like other new states, to sign a "minority treaty," which guaranteed all its inhabitants, including all ethnic and religious groups, equal rights and full protection under the law.[7] Pursuant to this pledge, in 1919 Yugoslavia's Jews were, for the first time, granted legal emancipation and full civil equality, "without distinction as to birth, nationality, language, race or religion." The constitutions of 1921 and 1931 reiterated these guarantees. The official attitude of the monarchy toward the Jews throughout its twenty-three years could be regarded as sympathetic.

Yet, the comingling of peoples in a political structure by itself neither achieves "unification" nor creates a "nation," and the South Slavs demonstrably lacked the *cultural* attributes and the sense of a common history that together could have provided a strong foundation for political unity. Not surprisingly, ethnic distrust, religious rivalry, language barriers, and cultural conflicts would plague the political entity that began as the Kingdom of the Serbs, Croats, and Slovenes, and after 1929 was known as the Kingdom of Yugoslavia.[8]

The Croats aimed from the outset to secure their culture, religious heritage, and territorial rights as a means of protecting their national integrity from "obliteration," not just by Serbia but also by Italy, which had ambitions to annex the Croatian coastline, in particular.[9] The leading proponent of a "cautious approach" toward unification was Stjepan Radić, the leader of the popular Croatian People's Peasant Party (CPP), which gained strength from the Croats' political awaking. Before any decision on unification was made, he insisted that the National Council meeting in Zagreb carefully debate the many unresolved issues he saw.[10] Because the nationalism espoused by Radić and his party focused on Croatia, they opposed centralization under a strong leader like Serbia's King Aleksander. Unless limits to a central government were established prior to unification, they feared, Croatia's national character would be endangered.

Despite the ethnic and religious heterogeneity of the Balkan Peninsula and the disputes between the Serbs and the Croats, there seemed to be surprisingly widespread concurrence both on the idea of South Slav unification and on the advantages of having some kind of centralized government. Yet it soon became apparent that there was no common agreement on what unification might mean. The communists, for example, viewed unification and centralization as means to combat differences based on religious affiliations, culture, and history.[11]

Similarly, intellectuals in general, as well as members of the pro-Yugoslav "revolutionary youth," maintained that Serbs, Croats, and Slovenes were by nature three tribes (*plemena*) that together constituted one entity. Nonetheless, the Croatian Diet had issued clear guidelines that its delegates to the National Council obtain the Serbian monarchy's guarantees of the continued sovereignty of each constituent state and of the equality of the three main partners within any new unified state.[12] The head of the Croatian National Council, Svetozar Pribićević, a Croat of Serb ancestry, argued on the other hand that there was no time for debates on the format for unification in the face of two urgent threats: irredentist Italian encroachment on Croatian and Slovenian territories and the spread of the Bolshevik Revolution into the region.[13] Pribićević's pro-Serbian position prevailed against the objections of his countryman Stjepan Radić, the leader of the Croatian People's Peasant Party (CPP). The decision to unite with the Serbian Kingdom demonstrated both the Croatian Council's weakness and the strength and confidence of the monarchy. But frictions and tensions between the Serbian monarchy and the CPP remained.[14]

Among the reasons for the difficulties in reaching reconciliation was the post World War I Yugoslavia's daunting economic problems. The agricultural sector, which employed 75 percent of the population, underwent radical pressure to modernize as Yugoslavia opened its borders to European markets. The illiterate and uneducated peasants did not easily adapt to the use of modern technologies or new agricultural practices, and agriculture continued to stagnate, making the country more dependent on imports. Despite significant strides in its industrial sectors, Yugoslavia remained underdeveloped due to insufficient capital resources, making the country reliant on foreign capital, much of which came from Germany, in line with that country's conscious policy.

To assuage this situation, the government sold mining rights to foreign companies, but this did not alleviate poverty and hunger. The heterogeneity and divergent interests among the constituent Yugoslav states also affected the national economy. In particular, Croatia and Slovenia were far more developed than Serbia and Bosnia-Herzegovina.

Not only did economic disparity exacerbate the tensions and animosity between Serbs and Croats, it reverberated to other ethnic groups.[15]

On December 1, 1918, the Serbian king proclaimed a unified Kingdom of Serbs, Croats, and Slovenes,[16] soon followed by a provisional government. On June 28, 1921, the Constitutional Assembly approved the kingdom's "Vidovan" Constitution, although the opposition boycotted the vote. The constitution was named after the feast of St. Vitus (Vidovan), a Serbian holiday. The adoption of a centralist constitution went against the wishes of Croats, who largely favored a federal state that would guarantee autonomy to the historic territories.

The efforts of the Serbian monarchy, as well as those of Yugoslav communists—each for their own reason—to create an overarching South Slav centralized nation-state were doomed to failure. In particular, they provoked intense resistance among the Croats throughout the 1920s.[17] Serb-Croat tensions flared in Belgrade during a session of parliament in June 1928. The newspaper, widely considered to be the mouthpiece of the prime minister, issued an invitation to the assassination of CCP leader Stjepan Radić. Days later, a Serb nationalist deputy shot him on the floor of the parliament.[18] In addition to further increasing ethnic tensions, Radić's assassination led to an alliance between the CPP and the Croatian working class against the Belgrade regime.

Croatian nationalist Ante Pavelić used the assassination as a pretext to form the Ustaše (insurgents) as an illegal paramilitary organization with the declared aim "with all possible means—including armed uprising—to liberate Croatia from alien rule and establish a completely free and independent state over its whole and historic territory."[19] Moreover, this would be a Croatia for ethnic Croatians. The Ustaše also incited peasants to kill their political opponents and Serbs.[20] On January 6, 1929, King Alexander dissolved the legislature, abolished the constitution, declared a royal dictatorship, and renamed the country the Kingdom of Yugoslavia. The declaration of a Serbian dictatorship blocked any hope of democratic solutions to Yugoslavia's problems. The Serb-Croat conflict was probably the most important single reason for the breakdown of the post-1918 Yugoslav state and for the escalation of brutalities during

World War II: "Ustaše genocide and internecine massacres and coun-termassacres by extremist Croatian, Serbian and Muslim nationalists."[21]

JEWRY IN THE INTERWAR PERIOD

To deal with its heterogeneous population, the new kingdom pro-posed that each ethnic and religious group establish its own central-ized federation to interact with the government on the group's behalf. To Belgrade's surprise, the Jews did not immediately act on this pro-posal, primarily because of the presence in Yugoslavia of two distinct branches of Judaism, each with its own language and religious practices. The Sephardim, whose origins are in Spain, had a longer history in the region; the Ashkenazim, whose culture emanated mostly from Hungary and Germany, were relative newcomers.

The first Sephardim arrived in 1398 and settled along the Dalmatian coast, predominantly in Dubrovnik and Split. However, their primary migration followed the expulsion of Jews from Spain by Ferdinand and Isabella in 1492. Their name derives from the Hebrew word *Sephard*, which refers to Spain. Arriving in large numbers in 1565, they estab-lished communities in towns that included Belgrade in Serbia, Sarajevo in Bosnia, and Skoplje and Bitola in Macedonia. Jewish Communities prospered in Bosnia, living side by side with their Bosnian Muslim, Serb, and Catholic neighbors. Jews in the Ottoman Empire were generally well-treated and were recognized under the law as non-Muslims. [22] As with other ethnic and religious groups, Ottoman law granted Jews full civil equality. Despite some restrictions, Jewish Communities prospered under the Ottomans; for example, they were allowed to purchase real estate and to conduct trade throughout the Ottoman Empire. They also had significant social, cultural and religious autonomy, including the right to build synagogues.[23]

Although the Ottoman Empire recognized members of all three reli-gious communities as legitimate residents,[24] each lived in its own des-ignated quarter granted by the Muslim authorities,[25] and each had its own internal cultural and religious life. In 1581, the Ottoman governor in Sarajevo gave the Jews a piece of land upon which he erected for them a special dwelling and a synagogue, which in his honor was named *Sijavus-paša daire* (the bequest of Siavus paša). The area where Jews resided, including the synagogue in which they prayed, was known as "Čifuthan" (the Jewish house). The Sephardim lived in extremely traditional and patriarchal communities. Their one-story houses built around large courtyards were suited for extended families. As a sign of the atmosphere of religious tolerance, parents, children, and grandchildren often wore Muslim garb.[26]

In return for the safeguarding of their lives and property and the right to worship unmolested according to their consciences, Jews had to pay special taxes and to conduct themselves with the demeanor befitting a subject population. This situation was perfectly suited to the Sephardim, who viewed segregation as a way to preserve the heritage they brought with them from Spain to the Balkans. They spoke their own Judeo-Spanish language, known as Ladino, and were preoccupied with their own culture and customs. They controlled all their internal affairs, including tax collection and a judicial system. They engaged in business with other ethnic groups, usually in special commercial areas of the city.

The balance between Sephardim and Ashkenazim in Bosnia-Herzegovina began to shift in the 1880s. In the Treaty of Berlin of 1878, which followed a period of Balkan unrest and decline of the Ottoman Empire, the Great Powers recognized Austro-Hungary's administrative control over Bosnia, including Sarajevo, and Herzegovina. It also recognized Serbia's independence as a state. The treaty recognized minority rights, which were also extended *de facto* to Bosnian Jewry. Although Austria-Hungary did not annex Bosnia and Herzegovina until 1908, the Hapsburgs viewed them from the outset as part of their multinational empire, which included a substantial Jewish population. By the eve of World War II, Ashkenazim comprised approximately 60 percent of Sarajevo's Jews.

Within the Austro-Hungarian Empire, the Ashkenazim arrived in Croatia as early as 1772, when the Croatian authorities granted them permission to live in Zagreb.[27] In Croatia, as well as in Bosnia, the Ashkenazim formed separate Jewish Communities, where they rapidly improved their living conditions. Their success was due in large measure to their emigration from countries that were technologically more advanced. In addition, they dedicated their energies and resources to the education of their children. Consequently, in relatively short time, they reached the highest economic strata and gained social recognition in the professions, greatly surpassing the Sephardim.[28]

The differences between the two Jewish Communities need to be explained and undersood because it is a key to understanding the precarious situation of Yugoslav Jews in the interwar period. Most Ashkenazim lived in northern Yugoslavia, which was more Europeanized than Serbia or Bosnia due to the Austrian influence and greater urbanization. Their more rapid acculturation was evidenced by the Croatian language spoken in most homes and by the Croatization of their surnames, often by translating them from German to Croatian; thus, for example, Stein (stone) became Kamenić with a customary suffix (ć) added. Their frequent intermarriages reflected a greater openness to assimilation, as did the large percentage who converted to Catholicism or to Serb Orthodoxy.

The Sephardim, who for centuries had lived their own private lives under the Ottoman Empire, took longer to adapt to the changes introduced by the Austro-Hungarian government. After the war, their acculturation to the new Yugoslav state was also relatively slow.

Jewish communal life in Yugoslavia in the first postwar decade was fragmented into some 110 to 115 self-governing communities, varying in their religious practices and affiliations with Zionist organizations.[29] The heterogeneity within the larger Jewish Community led to animosities and even harsh accusations against one another; nevertheless, interactions among individual Jews began, especially for those of similar economic and social levels. The most important factor contributing to the surprisingly high degree of unity ultimately achieved was that both the Sephardim and the Ashkenazim sought to establish a positive and constructive relationship with the government in Belgrade, as well as with their respective state governments.

After long debates, between and within the two communities, in 1929 the National Federation of Jewish Religious Communities came into being. For the first time, the more traditional Sephardic communities of Serbia, Bosnia, and Macedonia began to cooperate with the larger and mostly assimilated Ashkenazi communities of Croatia and Serbia; the Bosnian Jews were less open to this cooperation.[30] Although the Federation represented all Yugoslav Jews, each local community was responsible for such internal activities as levying taxes from its members for the community's use, providing education for its children, and engaging its membership in social, cultural, and charitable activities.

The success of Yugoslavia's Jews in gaining a higher standard of living was most notably manifested in their numerical growth. Between the Yugoslav government's first census in 1921 and a poll taken in 1924 by the National Federation of Rabbis, the Jewish population grew by 10.2 percent, from 64,753 to 73,266.[31] Population increases over these three years have been attributed to a higher birth rate and lower infant mortality as well as to immigration from Central European countries, in each case reflecting improved living conditions and nutrition. In 1857 there were 625 Jews (2.3 percent of the population) in Zagreb, the capital of Croatia; in 1941, just before Yugoslavia's demise, 12,315 Jews constituted 4.8 percent of the city's population.[32]

The number of Jewish students in higher education also showed remarkable progress. Although Jews were only 0.46 percent of Yugoslavia's total population, they constituted 4.6 percent of the enrollment in vocational schools; 2.75 percent of high school graduates and 16 percent of students in medical and law schools.[33] Upon completion of their studies, doors opened for Jews with expertise in social, economic, cultural, educational, legal, medical, and scientific areas. Data assembled by David Perera regarding the occupations of Jews in the interwar period indicates that the largest segment (44 percent) of the Jewish workforce, women included, were public servants; 33 percent worked in trade and commerce; 12 percent were skilled workers; and 8 percent were professionals, predominantly physicians, engineers, and lawyers. Only 1-2 percent of Yugoslavian Jews engaged in agriculture, as against 76 percent of Croats.[34]

The progress of Jewish students in institutions of higher learning quickly became manifest when they began obtaining positions in universities, hospitals, banks, and industry. Unfortunately their progress had negative ramifications, in that it provoked jealousy and anger. As early as 1920, some 340 medical students at the University of Zagreb signed a petition demanding the introduction of a *numerus clausus* in order to limit Jewish admissions in numbers above their percentage of the overall local population. Students made similar requests in Bosnia-Herzegovina,[35] where Muslim students demanded that the government establish a quota system that would curtail Jewish enrollment in order to give opportunities for advancement to other ethnic groups and minorities.[36] The Yugoslav government, which needed an educated and reliable workforce, forcefully rejected such petitions. Despite requests to limit Jewish access to institutions of higher learning, their progress in the fields of banking and commerce, in particular, was unstoppable at a time when the danger of antisemitism loomed on the horizon.[37]

The Yugoslavian government enacted provisions that allowed minorities to create their own charitable, social, cultural, and educational organizations. The freedom to form internal community organizations provided opportunities for Jews who had acquired substantial wealth to promote education among the disadvantaged and reduce misery among the Jewish poor.[38] Although the government did not financially support Jewish education beyond the first four years of public school, it allowed religious education to be subsidized by private individuals or organizations throughout the secondary and high school years.

The kingdom made sincere efforts to create an atmosphere of understanding and cooperation among the various religious and ethnic groups. It guaranteed religious freedom and frequently reiterated its citizens' full political rights. Despite the kingdom's attempt to fight bigotry and antisemitism, Nazi and other anti-Jewish propaganda was already on the increase by 1929 when Minister of External Affairs Vojislav Marinković declared:

> Our country does not suffer from the poison of antisemitism. On the contrary, we value and love the Jews. And this is not a coincidence.

The historical predicament of our nation was similar to the develop-
ment of the Jewish national identity. We experienced much suffering
due to our sacrifices for freedom; we have a full understanding for the
Jews, whose history knows pain and hardship.... We value the loyalty the Jews have for their faith; we do not scorn the Jews on this
account.[39]

After Hitler's assumption of power in 1933, the government's
attempts to fend off the rise of antisemitism were clearly doomed. The
Nazis targeted propaganda at what they termed "Germany Abroad."
Yugoslavia's ethnic German citizens (Volksdeutsche) zealously took on
the assassination of the Jewish character, stressing Jews' lack of integrity and loyalty. And as economic hardship deepened worldwide, and
Germany's political and economic influence in the country increased,
National Socialist antisemitic rhetoric spread like wildfire, threatening
the social gains Jews had achieved in the interwar period.[40]

Yugoslav intellectuals, in particular university professors, editors of
various progressive daily and weekly newspapers, supported their Jewish
comrades while leaders of most nationalist right-wing media demonized
them. Jews gained acceptance and support in the Communist Party in
general when they proclaimed support for "Unity and brotherhood"
(*Bratsvo jedinstvo*), but most religious leaders openly declared their hostility to Jews. The government's support for its Jewish citizens became
less forthcoming than it had been during the 1920s. The antisemites
no longer needed to fear official condemnation when they echoed Nazi
slogans and asserted connections among Bolsheviks, polyglots, and
International Jewry.[41] Their publications found a wide readership, especially inside church circles, both Serbian Orthodox and Catholic. In
1939, a Croatian right-wing newspaper editorial denied that Jews could
be Croatian citizens:

The Jews were not Croats, and they could never become Croatian
because by nationality they are Zionists, by race they are Semites,
their religion is Israelite... and in essence, I am asking the peoples of
the world, how long are we going to kill each other for the interests

of the Jews?. . . . if we are to kill each other, let us first kill the Jews and, only afterwards, can we ask ourselves if there is a justifiable reason for our mutual killing?[42]

Hostile propaganda directed exclusively against Jews was intended to legitimize racist antisemitism and to turn the concept of "purity of Croatian blood" into a legal category. Although the process of isolating the Jews was fostered from abroad rather than from locally-rooted anti-semitism, it was channeled primarily by the Volksdeutsche and by Muslim clerics. Although the Catholic media ostracized the Jews, the Catholic Church conducted vigorous missionary campaigns to convert them.[43]

JEWISH INTELLECTUALS AND COMMUNISTS IN THE INTERWAR PERIOD

With the end of World War I, Jewish youth took an active interest in causes outside their own communities and religious sphere. For many, this meant efforts to unify people of all religions under a universal banner and to proclaim international communism as the only way to improve the lot of mankind. During the 1920s, Jewish membership in the Yugoslavian Communist Party continued to grow despite the disapproval expressed by the Jewish leadership. In 1929 the Kingdom of Yugoslavia outlawed the party. Nonetheless, by 1932 the communists succeeded in consolidating their ranks and revitalizing the revolutionary movements of both the working classes and progressive youth. Many young Jews joined the party because of high unemployment and economic hardship caused by the failure of the capitalist system. They were also convinced that the economic difficulties gave rise to Nazism and other fascist movements and regimes.

Jews gained visibility and prominence in the ranks of the Yugoslav Communist Party during the 1930s. Thirty-nine Jews, from Croatia, Serbia and Bosnia-Herzegovina, joined the Spanish Republican Army and fought in the civil war. Fifty-three Jews, both men and women, held leadership positions within the party. Jewish intellectuals, particularly in Bosnia-Herzegovina, maintained that only communism had the moral

integrity to defeat fascism.[44] Young Jewish workers in ever-increasing
numbers also began joining labor unions in an effort to improve the
working conditions of laborers. The heterogeneity among Yugoslav Jews
is reflected in the fact that in 1938, while many were attracted to communism, with its anti-religious and international message, in Zagreb
alone, approximately 4,000 Jews, one-third of the city's Jewish population, converted to Catholicism, and a large number Croatized their surnames. The converted Jews often joined right-wing causes; even the top
Ustaše leadership had several Jews.[45]

Jewish youth were also drawn to Zionism, which they tailored to
their own brand of Social Zionism. Jewish students from Croatia who
were studying in Vienna had first introduced revolutionary Zionist ideology to Yugoslavia in 1902; it gained momentum in the 1920s through
two Zionist youth organizations, *Hashomer Hatzair* and *Thelet Lavan*. By
1940 some of these young people—hardly aware of what was happening
in their own backyard—were initially eager to immigrate to what they
called Eretz Israel (land of Israel). But with maturity, many put away the
dream and settled into a lifestyle carved out for them by their parents. [46]

Although the Jewish media reacted promptly to the first visible signs
of antisemitic propaganda, they sent mixed signals to their readers. For
example, editors failed to warn their readers of the possibility that Nazi
Germany might occupy their country, and that Jews should get ready for
such an event. They also belittled the threat of antisemitic propaganda;
some editors even suggested that its authors and propagandists were
merely trying to satisfy Hitler's loyalists and politicians in Yugoslavia.
The vicious antisemitic propaganda and journalism, the editors argued,
had little impact on public opinion regarding Jews.[47] Indeed, the government used the daily local papers to emphasize that the antisemitic editorials came from Nazi Germany, which the Ustaše and other right-wing
parties followed blindly.

The atmosphere in Yugoslavia changed drastically in 1940, with the
first anti-Jewish legislation. Unable to withstand German pressure to act
against the Jews, the unity government of the Serb Dragiša Cvetković
and the Croat Vladko Maček, the popular CPP leader, enacted two

decrees: a quota system that precluded Jews from enrolling in institutions of higher learning based on merit; and a prohibition against Jews' engaging in the wholesale trade of certain foods, specifically grains, an area in which they were prominent. Finally, although this measure was kept confidential, Jews were prohibited from serving in the elite air force units and from taking exams for advancement in the various branches of the army.[48]

Without ideas or plans for effectively coping with the threat from Nazi influence, Jewish intellectuals fell back on age-old frictions between the Ashkenazim and Sephardim. They were joined by rabbinical scholars, Zionist youth leaders, and various cultural groups, who displayed their internalized animosities in a number of weekly publications. The Ashkenazi weekly journal *Židov*[49] (Jew), for example, which appeared on Zagreb newsstands every Friday without interruption from 1917 to 1941, took an increasingly Zionist position.[50] From 1928 to 1941 Sephardic intellectuals in Sarajevo published the weekly *Jevrejski glas*[51] (The Jewish Voice), which advanced their conviction that the future of Judaism should forever be grounded in the diaspora, not in ephemeral ideology and hopes for a return to Zion.[52] The two groups shared one mutual goal: exposing Nazi lies and acts of injustice, while emphasizing that the equal status granted to Jews was a matter of their rights as citizens. This internecine strife troubled the Jewish Federation's journal *Gazette*, which tried to tone down the editorial controversies and reduce the tension between Sephardic and Ashkenazic intellectuals.

THE PROLOGUE TO WAR: RISING DISCONTENT IN THE 1930s

Ever since Yugoslav unification in 1919, Croatian nationalists were preoccupied with the idea of nullifying the union with Serbia.[53] In the 1930s the world economic crisis hit Yugoslavia hard: unemployment surged, mines closed, bankruptcies increased, and severe weather conditions brought rural starvation.[54] Croatian discontent manifested itself primarily in the rising membership of right-wing nationalist parties.[55] Heightened ethnic tensions thus provided a fertile climate for the Ustaše movement, which burgeoned in the mountainous regions of Croatia and Bosnia-Herzegovina.

The Ustaše expressed their discontent in the group's newspaper, *Vjesnik hrvatskih revolucionara* (Herald of Croatian Revolutionaries). Its editorials aimed especially at igniting hatred toward the Belgrade regime. The Ustaše's exiled unofficial leader, Dr. Ante Pavelić, bore the title *poglavnik* (leader). Assertive and boisterous, he often declared: "The dagger, revolver, machine gun and bomb, those are the bells that will ring the dawn and the resurrection of the Independent State of Croatia."[56] The combative spirit of poor Croatian villagers often led to their arrest and torture by the Yugoslav police. The objects of their protests included high taxes, a corrupt administration, and the harsh conditions of military service; they mistrusted the Serbian political and military elite, and by extension all Serbs.[57] In general, they lived in the hope that at some future date an independent Croatian state would emerge and the peasantry would be better treated. Despite widespread animosity toward the regime in Belgrade, a comprehensive Ustaše ideology did not exist in Croatia prior to the beginning of World War II.[58]

Pavelić began his career as a political novice in 1929 after the Serbs had murdered Stjepan Radić, the leader of the Croats in the Yugoslav Parliament. He was a violent Croat nationalist who subsequently fled from Yugoslavia. The Serbs retaliated by killing off all the members of his family. As a result, Pavelić became even more radical and rose to the leadership of the Ustaše movement in 1933 while living in Switzerland. Later that year, a Belgrade court sentenced him *in absentia* to death for publicly advocating the Yugoslav state's overthrow—thus increasing his popularity in Croatia.[59] For a time, Pavelić led a shady existence, living in third-class hotels throughout Central and Western Europe. He was in contact with political intelligence agents of Mussolini and Hungarian leader Admiral Horthy, in alliance against Yugoslavia with Balkan secret societies, and in league with the Roman Catholic Church in Croatia, combating the Serb Orthodox Church.[60]

In 1932, Pavelić moved to Mussolini's Italy, where he set up training camps for the few hundred Ustaše followers in exile. There was another camp in Hungary. Mussolini, who aspired to obtain a foothold in Croatia, provided support, including arms for a failed uprising attempt in Croatia. After the double assassination, however, Mussolini—as a head of state himself—became concerned. He shut down the camps, interned the Ustaše, and imprisoned Pavelić until 1936.[61] While in Italy, Pavelić learned the basic tenets of the fascist philosophy and formulated his views regarding the Jews, which he summarized in the statement that "all financial business and all trade are in Jewish hands; Communism and Judaism work together against the national liberation of Croatia."[62] Pavelić was aware that, despite the disappearance of capital and credit during the depression, Jews managed to establish national and international personal connections which allowed them without interruption to conduct trade and grow their enterprises. Except in Bosnia and Macedonia, Jews throughout Yugoslavia, and especially those in Serbia and Croatia, prospered during this period. Together with Nazi propaganda, jealousy at Jewish prosperity fed open but not yet physical and violent antisemitism.

After World War II, Dr. Samuel Pinto, at the request of the National Commission for the Ascertainment of Crimes Committed Against the Jews by the Occupiers and their Collaborators (hereafter National Commission), reported that from 1934 through 1939 Nazi clandestine activities and propaganda against Jews became more aggressive.[63] Pinto attributed Germany's rising importance in Yugoslavia to the economic weakness of France and Britain: When their financial support "dried up" and the Belgrade government urgently needed credit advances, Nazi Germany was the only viable source of capital. The monarchy was hesitant to turn to the Third Reich for assistance, knowing that a credit line would have strings attached: interference in the country's internal affairs and an influx of spies and Nazi party activists. But the situation became so grave that the government succumbed to Nazi overtures of friendship and cash.

In the early 1930s Nazi interests in the region were threefold. First, by clandestinely mobilizing and organizing Yugoslavia's 500,000 Volksdeutsche, who were strategically spread throughout the country, the Nazis aimed to make them fully operational in the service of the fatherland for the eventuality of war.[64] The Volksdeutsche were exceptionally well organized because all religious and ethnic groups in Yugoslavia were united by their own federations. After several years of Nazi training, within a day's notice each person was ready to assume his predetermined post should Germany occupy the country.[64] Second, German spies recruited individuals to serve as a fifth column, while in the meantime they scouted Yugoslavia's territories and gathered useful information on such subjects as the location of natural resources, Jews and their organizations, and potential enemies. Third, the Nazis activated their lethal propaganda machine against Jews and introduced antisemitism in a country that had experienced little or no racial discrimination. Historians have attributed the success of German propaganda to the heterogeneity of Yugoslavia's population, economic hardship, and political instability.[66]

Bosnia-Herzegovina also offered an attractive market for right-wing fascist movements. Sarajevo, the capital of one of Yugoslavia's poorest states, was an ideal location for breeding a fifth column.[67] Daily newspapers and weekly magazines such as *Svoj svome* (Each to his own) dealt exclusively with the incitement of the population against the Jews. The *Katolički List* (Catholic Page) and *Glasnik sv Ante* (Herald of St. Ante) began sporadically interjecting antisemitic editorials. Belgrade newspapers such as *Balkan* and *Vrme* (Time) mounted more sophisticated attacks against the Jews: For example, *Balkan*'s assertion in June 1938 that "the Sarajevo Jews are the subject and the source of all the city's hardship and agony... is there any chance of inventing a fumigator with which to annihilate the Jewish scourge"?[68]

The Roman Catholic Church in Sarajevo staked its own position in support of the German invasion. *Katolički Tjedan*, (Catholic Week), Sarajevo's main paper, published several articles deriding an American-Jewish conspiracy, citing in one a quote from Berlin alleging that "Jews will have no place in the New Europe." Božidar Bralo, a priest and a close associate of Sarajevo's Archbishop Ivan Sarić, participated in secret meetings with other Catholics and Muslims in support of the German cause.[69] The Bosnian Croats wished to rid the state of both Serbs and Jews in order to seize their assets and establish their own Croat-Catholic *Lebensraum*. In Sarajevo, more than in other parts of Bosnia-Herzegovina, Croat nationalist/anti-Jewish media attained high visibility and circulation.[70]

In early 1934, Sarajevo's Nazi sympathizers provoked an incident that greatly distressed the Jewish population. A few Jewish opera singers who had fled Germany and were en route to Eretz Israel (land of Israel), received an official invitation from the city to perform in the National Concert Hall. As the curtain rose, young supporters of one of the right-wing parties began throwing eggs and rotten oranges at the singers.[71] Incidents of heightened hatred toward Jews thereafter became increasingly frequent.[72]

The strongest anti-Jewish sentiments were voiced by Palestinian clerical emissaries sent by Hajj Amin el Husseini, the Mufti of Jerusalem,[73] and by the Volksdeutsche.[74] In Sarajevo, probably more than in any other territory of Yugoslavia, these two groups strove to segregate the Jews from other citizens by identifying them as a foreign element in their midst. The Muslim emissaries read passages from the Koran to demonstrate that the Prophet had excluded the Jews from the community of believers.[75] The Muslim leadership recognized Nazi Germany's interest in anti-Jewish propaganda, and they hoped to be rewarded for their cooperation with a Muslim protectorate for Bosnia-Herzegovina. The Muslim leadership also sought to exterminate the Jews and seize their assets, as well as to prevent the young Jewish men from immigrating to Palestine. These goals dovetailed with those of the Volksdeutsche and right-wing Croatian elements.[76]

Mussolini was also preparing for war. In June 1940 he decided that *rapprochement* with Pavelić might serve Italy's objective of annexing a large part of the Dalmatian coast. In exchange, Mussolini would help Croatia achieve independence from Serbia.[77] As a result of this agreement, the Croatian right-wing parties agreed, in the case of war, not to side with the Kingdom of Yugoslavia against the Axis powers.[78] Rumors of this agreement unsettled the borders between Croatia and Serbia because it signaled a split within Yugoslavia. Indeed, several public protests against the kingdom's policies took place in major cities across Yugoslavia. The division in public opinion foreshadowed later battle lines: liberals and communists against right-wing fascist forces.[79] In the meantime, the realization that Croatia might secede from the Yugoslav union, compounded by the economic hardships, strengthened the control Nazi Germany exercised in the region.[80]

WORLD WAR II COMES TO YUGOSLAVIA

Although invasion by foreign troops was some six months away, for all intents and purposes, World War II began for Yugoslavia on September 27, 1940, when Germany, Italy, and Japan signed the Tripartite Pact. The three Axis powers recognized German hegemony over most of continental Europe, Italian hegemony over the Mediterranean, and Japanese hegemony over East Asia and the Pacific. The Axis partners shared two key interests: first, territorial expansion of their respective empires based on military conquest and the overthrow of the post-World War I international order; second, a goal of neutralizing and eventually obliterating Soviet Communism. At the time Germany signed the agreement, the Nazi government expressed no interest in either annexing or directly governing Croatian territories; indeed, it seemed to concede that they lay in Italy's sphere of influence.

By November 1940, Hitler began to relentlessly pressure Yugoslavia to join the Tripartite Pact and align with its neighbors Bulgaria, Romania, and Hungary. After several months of negotiations, the Yugoslav government recognized that it had neither the military nor the economic foundation to sustain a prolonged military offensive against the Axis. On March 25, 1941, the government of Prince Regent Pavel Karadjordhević reached the momentous decision to abandon its historical ties with France and England in favor of alignment with the Axis powers. In return, Hitler guaranteed that Germany would not force Yugoslavia to provide military assistance; neither would it move its army into Yugoslav territory nor violate the country's sovereignty.[81] On March 26, 1941, Yugoslav Prime Minister Dragiša Cvetković and Foreign Minister

Cincar Marković departed for Vienna to sign an agreement to join the Axis powers. Immediately upon the conclusion of this agreement, German Foreign Minister Von Ribbentrop and his Italian counterpart, Galeazzo Ciano, gave their governments' guarantees to their new ally's foreign minister that they would respect the sovereignty and integrity of Yugoslavia.[82] Nonetheless, vocal objections to Yugoslavia's joining this pact arose from all strata of the society.

Devastated by news of the alliance, Great Britain and the United States urged the Yugoslavs to "save their souls" by defying Hitler. On March 27, 1941, Belgrade awakened to news of a coup d'état initiated by military officers and politicians opposed to the pact. The city's citizens responded by parading through the streets shouting slogans such as: "Better grave than slave" and "Better war than pact."[83] Serbian military officers overthrew Prince Regent Pavel's government and declared the minor Prince Peter the rightful king of Yugoslavia. The new rulers thought that they could avoid antagonizing Berlin, but anti-German euphoria swept Belgrade: Yugoslav, British, French, and United States flags flew, and crowds shouted anti-Axis slogans.[84] The Jews were overjoyed by the military's revolt and the new king. But all these hopes were soon dashed.

The demonstrations unnerved the new king and his cabinet, under General Dušan Simović. The government—also troubled by the country's perilous economic and military position—soon reaffirmed Yugoslavia's loyalty to the Tripartite Pact. Hitler reacted forcefully and decisively, intending to destroy Yugoslavia militarily and thus eliminate the threat of British air power against the southern flank of the German armies. Yugoslavia's Jews could not comprehend how their country could so betray them. At the same time, Hitler decided to dismember Yugoslavia politically, using not only Axis military forces but also right-wing Croats and Yugoslavia's national minorities, especially the compliant Volksdeutsche.

On March 31, 1941, at a conference in the Wehrmacht's Abteilung Landesverteidigung (Division for Homeland Defense), Germany abruptly decided that Croatia should become an independent state.[85]

Driving this decision was the recognition that Croatian troops could be an effective force once the Luftwaffe bombed Belgrade. From that decision onward, German agents stepped up their subversive activities in Zagreb in preparation for the Wehrmacht's entrance into the city.[86] On April 5, 1941, the kingdom signed an agreement of friendship with the U.S.S.R., with whom Nazi Germany itself had signed a pact in 1939.[87] Despite Yugoslavia's signed allegiance to the Axis and his own pact with the U.S.S.R., Hitler—who viewed Slavs in general as an inferior race—questioned the intentions of the Yugoslav monarchy. On April 6, 1941, the Luftwaffe bombed Belgrade, killing thousands.

Nonetheless, the force of Germany's military invasion on April 10, 1941, and the subsequent capitulation of the Yugoslav kingdom left no doubt as to which Axis partner was in control. Italian Foreign Minister Galeazzo Ciano sought a territorial agreement with Pavelić, who had lived in exile in Italy for a decade prior to the declaration of war against Yugoslavia.[88] But Croatia's nationalists realized that their country's independence—given Italy's history of irredentist designs on its territory—required the support of the Nazi regime.

On April 10, 1941, German troops equipped with heavy armor poured into Zagreb; in parallel the Nazi agents stationed there decided to orchestrate the declaration of an independent Croatian state to coincide with the entry of German troops. Hitler, who knew of the agreement between Mussolini and the Ustaše, was determined to control the government by dominating the economy as well as through military strength, thus driving a wedge into the agreement reached between Italy and Pavelić.

The same day that German troops entered Zagreb, Nazi Germany and Fascist Italy proclaimed the Independent State of Croatia (Nezavisna Država Hrvatska—NDH), carved out of the dismembered Yugoslavia. The new state comprised the territories of Croatia and Bosnia-Herzegovina. To lead this new entity, the Axis partners installed the returned leader of the Ustaše, Dr. Ante Pavelić, who named himself *Poglavnik* (leader). Hitler readily agreed with the choice of the man whom Mussolini had groomed for the role, first, because many of his Ustaše were Nazi supporters, and second, because he assumed that Pavelić's political weakness in the country would make him easily manipulated.[89]

Meanwhile, the Wehrmacht and SS troops continued their march through Yugoslavia, on April 15 reaching Sarajevo, the capital of Bosnia-Herzegovina. As they had in Zagreb, they entered the Bosnian city amidst a display of military might. The Yugoslav Army collapsed on April 17. King Peter II and his government fled to Palestine and then to London, and the remaining resistance forces surrendered unconditionally.[90] On April 18, all was over for the union of the South Slavs, as well as for the Federation of the Jewish Communities of Yugoslavia. Under Axis occupation, Yugoslavia once again became a collection of disparate governments, all of them plagued by chaos and civil war. Axis forces spread throughout the country.

THE JEWISH POPULATION ON THE EVE OF WORLD WAR II

In the opening section on Yugoslavia in his book *The Final Solution*, Gerald Reitlinger wrote: "In no country of Axis-occupied Europe is the fate of Jewry more difficult to assess."[91] Indeed, to this day historians have found it difficult to determine even approximately the number of Jews living in pre-World War II Yugoslavia. As a result, one encounters estimates ranging from 70,000 to 82,000; a difference of 17.14 percent. The absence of accurate birth and death records began centuries ago, especially in Sephardic communities. As mentioned earlier, the Jews lived in 115 separate communities under various foreign powers, none of which required periodic and accurate censuses of Jews for administrative purposes. The problem was further exacerbated after 1933 by the influx of 55,800 Jews fleeing Nazi-occupied Europe. Most of these Jews were transient and left the country before the outbreak of war, but a few thousand remained, and it is possible that some historians and demographers may have included them in their estimates of the Jewish population in Yugoslavia on the eve of the war. Thus, the numbers of those lost as well as of those who survived are necessarily imprecise.

With the creation of the NDH and the German and Italian occupations, the political union represented by the Kingdom of Yugoslavia was
dissolved, and with it the Federation of Jewish religious communities,
thus driving these communities further apart. Under Axis occupation,
Germany's ally Hungary gained territory east of the Danube: Bačka,
with 16,000 Jewish residents, and Banat with 4,200 Jews. The German
Army occupied old Serbia, Vojvodina, and Northern Slovenia, with a
combined Jewish population of approximately 12,500. Italy annexed
the Dalmatian coast, with 400 Jews. Montenegro, with thirty Jews, and
Kosovo, with approximately 550 Jews, were divided between Italian
and German occupiers. Finally, Bulgaria annexed Yugoslavia's part of
Macedonia, with its 7,762 Jews, parts of southern Serbia, and a small
eastern part of Kosovo.[92]

The NDH inherited the largest Jewish populations in Yugoslavia:
25,500 in Croatia-Slavonia and 14,000 in Bosnia-Herzegovina. The fate
of this group of Jews will be the subject of the following chapters.

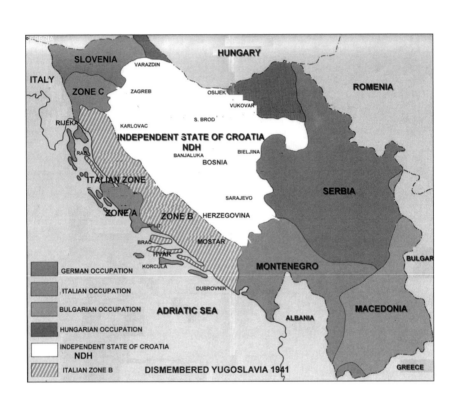

SLOVENIA

HUNGARY

ITALY

ZONE C

ROMENIA

VARAZDIN

ZAGREB

OSIJEK

VUKOVAR

RIJEKA

S. BROD

KARLOVAC

INDEPENDENT STATE OF CROATIA
NDH

RAB

BANJALUKA

BIELJINA

BOSNIA

ITALIAN ZONE

SERBIA

SARAJEVO

ZONE A

ZONE B

HERZEGOVINA

SPLIT

BRAC

MOSTAR

HVAR

MONTENEGRO

BULGAR

KORCULA

DUBROVNIK

GERMAN OCCUPATION

ITALIAN OCCUPATION

ADRIATIC SEA

MACEDONIA

BULGARIAN OCCUPATION

ALBANIA

HUNGARIAN OCCUPATION

INDEPENDENT STATE OF CROATIA
NDH

ITALIAN ZONE B

DISMEMBERED YUGOSLAVIA 1941

GREECE

2

The Ustaše Rule of Terror Against Jews and Their Rescue by Ordinary Citizens

THE USTAŠE AND THE IMPOSITION OF AN ANTISEMITIC REGIME IN CROATIA

On April 10, 1941, Nazi Germany and Fascist Italy proclaimed the Independent State of Croatia (Nezavisna Država Hrvatska—NDH), carved out of the dismembered Yugoslavia. Pavelić arrived in Croatia on April 15, the same day that German troops entered Sarajevo, accompanied by a force of 250 to 300 hard-core Ustaše supporters. Following Germany's instructions and expectations, his first objective—after taking control of the government—was to mobilize the manpower to deal promptly and decisively with the Jews, along with Serbs and Roma. To engage local citizens as collaborators and motivate them to commit acts that had hitherto been regarded as crimes, the Nazis and the Ustaše government relied on the philosophy of divide and rule, the distinction between "them" and "us," and the doctrine of "inferior races."

After the NDH's creation, the Ustaše regime was directly dependent on Germany for financial and military assistance; the NDH reciprocated with ideological concessions, among them vigorous implementation of the Final Solution.[1] Nazi Germany provided the template for accomplishing this task: first, confiscate all Jewish assets and use them to rebuild the NDH; second, exterminate the Jews in its territories.[2] The Ustaše, following the Nazi blueprint, on April 17, announced their first legislative ordinance, the "Protection of the Croatian People and the State Act,"[3] which stated that,

> ... Anyone who damages, or has damaged, in any way, the honor of the Croatian people and their vital interests, or who endangers in any way the existence of the Independent State of Croatia and its ruling authorities stands accused of the crime of high treason (*veleizdaja*).[4]

This act could be construed to legitimize the annihilation of Croatia's Jews and the punishment for treason of those who assisted them. In order to reinforce the law's urgency and intent, on April 18 the Ustaše placed a notice in *Novi list*, the official daily newspaper, stating that:

> Since many Croat citizens individually and in groups are engaged in the rescue of individual Jews and their families, the Ustaše Office for Law and Order sent instructions to the State Regulatory Board forbidding lawyers and solicitors from being involved in political matters, particularly on behalf of the Jews. Those who fail to uphold this law will bear penalties.[5]

On April 30, 1941, the Ustaše enacted a second statute that more explicitly accused the Jews of collectively "disseminating lies about the conduct of the government and thus disturbing the public peace and order." This "crime" carried a penalty of death.[6] From April 1941 to May 1945 the Croatian national daily newspapers published 589 editorials and decrees against the Jews, including the one imposing the infamous "Z" identification mark for Židov (Jew). These decrees further denied Jews the right to earn a living, to reside in certain areas from which they were evicted, and to appear in most public places. The NDH also confiscated and looted Jewish real estate and bank accounts and Aryanized Jewish-owned businesses.[7]

Nonetheless, in May 1941 Pavelić was informed that "many Croat citizens individually and in groups are engaged in the rescue of individual Jews and their families." Determined to prevent all such assistance, he announced that the Ustaše Office for Law and Order had instructed the State Regulatory Board to forbid all government and private entities from involvement in political matters, particularly on behalf of the Jews. Derivation from this law would entail heavy penalties.[8] Under Nazi tutelage, the Ustaše aimed to provide a radical solution to the "Jewish Question." From April 1941 until the end of July 1942, the Ustaše carried out this program under the watchful eye of the Gestapo and the SS. Using the kingdom's prisons and erecting their own concentration camps, the Ustaše carried out the internment, execution, and annihilation of Jews on Croatian soil. From mid-1942 until the end of the war, Jews were being deported, with the help of the Ustaše, to Nazi labor and death camps, mostly to Auschwitz.

On May 2, 1941, less than a month into the NDH's existence, U.S. Secretary of State Cordell Hull received alarming news from Berlin regarding the NDH regime, which had just introduced "energetic and immediate measures to solve the Jewish question." The dispatch continued: "The new ordinances and decrees were to alter the lives of nearly 40,000 Jews and of the country since the Jews occupied important positions in economic life…. one should expect the same outcome as that inflicted upon Jews in Nazi-controlled Slovakia and Poland."[9]

On June 13, 1941, John James Meily, the U.S. consul in Zagreb, reported to the secretary of state: "Pavelić's Ustaše had struck with such consistent intensity that today the Jew is stripped of practically all the rights accruing to a citizen of this State," such as:

1. Definition of the Jew "by race" and assessment of his private fortune
2. Definition of what constitutes a "Jewish firm" and assessment of its assets
3. Establishing a mechanism for the confiscation of Jewish assets
4. Adopting confiscatory measures

On June 6, 1941, Pavelić met Hitler at his Berghof retreat in the Bavarian Alps to discuss Croatia's national policy, in particular its attitude toward minorities. Initially, Pavelić planned to execute only those

Jews who had arrived in Croatia after 1933. Hitler had a different opinion: "After all, if the Croat state wishes to be strong, a nationally intolerant policy must be pursued for fifty years, because too much tolerance on such issues… could bring hardship."[10] In 1942, the German plenipotentiary in Zagreb, Edmund Glaise-Horstenau, recounted to a fellow diplomat Hitler's views on the Jewish Question in Croatia. Rejecting any notion of acting only against recent Jewish immigrants, he had argued that the NDH must act harshly against all Jews because they hold the economy's purse strings.[11] Hitler convinced Pavelić to pursue a thoroughgoing policy of "intolerance," one that included the mass persecution of Jews and all other dissidents and ethnic groups that stood in the way of the NDH's rise to power. Hitler's tactic of "divide and rule" appealed to Pavelić, especially in his dealings with Italy and even his cabinet ministers.[12]

In June 1941, approximately three months after Yugoslavia's dismemberment, one of history's bloodiest civil wars broke out. Four different factions took part in this struggle for domination over the former Yugoslavian territories: the Croatian and Bosnian Ustaše; the 500,000 Volksdeutsche; the Četniks (Serbian Royalist paramilitaries); and the Partisans (a resistance force comprising individuals from all ethnic and religious groups).[13] Apart from the Partisans, these groups all worked vigorously to rid Croatia of its Jews.

JEWS PARALYZED BY THE DISMEMBERMENT OF YUGOSLAVIA

While the fate of Jews during World War II was devastating throughout Yugoslavia, there were marked differences in their treatment, depending in particular on their location and the local occupation power or collaborationist regime. In NDH, for example, the Ustaše followed Germany's model in terms of antisemitic legislation and participated directly in the persecution of Jews. Nonetheless, as discussed in the next chapter, officials shielded Jews in mixed marriages and those deemed important to the Croatian economy. Bosnia-Herzegovina, although annexed by Croatia, experienced a very different occupation regime.

The Wehrmacht had its headquarters in Sarajevo, the capital of Bosnia, and both Croats and Muslims in the Ustaše, as well as the large population of Volksdeutsche, collaborated closely with the occupiers.[14] In the final analysis, however, Nazi Germany was the primary force behind the atrocities committed against Yugoslav Jewry during World War II. They invented the model of anti-Jewish measures, and they had the will and the power to impose them, regardless of public sentiment.

Testimonies by survivors—such as those recounted later in this chapter—make clear that many Jews held on to the idea that they would survive and return to their homes, even after Yugoslavia's dissolution and occupation. Did they perhaps think that Hitler's invasion of Russia would require him to remove German troops from the land of the South Slavs? Were they eternally optimistic about the survival of the Jewish people after so many earlier disasters, or were they sadly aware that the world at large did not wish to deal with thousands of Jewish refugees? In any case, most Jews chose to remain in their homes, and those Croatian Jews who had obtained special NDH protection believed they were safe. Bosnian Jews, many of whom had never left their homes and who feared change more than they did the Ustaše, also remained. Croatian poet Viktor G. Rosenzweig eloquently expressed this fateful truth in his "Dilemma":

> Should I hold my head up or should I keep it down?
> Where should I walk? Where can I go?
> To run away, to swallow a poisonous bitter flower;
> Stare death straight in the eye in this hard moment.
> No, no, here to stay, standing firmly on the feet
> Firmly clenching the fist, not to run away."[15]

THE JEWS OF ZAGREB PLAY FOR TIME

Although Stephen Wise of New York alerted the Jewish people of the impeding danger of destruction, most Jews did not understand the threat Hitler's philosophy posed for them, despite revealing to them his intentions and the manner of execution. We cannot blame our people for not foreseeing the Final Solution, said Nahum Goldman, "only someone endowed with Hitler's devilish brutality could believe in the possibility of an Auschwitz or a Majdanek in the twentieth century."[16] Why then would we expect the Jews of NDH to act differently, especially in light of their experience of a moderate rate of antisemitism? Ivo Goldstein, Croatian historian, suggests that Yugoslavia's Jews might have had reason to believe that World War II would not have life-threatening consequences for them.

> There was nothing in previous Croatian history to indicate that such crimes might be committed. It is true that there were antisemitic pamphlets and incidents. In Croatia in the 19th century and the first half of the 20th century, various political parties, in their ideologies and programs, used antisemitic slogans, but it was mostly to gain political power. But antisemitism had never reached the kind of extreme forms of pogroms and murders that were seen, for example, in Poland and Russia.[17]

On the eve of the war, most Croatian Jews were assimilated; some had converted to Catholicism; still others legally Croatized their surnames as a sign of membership in the Croatian nation and most socialized with Croatian friends and neighbors. By acquiring a new, so-called Aryan identity many assumed that escape was unnecessary.

Zdenka Steiner-Novak eloquently described the state of mind of those Jews who refused to believe that their people would be targeted in Croatia as they had been in all the other European countries under German occupation. Zdenka's father, Lavoslav Steiner, a successful industrialist, refused to heed the warnings of his friends in England and the United States. They urged him to flee, but he and his family decided to stay put. Zdenka recalled how some good Christian friends offered to provide the family with false papers that would identify them as belonging to the Greek Orthodox Church. Steiner thanked them, but graciously refused to take this precautionary measure. In her memoir Zdenka wrote:

> From today's perspective, it is clear to me that our fatal mistake was that of not taking Hitler seriously. During all those years he announced

his plans to the world, shouting so loudly that heaven and hell could shake, yet we did not hear or did not want to hear. When it did happen it seemed so unexpected, like a whirlwind destroying everything in its way with violent blows.[18]

When Zdenka's father finally considered leaving Zagreb and hiding in the mountains of Bosnia time was no longer on his side: "We failed to recognize that we were no longer masters of our time; it was controlled by others." One day while Zdenka was running home, their neighbor shouted: "Zdenka, quick, hurry, the Ustaše are snatching girls and young women in the streets." At first, she thought he was joking, but he was not. Waiting for her at home were two men, with orders to arrest her and her husband Fritz and bring them to the Zagreb detention center (Zagrebački Zbor). The detention center was crowded, mostly with young people. Suddenly, from a distance Zdenka recognized a familiar face among the Ustaše; it was Jedvaj, one of her father's former employees, who had come to seek her release. Although Zdenka was not listed among those slated for release, Baraković, a high Ustaše official and a family acquaintance, motioned with his hands and exclaimed: "Go, go quickly." She left immediately, without even saying goodbye to Fritz. Jedvaj promised to bring her husband home the following day, but in those days tomorrow never happened for some. Zdenka never saw Fritz again.

After this experience, Zdenka beseeched her father to leave Zagreb. Her younger sister Mirica wanted to go to Split, where her fiancé waited. But Zdenka's father still procrastinated. Unwilling to let his daughter go alone, he reassured his family that once his finances were in order they would all flee Zagreb. But trying to buy time proved disastrous: His entire family, except Zdenka, was captured in mid-1941, detained in Zagreb for a few days, and deported to one of the Ustaše concentration camps. Zdenka escaped this fate because, finally, her father, in a note he wrote in the detention center, had urged her to leave Zagreb and go to Sušak, in the Italian occupation zone.

In leaving Zagreb, Zdenka again called on a family connection—this time, a railway official named Pašić, now an Ustaše. Before the war, he worked for Zdenka's father-in-law, who had come to his aid many times.

In gratitude to him, and for a fee, Pašić arranged for Zdenka to travel, with the proper identity card, as his teenage daughter Olgica. As a precaution, several miles short of the NDH-Italian border zone, Pašić asked Zdenka to lie down, and he covered her with a blanket. At the Plaše border control, to his great surprise and dismay, the Ustaše guard was Olgica's former gym teacher, who wanted to see his former student. Pašić refused, on the grounds that his daughter was feeling ill and should be allowed to sleep. It was a stressful and dangerous moment for both Pašić and Zdenka. However, they crossed the border and headed toward Sušak. Although Pašić received payment for his help, he nevertheless took a great risk by transporting Zdenka out of NDH territory. Had he been caught, the money he received would have been insufficient to pay for his life.[19]

Since the outbreak of war in 1939, Yugoslavian Jews had the opportunity to see what was happening to Jews in other countries occupied by Nazi Germany. Although few of them made any preparations for the eventuality that their country might became a target of German aggression, they worked assiduously to accommodate and assist the thousands of Jewish refugees from Germany, Austria, Romania, and Czechoslovakia who fled to the kingdom. This tide of refugees began in 1933 with Hitler's seizure of power, then accelerated in 1938 with the Anschluss of Austria, and again after 1939 as German troops pushed eastward. The Yugoslav Jewish Communities did the best to help the refugees, but only with the sizable help of the JOINT, contribution of 21,650,000 dinars ($386,607), and HICEM's contribution of 15,520.000 dinars ($2,777,142).[20] In cities and towns all across Yugoslavia, these refugees related horror stories of Nazi atrocities against Jews in Eastern and Central Europe. Some advised their hosts to flee to Italy in case Yugoslavia should fall prey to the Axis powers. But even after the occupation troops arrived, Yugoslavian Jews for the most part held to their conviction that "nothing bad will happen here."

The available evidence indicates that from 1933 to 1941 only 5,200 of the 82,000 Jews living in Yugoslavia left the country. Those who were so poor that they had little or nothing material to lose frequently argued that no harm could come to them. They derived their flawed logic from antisemitic propaganda that primarily targeted the wealthy. Some Jews hesitated to leave because of family connections and obligations. Žuži Jelenik, a survivor, recalled how she and her husband made an early decision to leave Zagreb and head toward the Adriatic coast. But once there, she felt terrible for leaving behind her disabled parents. After securing documents from the Italian authorities that would enable her to return with her parents, Žuži's stay in Zagreb was short, and before leaving Zagreb she urged her two brothers to join her; they refused, contending that they were poor and the Ustaše were only after the "big fish." Neither brother survived.[21]

Branko Polić, a Croatian survivor, asked me as soon as I entered his home whether I had heard about "the stadium incident." I shook my head to indicate "no," sensing that he was eager to tell me about an event that must have left a lasting impression on him. He recounted the story:

> All secondary school kids were requested to participate in an event that had to take place in the Zagreb Maksimir Stadium. We did not know what to expect. We were lined up and standing, listening to a speech addressed only to the Croatian children. Immediately thereafter a loud command was given: All Jews and Serbs step forward. No one moved. I [Branko] looked around and uttered, 'I am stepping forward'; my comrades urged me to ignore the command. But when the orders grew louder and louder, I was ready to obey; it was clear that unnecessary delays would place my friends in jeopardy. As I stepped forward, something miraculous happened: All the participants, Croats, Serbs, Muslims and Jews, stepped forward as one, totally oblivious to police threats and possible brutalities.[22]

Branko—and probably many others who experienced this event—were deeply touched. However, Branko's father, Artur Polić, a savvy banker, realized that neither the stadium incident nor their conversion to Catholicism guaranteed survival. Polić was convinced that their only chance to live was leaving everything behind and exiting NDH territories. The Polić family, suitcases packed and ready, waited for an opportune moment. That moment came when Vilko Kuhnel, in a story that will be told in detail later in this chapter, issued 2,000 exit visas to Jews wishing to leave.

THE JEWISH LEADERSHIP IN SARAJEVO RECOMMENDS STAYING PUT

In late 1940 and early 1941 the debate relative to Nazi ideology in the Yugoslav Jewish press subsided. As danger loomed, the Jewish press became introspective in trying to determine whether Zionism was a viable solution to their problem. Dr. Željko Lederer of Zagreb, in four articles, undertook to analyze the relevance of Zionism to questions of everyday life, which seemed a wasteful activity considering the British position regarding the issue of Jewish immigration to Palestine.[23] Rabbi Šalom Freiberger, the chief rabbi of Croatia, in his article "Assimilation and Segregation" dealing with dual forces operating within and without, discusses the disintegrative power of assimilation by emphasizing its "vanquished spiritual independence of Jewry." In these trying times, facing the Jews, his only advice was "learn to live."[24]

With the occupation of Yugoslavia and its dismemberment, the Jewish leadership in Zagreb and in most parts of Croatia had no specific advice or instructions for their members in light of the growing danger. In Sarajevo, however, the community's leaders requested that Jews remain where they were and listen to instructions from the Ustaše. Michael (Mišo) Montiljo recalled how his parents frequently asked their rabbi what to do. His answer was always the same: "Stay where you are; it is possible that they may send you to a labor camp, but eventually you will return to your homes."[25]

Although the Jews of Sarajevo, with a shared memory of four centuries, had known some discrimination, they had never encountered life-threatening situations. So it seemed inconceivable that they would be expelled from a city they helped build. Or was their earlier history now repeating itself? Would they experience what their Spanish ancestors had gone through during the Inquisition and the reign of Ferdinand and Isabella?

The Ustaše appointed Srečko Bujas, a Supreme Court judge, as a trustee responsible for overseeing the day-to-day affairs of the Sephardic Jewish Community in Sarajevo. Shortly after his appointment, Bujas visited Zagreb, where he learned of the Ustaše's plans to rid Sarajevo of its Jewish population. Immediately upon returning home, he let the Jewish leadership know what to expect, and urged them to encourage their members to leave Sarajevo. Despite Bujas' warnings, the leadership had the one same mantra, encouraging the city's Jews to remain.[26]

Nonetheless, within a few weeks of the occupation of Yugoslavia, many of the wealthier and more independent-minded Jews—who had always assisted the disadvantaged—had left the city. Those who remained were bullied and physically attacked, and in September, five months into the Nazi occupation and the Ustaše regime, some 70 percent of Sarajevo's Jewish population was deported to the NDH concentration camps. The situation of the remaining Jews was appalling. As Ivo Andrić, the Yugoslav 1961 Nobel Laureate in literature, described their centuries-old plight:

> During the Second World War, however, the dark, murderous onslaught of racism managed to disperse and destroy the Bosnian Sephardim, unprepared and unaccustomed as they were to this sort of fight. They had always wanted simply to live their lives, yet throughout their tortuous history they had always been deprived of a part of life. This time they were deprived of life itself.[27]

It is quite possible that most of these Jews, who had never on any occasion left Sarajevo, would have remained, even if given the opportunity to leave. It is also likely that many were overwhelmed by sentimental attachments to home and family and by their affection for Sarajevo. If leaving seemed worse than death, they would opt to stay.

Mišo Montiljo, a twelve-year-old boy, recognized that escape was the only way to survive. He recalled clearly the events of the night of June 1941, when the Ustaše, in the middle of the night, appeared at his family's home, began knocking on the door with their guns, and then in five dark and short moments whisked away his father and older brothers.

The comforting words of their rabbi no longer sounded reliable or reassuring. When, a few weeks later, the Ustaše took him, his mother, and sisters to a detention center, he realized that it was not too late to act. Pointing out to his mother an opening in the center's fence, he told her: "There are only two guards and many of us, we should leave." But his mother's warnings were loud and clear: "Do not dare do anything foolish, you will be punished." At that moment, he kissed her, bade her goodbye, and swiftly leaped the fence.

Unsure where to go, Mišo returned home. The door was already sealed, but he managed to enter through a broken bathroom window. In his heart he knew that what he had done was right and that he would survive.[28] When the Muslim next-door neighbors heard movements coming from the Montiljo's apartment, they cautiously knocked on the door and called his name. Mišo asked them to go to the rear of the house, where the broken window was. The neighbors handed him a tray of food and promised to get help. The following day, a woman whom Mišo had never met came to the house. She took him with her on a local train to Mostar in the Italian military zone. With a few words, the woman handed him a piece of paper on which was written the name and address of a person who would help him. Mišo thanked her and left on his own to find the address, which was a workshop in a shipyard. The name he had been given belonged to the workshop manager, who arranged for Mišo to apprentice. He also pointed him to a secluded corner where he could sleep. After six months or so, sometimes in mid-1942, the manager quietly informed Mišo that he should leave because the place was no longer safe. He also let Mišo know that Italian motorboats were transferring Jewish refugees from Mostar to the Adriatic coast. Mišo was lucky to have had several people—both friends and strangers—who cared for him and helped him reach safety in the Italian zone.

PETITION LETTERS ON BEHALF OF JEWS

Groups of individuals from all walks of life and diverse residential areas showed their discontent with the government's dissemination of antisemitic propaganda, its harsh decrees, and above all, its implementation of racial laws. They often did so by sending letters to the authorities expressing objections to the injustices they saw taking place around them. In the Croatian National Archive (HDA), I found 412 such petitions written by ordinary citizens and signed by many hundreds and possibly thousands. There were also 120 recommendations given by high officials, clergy, and professionals on behalf of Jewish friends, colleagues, and neighbors, with whom they had coexisted amicably for years. The thousands of Croatians who signed these letters aimed to reverse the injustices inflicted upon one segment of the population not because of wrongdoing but rather because they belonged to a particular religion. The letters clearly manifested the petitioners' naïve belief that their government was ethical, if also misinformed. Accordingly, the petitioners steadfastly tried to set the record straight by, for example, pointing out the positive attributes of those on whose behalf they were writing. Initially, villagers and those living in smaller cities were oblivious to the fact that the new Croatian government—like other totalitarian regimes—had abolished the rule of law and turned to mob rule.

Most of the petitions originated in Croatia; very few came from the annexed territory of Bosnia-Herzegovina. The level of collaboration with the Nazi occupiers was higher in the multi-ethnic and multi-religious Bosnia-Herzegovina, where the various groups vied for favors and recognition. Thus, petitioning the authorities on behalf of a Jewish neighbor or friend could result in the death of an entire family. This concern was especially evident among Catholics in Sarajevo and Muslims. Archbishop Ivan Sarić and other priests openly sided with the Nazi-Ustaše ideology. Similarly, the Bosnian Muslims, with the help of Hajj Amin el Husseini, the Grand Mufti of Jerusalem, sought to convince Hitler that Bosnia-Herzegovina should be a separate Nazi Protectorate on the Croatian model. Hajj Amin's objectives regarding the fate of Jews in the region coincided with Hitler's. On November 28, 1941, Hitler told him that Germany had declared an uncompromising war on the Jews, while at the same time opposing a Jewish homeland in Palestine.[29] As a consequence of the Muslims' eagerness to please Hitler and his officials, more than 100,000 Muslim conscripts were raised to fight in special units alongside the Wehrmacht and SS troops.[30] While the upper echelon of the Muslims in Bosnia-Herzegovina worked closely with the Ustaše, many ordinary Muslims risked their lives by helping Jews escape from detention centers, cross borders, and find temporary shelter in Muslim villages. They did not, however, seek justice for the Jews in the form of petitions to the authorities.

There is evidence of some correlation between the citizens' petitions and the release of Jews from concentration camps. It is possible that certain individuals were released without knowing that letters had been written on their behalf, just as others went to their deaths never knowing that friends and neighbors had made an effort to save them. The following letters are evidence that some Croatians acted out of conscience and compassion in the face of government persecution of their fellow citizens, even at the risk of their own well-being.

In the small village of Velika Kopanica, in the district of Slavonski Brod, 103 residents signed a petition:

To the Minister of Finance, Zagreb   May 5, 1941

In our village reside a Jewish family and their daughter Branka Špicer, [who] owned a store. The Špicer family has lived in Velika Kopanica for approximately 50 years and during all this period they established friends and customers due to their honest conduct. But in recent days, the government has appointed a trustee over their store. This individual expects to be paid and he also has to set aside a portion of the profits for the commissariat. Since the Špicer store can support only one family, we the farmers of Kopanica request that the store be returned immediately to Branka and the trustee removed. We, the citizens' committee, who worked with the Špicer family, recognize that these good and loyal people, though Jewish, managed to live in our midst without ever harming any of us, yet always ready to extend help to all of us.[31]

Another letter, dated August 29, 1941, and addressed to the Head of the Zagorje District in the city of Varaždin, bears the signatures of seventy-two individuals who requested the release of neighbors from a concentration camp:

> The couple Josip and Josipa Klein and their two sons Ivica and Miroslav, [and] the brother of Josipa, Ljudevit, lived in a house in Dolić, a village near Krapina. The couple had a guesthouse and a local pub and they engaged in commerce. They were all born in Croatia and most of them lived in the same district for all of their lives. Their commerce was conducted honestly and efficiently; it was of great value to the local peasants to whom they gave food during the winter on trust and under most favorable terms. Because of their generosity, they had nothing else but the house they lived in and the plot around it. Josip Klein and his family acted no differently than any other Croat, they were socially accepted in our midst. Also, both are approaching 60 and are in poor health. Thus due to all the reasons mentioned above, we their neighbors and peasants, who know these decent people well, are asking for their release from the concentration camp and their permanent return to their home.[32]

The petitioners most often complained that the government was arbitrarily taking punitive measures against innocent Jews who lived by the law and contributed to the well-being of their communities. For example, the petition below concerned an apparent attempt by the Ustaše to deport the widow of Ljudevit Bauer. Eight neighbors signed a letter sent on July 14, 1941, which declared:

> The undersigned citizens of Croatia, residents of Podravska Slatina, state that it is true that in 1939, Ljudevit Bauer, a printer and an owner of a paper goods business for forty years, passed away. His upright conduct is still remembered fondly by the citizens of Slatina. … His wife is very ill and is currently in the care of the nuns in the hospital of Sestara Milosrdnica in Slatina. For all the reasons mentioned above, the undersigned citizens of Slatina recommend to the Ministry of the Interior to resolve the issue favorably by allowing her to remain in the nuns' care.[33]

In the case of Adolf Švarc, an officer with the Austrian forces in World War I, eleven of his comrades-in-arms attested to his heroism and loyalty to Croatia's national causes in a petition sent from Zagreb on July 23, 1941:

> Adolf Švarc, a commercial assistant, born in Vaska-Podravska-Slatina on 24.I.1899, son of Jakob Švarc, current resident of Zagreb. By the orders of the Ustaše he was sent to a concentration camp. The police, with no consideration that Adolf Švarc was an officer in the former 53rd infantry division in Zagreb and on 5.XII.1918 was awarded the highest Medal of Honor, took him to an unknown destination. Švarc fought valiantly against the Serbs in Zagreb. He fought for our country and he was sentenced by the Serbs to a prison term of 3.5 years. Since throughout the war, he was an outstanding soldier known for his bravery, we request that the Ministry of the Interior release Adolf Švarc from imprisonment and measures taken against the Jews should not be applied to him.[34]

And a letter of September 23, 1941, to the Ministry of the Interior bore signatures of seventy-two residents from Donja Lomnica. These neighbors requested the release of Alexander Šandor Loyi from the Jasenovac concentration camp. While Loyi was not described as a war hero, its signers recognized that, besides having lived in their community for thirty years and being known as a good friend, he was a loyal Croat.[35]

One surprising letter, written on September 23, 1941, by the mother of a loyal Ustaše, Matija Gubc, was sent directly to Ante Pavelić. Mrs. Gubc was distraught because of the regime's actions against honest, educated, and loyal citizens of Croatia who happened to be Jews. She explained that, from the very beginning, she had wholeheartedly supported the Ustaše cause: freeing Croatia from the clutches of the Serbian Kingdom. However, she could not understand why the Ustaše were sending educated and loyal citizens such as Dr. Kazimir Donner and his family to concentration camps. The Donners had always helped the poor and contributed to all of Croatia's important causes. Thus she implored Pavelić to protect, treasure, and rescue such people, who would be needed to help build a new and independent Croatia.[36]

In the first several months of the NDH, such letters, as well as other courageous and risky efforts to rescue individual Jews, were daily occurrences. Dr. Stjepan Steiner related one such incident that took place in Zagreb when the Ustaše captured his father and sent him to a detention center. His father, an admired and respected veterinarian who worked closely with the local peasants, was also a friend of Dr. Vladko Maček, the former head of the Croatian Peasant Party. When news of Dr. Steiner's arrest and incarceration spread, Dr. Maček, together with one thousand rowdy peasants, descended on the detention center on Savska Street, where they shouted: "We want our veterinarian [they called him Tasta] to be released." The next day their Tasta was released, along with all the others in his cell.[37]

The actions of thousands of Croatian citizens who petitioned on behalf of their Jewish neighbors, friends, employers, managers, husbands, and wives demonstrated widespread contempt for the Ustaše's treatment of Jews. Pavelić and his Ustaše were chosen by Nazi Germany and Fascist Italy, not elected by the Croatian people. Before they experienced the full scale of the regime's cruelty, Croats dared to protest and vocally denounce the injustices committed against innocent people. When they learned who their true enemies were, they began to join the Partisans in large numbers. The first secretary of the Italian embassy in Zagreb noted this widespread dissatisfaction with the NDH regime in 1942 in a dispatch to Rome:

> The general public in Croatia feels great distrust toward the new regime and is adversely affected by the repeated illegal activities of the unscrupulous Ustaše officials. The Croatian people are reacting very negatively to the anti-Jewish measures and are very skeptical about the further course of events.[38]

In fact, resistance came from all strata of society, and ordinary citizens dared as late March 12, 1943, to stand up for a neighbor:

Srečko Breyer, a Jewish merchant, who resided in the District of Jastrebarsko, near Zagreb, wrote a letter to the Minister of the Interior requesting Aryan rights for his mother, sister and for himself. He considered his family to be honorable and equal to any other citizen in the region. Brayer's request was seconded by 151 Croats.[39]

Brayer felt the confidence that he was wanted in the village and that his family had many supporters. I had no way of finding his whereabouts and fate.

TWO THOUSAND EXIT VISAS FOR THE JEWS OF ZAGREB

Dr. Vilko Kuhnel's story is known primarily to historians researching the history of Croatia during World War II. Yet his name would also be recognized by the surviving recipients of 2,000 exit visas he issued to Jews of Zagreb who wanted to leave the NDH. Kuhnel's connections with individual Jews began in mid-1941 when the Ustaše imposed on well-to-do Jews, particularly in Zagreb, a so-called "voluntary contribution." The basic assessment was 1,000 kg (2,200 lbs.) of 24K gold for the wealthiest Jews, with a sliding scale for those of somewhat lesser means. Since few would have access to so much gold, the contribution could also be made in works of art, porcelain, silver, or fine imported furniture of equivalent value. An initial deadline of eight days for the contribution was set.[40] To encourage compliance, the Ustaše first took hostage family members of the wealthiest Jews, promising life and security for their families in exchange for their "gold."[41]

The Pavelić government assigned the task of collecting the payments to Dido Kvaternik, the director of the Ustaše Office for Security and Public Order, and to his three deputies, one of whom was Kuhnel.[42] In June 1941, Kuhnel was promoted to head the Jewish Division of the Ustaše Surveillance Service (Ustaška nadzorna služba; UNS). In this position Kuhnel headed a department that dealt with everything that pertained to Jews. This job required daily interaction with the Jewish Community, whose involvement in the collections expedited the process. Because the regime lacked the professional know-how to determine the value of non-currency assets "donated" in lieu of gold, it released a number of Jewish lawyers who had been sent to concentration camps.

On August 6, 1945, Dr. Robert Glucksthal, one of these lawyers, testified before a National Commission,[43] that he and Dr. Milan Brihta, among others, had been released from Kerestinec, a Ustaše concentration camp. Although the lawyers were initially overjoyed to get this new lease on life, when back in Zagreb, they learned that they would be working with the "voluntary contribution board." Since few of these contributions were delivered as pure gold, most of their work consisted of appraising the value of foreign currencies, works of art, precious stones, silver, and the like, and determining their equivalency in gold. Many of the lawyers who were fortunate enough to be recalled from concentration camps, and who later seized the right moment to flee Zagreb, survived.[44]

In 1945, Hinko Mann submitted written testimony to the National Commission describing the circumstances that led him to work with Kuhnel. His invitation to join the collections board came from Julius Koenig, one of the wealthiest Jews in Zagreb and head of the Jewish Community board in charge of encouraging the "voluntary contributions."[45] Although the first few days' receipts seemed promising, the response slowed down by the end of the first week. Many Jews had no intention of paying the enormous sums assessed by their own community, and the Ustaše insisted on prompt delivery.[46] Not wishing to forfeit further "contributions," the Ustaše extended the deadline repeatedly until the end of January 1942.

Soon after Kuhnel's appointment to head the UNS in June 1941, Dr. Laufer, another board member, and Mann, paid him a visit, ostensibly to discuss the "contributions." Finding Kuhnel surprisingly hospitable, Mann decided to seize this moment of "good will" to ask his opinion on the Ustaše's harsh measures against the Jews. Kuhnel responded: "I am in the first place a human being and then a lawyer. I think that with this statement I answered everything."[47] Realizing that Kuhnel might be amenable to extending assistance, Mann subsequently inquired whether he, as head of the UNS Jewish division, might be in a position to issue exit visas to

Jews who had already paid their assessments, or to those who might be encouraged to do so, knowing that they would then be able to leave.

Kuhnel claimed that he had no jurisdiction over visas, but said he was willing to try. Thus he delegated an assistant to ask the NDH Passport [Travel] Division for visa applications. When the assistant received the documents, Kuhnel realized that he did have the authority to issue exit visas. Once supplied with the official forms, the UNS Jewish division began distributing exit permits stamped with its own seal. When that aroused suspicion, Kuhnel began issuing visas stamped with a generic seal that did not identify the issuing agency. Mann claimed that this ruse granted more than 2,000 Jews the document that allowed them to leave Zagreb and the NDH territories.[48] While Mann's initial proposition linked the visa to fulfilling an assessed "contribution," many of the Jews who met their payment had no desire to leave Zagreb, in some cases because they understood that they had effectively purchased a guarantee of protection from the NDH. Branko Polić and his parents were among the Jews who used one of the visas to flee. In an interview, he explained that since more visas were issued than there were takers, Kuhnel's office and the Jewish board began distributing them to Jews like his family who had little or no money to contribute, but who wanted to get out.[49]

As they continued to work together, Mann reported to Kuhnel on the terrible sufferings of Zagreb's Jews. Kuhnel routinely responded that his hands were tied and that he was powerless to change their conditions. Nonetheless, he warned board members about anticipated round-ups and also suggested to Mann and possibly others how the Jewish Communities could improve conditions for Jews in concentration camps. Knowing that they would have greater concern for their own people than would the Ustaše camp officials, Kuhnel suggested they deliver food to the camps themselves rather than giving it to the Ustaše to deliver. Moreover, if the Jewish Communities of Zagreb, Osijek, and Sarajevo were to assume responsibility for camp maintenance, they would ensure that such facilities as bunk beds and toilets were refurbished before inmates arrived. Kuhnel was also instrumental in closing the Kruščica concentration camp, which was in deplorable condition.[50]

Despite Kuhnel's high position, he risked his life by cooperating with the Jews beyond what his position required. In his testimony to the postwar commission, Mann stressed that Kuhnel had never asked for payment for his deeds.[51] Naturally, the Jews who obtained exit visas from Kuhnel were eternally grateful to him. Nonetheless, the same man who helped these Jews to escape also obeyed orders that sent thousands of other Jews to concentration camps. In this duality, Dr. Vilko Kuhnel resembled a number of other Croatian officials historians encounter from this period, as will be discussed in Chapter 3. Kuhnel, unlike other officials, vacillated between universal values of humanity and decency, on the one hand, and the desire for power and greed on the other. His fear of punishment from those in more powerful positions apparently drove him to commit heinous crimes, while some second nature or learned values led him to extend humanitarian help. Toward the end of the war, Kuhnel committed suicide, recognizing his fate if captured by the Partisans.

After the war, because of his dealings with Kuhnel, the Allied occupation authorities in Bari, Italy, incarcerated Hinko Mann on charges of corruption and suspicion of collaboration with the enemy. After scores of witnesses were questioned, he was released without charge and exonerated on September 20, 1945. Mann observed that he had never expected gratitude for his deeds on behalf of many of Zagreb's citizens, but he did not expect "that his name would be dragged into the mud." Thus the purpose of his subsequent testimony to the inquiry commission was not just to praise Kuhnel; rather he also wanted both to clear his name of any taint of collaboration and to let Zagreb's surviving Jews know about the instrumental role he had played in enabling many of them to escape.[52]

WHO WAS LIKELY TO SURVIVE

Historians of the Holocaust in Germany have used the term "social death" to describe the progressive disassociation by ordinary Germans from their former Jewish friends and neighbors.[53] Yugoslavian Jews might have experienced a similar process had the transition from peace to war taken six years, as it did in Germany. In the NDH, however, the period of intense and aggressive antisemitic propaganda was brief, beginning in earnest only in April 1941, when Germany occupied the territories of Croatia and Bosnia-Herzegovina. Many ordinary Croatians expressed no hostility toward their Jewish employers or neighbors, and many had Jewish family members through intermarriage. Thus, efforts by the Nazis and Ustaše to demean and vilify the Jews apparently had a moderate effect on the opinion of individual Croats, although a considerable number succumbed to greed and took advantage of the opportunity to loot Jewish assets.

The circumstances differed considerably in Sarajevo and in Bosnia-Herzegovina. Not only did the Muslim elite join the Ustaše, they also wished to please the Germans, who established their headquarters in the city. The large German presence made it much harder for local citizens to act on behalf of their Jewish friends and neighbors once the racial laws and related ordinances were implemented. Those who dared to show even the smallest measure of kindness toward the Jews faced immediate accusations of assisting the enemy. The SS, the Gestapo, the Ustaše Catholics and Muslims acted together to make the Jews social pariahs, culpable for whatever ills plagued Sarajevo's residents.[54]

It is difficult to determine from testimonies and other records the extent of help Sarajevo's citizens provided to the city's Jews. Nonetheless, most of the survivors, numbering approximately 2,500 to 3,000, surely received assistance in varying degrees from non-Jews. Regina Perera, for example, described how, on October 24, 1941, her mother Ella, along with Regina and her older brother Isak (ages 2 and 4), left Sarajevo accompanied by a Muslim acquaintance of their father. He brought them to his village, where they formally converted to Islam. They took new names—Ermina for Ella, Ibrahim for Isak, and Sadika for Regina. They chose to keep their surname Perera, but from then on, they adopted Muslim dress and customs.

Since Ella had received no news from her husband, at an opportune moment she decided to take her children and leave the village.

Accompanied by a Muslim friend, they proceeded to Mostar, where they joined up with other family members. From Mostar, they reached the Adriatic coast, where they found passage aboard a private ship, landing in Italy in December 1941. The Italians offered them protection as "enemy civilian internees." They were no longer acting as Muslims; they reverted to Judaism when in Italy.[55]

Regina's father, Mojse Moric Perera, a merchant and industrialist, planned to join them once he settled his affairs in Sarajevo. However, despite his many business connections, he was captured on October 25, 1941, and deported to the Jasenovac concentration camp. Miraculously, his family—by then in Italy—received several postcards that he mailed while incarcerated. The first, dated March 31, 1942, was from Jasenovac; the second, dated May 22, came from the Stara Gradišk camp. He had been transferred back to Jasenovac when he mailed the third postcard eighteen months later, on December 12, 1943, and he remained there until June 9, 1944, the date on the last postcard his family received. Their hopes were high that if he had survived this long in Jasenovac, he might live to see the peace. However, evidence points to his having been killed toward the end of the war.

In an interview, Šarika Kaveson reminisced about her time as one of the first Jewish victims of the Ustaše regime in Sarajevo. She recalled in particular that many of the city's residents came to the detention centers to visit their friends and neighbors. In Šarika's case, it was Hakya Gengić, a former housekeeper, who came to ask how she could help. Since only a few guards were around, Šarika replied: "Please, take my two children out of here, and in a few days I will manage to escape." Because the housekeeper knew the children well, it was natural for her to hold their hands as if they were her own. After a few days, Šarika—disguised as a Muslim woman and accompanied by a former employee Arif Pozdar who was Muslim—left the detention center and rejoined her children in Maria's home. For six weeks they hid there until Maria was able to obtain forged visas for Mostar. Many were not as lucky as Šarika, who had loyal and brave employees as well as the courage and optimism to voluntarily surrender her children in the conviction that she would soon find a way to rejoin them.[56]

The rescue narrative of Leon Kabiljo, a Sarajevo industrialist in wool and silk, began with the confiscation of his factory a few days after the German forces entered Sarajevo. One of Kabiljo's many workers was Josip (Jozo) Eberhardt, a mechanic of German (Volksdeutsche) ancestry. The two men had bonded in friendship and trust; for example, Kabiljo had helped Eberhardt set up a home when he married Rozika, another factory worker. Shortly after Kabiljo's factory was nationalized, the Nazis recruited Eberhardt as a translator for a Gestapo unit. He did not want to serve in this capacity, but after consultation with Kabiljo, they concluded that he had no choice.

On the night of September 3, 1941, the Gestapo and the Ustaše planned a major roundup of Jews on two of Sarajevo's main streets, on one of which Kabiljo and his family lived. When Eberhardt learned of the plan, he ran to Kabiljo's home and told him to be ready to leave with his family before dawn. As planned, the Kabiljo family arrived at Eberhardt's apartment, whereupon it was decided that the Kabiljos would remain in hiding there as long as it took to obtain four authentic-looking travel visas for Mostar. In the end, they remained there for two months before they could leave Sarajevo. This story, while not unique in a time of war, is nevertheless special, attesting as it does that human bonds are frequently stronger than religious affiliations, loyalty to a country, and even danger.

Escapes such as those recounted required the courage to leave everything behind as well as the ingenuity to elude a network of informers, Ustaše, SS, and Gestapo. Those trying to flee had to have faith that they could detect who might betray them and who would be willing to help them, whether for a fee or as a matter of conviction, religious belief, compassion, or friendship. Most individuals who offered their help knew that both the Ustaše and the Nazis defined assisting Jews as an act of treason, punishable by death. Nevertheless, many took on the responsibility and hid or brought Jews to the border separating the NDH from the Italian occupation zones.

One morning in early September 1941, Regina Kamhi awakened and discovered that during the night the SS and the Ustaše had taken away her extended family. Her husband had already escaped to the Italian zone. Now she had to decide on her own next move. Luck had so far been on her side, since she had only by accident escaped her family's fate. A few weeks earlier officials had requisitioned her apartment to house two Aryan families, with whom she shared the space. Since it was no longer registered in her husband's name, it was not searched. Penniless, with a two-year-old, and expecting a second child any day, Regina anxiously considered what a woman in her condition should do. Following a certain logic, she decided to go to the hospital where she was registered to give birth. Regina's physicians, Dr. Jelka Knezević-Švarc, who was Russian Orthodox, and Dr. Bokonjić, a Muslim, reassured her that as long as she was in their care, her own and her children's safety were guaranteed. Although the Ustaše frequently made unexpected visits to the hospital, the staff of the maternity ward kept silent about her presence.

After the birth of Regina's second son, the physicians suggested that she should remain in the hospital for at least two additional weeks. In the meantime, her former maid Marica Odobašić, a Catholic, learned of Regina's whereabouts. A day before Regina was to be discharged; Marica was notified and brought the three of them to her home. While Regina was recuperating, Marica established contact with her relatives who lived in Mostar. They arranged for Regina to obtain forged travel papers in the name of a Muslim woman and her two children.

When the documents finally arrived, they came with a note from the relatives suggesting that Regina avoid showing them to border control because of their poor quality. On the train to Mostar, dressed as a Muslim woman, Regina covered herself and the baby with a large blanket and pretended to nurse him, whenever she encountered border inspectors. To Regina's relief, most inspectors paid scant attention to her. The one time they did begin harassing her, a Muslim gentleman, whom she had never met before, but who recognized her plight, came to her rescue by firmly telling the inspectors: "Don't you see that she is nursing; come later." Regina thinks the man recognized from the way she acted that the Muslim garb was a cover-up. She never learned who the man was, or why he chose to take an enormous risk to save a Jewish woman and her children.[57]

Even some of the Ustaše acted first and foremost as friends and neighbors, for example, letting Jews know of impending roundups or urging them to move to areas where it was safer to spend the night. Both Eva Grlić and Nada Grgeć,[58] from Zagreb, related that for weeks, because of such warnings, they and their families had moved daily from one neighborhood to another to sleep at night. Such actions might not have offered permanent safety, but in some cases could have allowed time to organize other escape plans. In addition to the two cases from Zagreb, Lotika Papo from Sarajevo related how a Muslim Ustaše activist, Mohammed Mahtević, would frequently appear in their neighborhood and tell her father, who was Jewish: "Albert, it is time for you to climb to the attic for a few days." Mahtević's information was valuable, but for both men the experience was traumatizing.[59] The rest of Albert Papo's ordeal is told later in this chapter. There are no data to determine how many Ustaše members helped Jews, but I intend that the many such cases I discovered during my interviews become a part of our oral history.

Slavko Goldstein's story, mentioned previously, also includes a Ustaše who helped his brother survive. Slavko was thirteen, and his younger brother nine, when his parents were captured and deported to a detention center in Zagreb. When their mother was released, she wanted her sons with her. Slavko's brother was staying with his grandfather in Tuzla, Bosnia. It would have been almost impossible, if not outright dangerous, for his mother to go and fetch her son. A young Ustaše, a son of an acquaintance, volunteered to travel, in uniform, to Tuzla and bring the boy to his mother.[60]

Such rescue stories, where friends, acquaintances, and even strangers freely or for a nominal price offered shelter and assistance to Jews, happened frequently. Every survivor could probably tell similar narratives. In fact, these accounts are much more than stories; they are vitally important lessons of survival in extraordinarily dangerous times. Both rescuers and rescued had to seize opportunities to act, aware that each one was ephemeral and that there might not be another. Survivors frequently commented that rescue was a state of mind, meaning that the process of rescue began when individuals made up their minds to escape and live, and then, with courage and without hesitation, took a leap of faith on the path to survival. Such courageous leaps are present in every survival story, such as the one Šarika Kaveson took when she handed over her children to her former maid with the conviction that she would somehow escape from the detention center. Or when Leon Kabiljo decided to trust his former employee and placed his entire family under Josip Eberhardt's protection, although he knew that the man was a Volksdeutsche employed by the Gestapo.

In addition to good friends and neighbors, or connections to those in power, ready cash could increase one's odds of survival. As Ella Finci-Koen recalled in an interview: "In those days of World War II, one had to have a lot of money, or else."[61] Without extraordinary determination and a willingness to take great risks, chances of survival for those without money depended mainly on luck. Those who wished to escape Sarajevo with professionally faked exit visas paid the going price, and knowledgeable guides cost even more. Most of the early escapes in Bosnia used Muslim disguises, a major expense if it meant purchasing clothing for the entire family.

Ella Finci-Koen, whose father was a well-known businessman, knew the importance of money first-hand. With the exception of her older brother, her entire family was captured on October 21, 1941, and sent to a detention center in a former military building in Sarajevo. After a few days locked in a shoddily constructed cell, a Ustaše named Sokol approached them. He knew Ella's father because he had been a local policeman before the war. Sokol asked straightforwardly if they wanted to escape. Their answer of course was positive, whereupon he opened the cell and they walked out, no questions asked. Ella had no idea how much and in which currency her father paid their helper; the transactions took place in great secrecy.

Before their departure, Sokol's warnings were clear: "Do not go to your apartment and do not visit the neighborhood. Disperse immediately." Ella, age ten, and her mother left Sarajevo dressed in Muslim garb, with authentic identification and travel documents purchased from a

Muslim woman who, along with her daughter, planned to return to her native village. This was a mutually valuable exchange. The woman did not need the identification cards, but she did need money for food; Ella and her mother needed documents on which professionals could affix their photographs. Without a hitch, Ella and her mother reached the safety of Mostar.

The rest of the Finci family remained in Sarajevo. Ella's twin brother and her older sister were captured and deported to the Stara Gradiška concentration camp. Luckily for them, that camp was overcrowded, so their transport returned to Sarajevo. Knowing the whereabouts of Ella's father, Sokol informed him about the transport on which his two children were returning. As soon as the train arrived in Sarajevo, Sokol again appeared, and this time he managed to whisk away the two teenagers. Ella later heard her father say that Sokol was paid handsomely. But she immediately added: "There was nothing for free, and we had to pay for everything." She expressed no anger about this:

> After all, these people were poor and they risked their lives, they needed the money to feed their own families. The Fincis felt fortunate that they had the money to exchange for their lives.[62]

According to available data, approximately 25 to 30 percent of Sarajevo's Jews survived—most of these survivors had escaped from the city. Those who remained had little hope of survival unless they were married to Aryans, a category that included Muslims and Catholics, or worked for the railroad—now run by the NDH—which employed many Jews. Especially in Sarajevo, women, children, and the elderly were the main categories of Jewish victims. The reason for this demographic imbalance was that the first transports from Sarajevo, in the early days of the war, intentionally targeted males ages thirteen to sixty. The Ustaše sought to rid the city of potential enemy fighters, and the Muslims wanted to prevent men from leaving for Palestine. As a consequence, most families made a particular effort to first send their men to the Italian zones. In addition, although women joined the Partisans, males in the ages targeted by the Ustaše for transports predominated.[63]

Of course, each Jewish family had to make its own existential decision. who should be the first to leave. Jakica Danon related how families had to make very painful decisions regarding what to sell for cash and whom to send with the proceeds. In his family it was decided that the father should be the first to leave; however, when the time came for his departure, he refused to leave his family behind. That same night he was deported. Nonetheless, Jakica and his two older sisters, all teenagers, managed on their own to escape through the mountains. Along the way they met other young people who, like them, carried only one backpack, walked during the night and rested by days.[64] All three reached Mostar.

Zlata Romano, another survivor from Sarajevo, repeatedly emphasized: "In those days, timing was everything." In October 1941 she and her husband, Moric Romano, had been married less than a year and were expecting their first child. They made all the necessary preparations to depart Sarajevo; their packed suitcases were waiting by the door, but so were the Ustaše, who came at dawn. Along with several hundred others, the Romanos were deported to Kruščica, a Bosnian concentration camp. After a few days, the men were all transferred to Jasenovac. Zlata, with many other women, was deported to the Loborgrad concentration camp. She was fortunate that a Ustaše woman guard took a liking to her, possibly because of her pregnancy or because of her remarkable beauty. Whatever the reason, Zlata never learned why this woman risked her life by letting her escape. Moving cautiously on foot and by hitchhiking she finally found her way to Zagreb and the Jewish Community. With their help she reached the Community Hospital, *Opća Bolnica Sestara Milosrednica,*[65] where she gave birth to her son Miro (meaning peace). After a short recuperation, the nuns let Zlata leave the hospital without notifying the authorities. Having no news from her husband, she strapped Miro on her back and, with a few belongings donated by Zagreb's Jewish Community, headed toward the Adriatic coast.

After the capitulation of Italy, in October 1943, from a small island near Korčula, Zlata reached Bari, Italy. In an operation discussed in Chapter 5, she along with thousands of other refugees, many non-Jews, crossed the Adriatic in a rescue operation that involved both the

Partisans and the Allies. Once in Italy, again like many other survivors, she received aid from several humanitarian organizations, among them the Red Cross and DELASEM (Delegazione per l'Assistena degli Emigranti Ebrei; Delegation for the Assistance of Jewish Emigrants). Returning to Sarajevo in May 1945, Zlata Romano was reunited with her husband Moric, who had escaped Jasenovac and joined the Partisans. He returned as a decorated officer in Tito's Army. [66]

Jews who had joined the Communist Party before the war received assistance from their comrades. Before they organized into a fighting force popularly known as the Partisans, the communists had secret locations in mountainous regions throughout the NDH, where members congregated in preparation for war. From their cells, individual members were either sent into the mountains or assigned to reach the Italian zones. Initially they offered help only to those who were known party members and single, in other words, those who were considered trustworthy and able to fight without the impediments of family. Months into the war, however, they began to accept anyone who managed to reach them in the mountains and forests. [67]

Eva Grlić and her husband were communists. He was captured and killed in Zagreb. Although their apartment was confiscated at the beginning of the war, Eva remained in Zagreb with her mother and infant daughter, Vesna. [68] Every day, they searched for a place to spend the night, a procedure that was both physically and psychologically exhausting. When Eva and her mother decided to join the Partisans, they first had to find accomodiations for Vesna. A few days after their decision, while Eva was walking about, she met a good friend, Ruža Gregorovich Fux, whom she knew well from their days in the party's youth group. Ruža was of German ancestry and married to a Jewish man. As soon as she learned of Eva's plan to join the Partisans, she responded: "Please, do what you feel is right; I have only one child, a few months older than Vesna, leave her with me." [69] With a heavy heart, but knowing her daughter was in good hands, Eva left Vesna in Zagreb. The Ustaše did not target the offspring of mixed marriages. In May 1945, Eva returned to Zagreb to reclaim a child whom she barely knew.

Edit Armuth, along with her parents and two hundred other Jews, decided to stay on the Island of Rab after Italy's capitulation in September 1943, opting not to be evacuated by the Partisans. In written testimony to the National Commission, she recalled how, on March 19, 1944, the Nazis—having encountered no resistance—had invaded the island from five different landing sites. The local population risked their lives by hiding the Jews. Edit was among 180 Jews whom the Nazis captured, took to the port of Rijeka, and then deported by train to Auschwitz. While on Rab, Edit had joined the Partisans. Because of this connection, Edit was welcomed into the inner circle of the Association of Anti-Fascist Women (AFŽ) incarcerated in Auschwitz. She recalled that these women's "boundless support, nurture and protection" while she was ill for six weeks "delivered me out of Auschwitz."[70] Her experience should be of great importance to scholars and others interested in the survival of Jews in concentration camps.

The stories recounted here, augmented by many not mentioned in this chapter, make it clear that the decision to leave everything behind and flee was a prerequisite for survival. Youth, connections, and money were equally important factors. Most survivors I interviewed stressed timing, being in the right place at the right moment, as well as sheer luck, as essential to survival.[71] Those who made up their minds to leave early in the war, when there was considerable confusion due to the change of regimes and when instructions were still unclear as to who should be captured and detained, fared better than those who attempted to flee later. In the case of Bosnia, it took the Nazis and the Ustaše some time to realize that many Jews were either accompanied by Muslims or used Muslim clothing as protective shields.

RESCUE OF JEWS BY INDIVIDUALS IN HOSPITAL

On September 1, 1944, SS Sturmbannführer Korndorfer delivered a list of forty names, twenty-four of which belonged to Jews, to Einsatzkommando SS Obersturmbannführer Hans Helm in Zagreb.[72] Helm opened a new file: *Notification Number 20*, Dr. Juraj Vranešić sanatorium for the mentally ill. It was alleged that Vranešić's sanatorium primarily sheltered Jews and Serbs who were not mentally ill. Korndorfer's document indicated that these so-called "patients" had been enjoying "the good life," regularly receiving visitors or even venturing into the center of Zagreb for coffee. Because there is no indication that the list was updated, it is assumed that most of the "patients" remained in the sanatorium at least until the fall of 1944. Although it is not clear how many of them survived, at least two Jews, Milan Sachs, the conductor of the Zagreb Opera, and his wife, stayed there from 1941 until the end of the war in 1945.[73]

The Belgrade Jewish Historical Museum (JIM) contains hundreds of documents dealing with Jews who were hidden in a variety of hospitals in Zagreb and its environs. Such acts of rescue usually depended on the will of one or a few people who took great risks by assisting Jews in their battle to survive. In some cases hospitals received payments for their services via the Jewish Community in Zagreb, which settled most of the accounts from funds they received from abroad or from local and international humanitarian organizations. Whether to protect the identity of those who sent money to support relatives and friends or because the hospitals did not want to depend on individuals for payment, in most cases the Jewish Community served as a liaison between the payee and the hospital.

The Zagreb hospitals that most frequently appear in archival documents are: the Community/General Hospital of the Sisters of Mercy (Opča Bolnica Sestara Milosredinica);[74] the State Hospital at St. Duhu (Državna Bolnica na Sv. Duhu);[75] the Municipal Hospital for Contagious Diseases (Bolnica za zarazne bolesti);[76] the Clinics of the Medical Faculty, Zagreb (Klinika med. Fakulteta Zagreb);[77] and the Regional Hospital at Rebro (Uprava zkladne bolnice na Rebru). Individuals who found shelter in these hospitals, however temporary, were probably saved.

On June 16, 1943, Zagreb's general hospital run by the Sisters of Mercy sent a bill to the Jewish Community totaling 8,440 kunas for three patients: Leo Braff, who had been hospitalized for sixty-two days; Oskar Scheiber, for nine days; and Berta Dorner, for fourteen days, at a rate of

100 kuna per day.[78] A bill of 15,700 kunas on August 4 again covered Leo Braff, as well as Salamon Hochstader. In another case, the Jewish Community, when sending Osias Ringl to the hospital for surgery, asked to be billed for thirty days.[79] It is not clear why the community specified the number of days of hospitalization before the patient was operated on; is it possible that it had to be done for accounting purposes or for the safely of the patient?

Even from documents that deal primarily with accounting matters between the Zagreb Jewish Community and the city's hospitals, one can glean relevant information on hospitals as places of refuge for Jews. They and their personnel clearly provided shelter and care for hundreds of endangered individuals. While for some they provided long periods of shelter, a reprieve of a few days might make a difference between life and death. Earlier chapters related three rescues in which hospitals played key roles. Two of these cases—those of Zlata Romano and Regina Kamhi—involved women who sought hospitals to give birth, but who then found medical help and protection from brave physicians. The third case was that of Albert Papo from Sarajevo, whose state of health was revealed by his daughter Lotika Papo Latinović. Physicians in the general hospital in Sarajevo sheltered Albert for six months until he was cured of a serious lung infection. Despite the anecdotally high rate of rescue in hospitals, the actual survival rate of Jews in hospitals is unknown, and the subject needs further investigation.

In the many cases when a hospital did not charge for its services, it is likely that the administrators were unaware that some of their physicians were shielding Jews. In an interview, Dr. Ante Fulgosi revealed how, as a medical student assigned to a hospital in Gospić, he had rescued fifteen inmates who had been sent for treatment from the local concentration camp, Maksimović-logor. Fulgosi attributed his success to the cooperation he received from several nuns who worked in the hospital. For example, after the physical examination of inmates, Fulgosi recommended that some of them required further treatment. He also obtained forged documents and travel papers for some of the people in his care. The patients whose lives Fulgosi's actions saved included Dr.

Emil Freundlich, Elza Polak, Eva Krajanski-Akerman, and Davor Band (mentioned in Chapter 5).

In the case of his friend Davor Band, Dr. Fulgosi even offered his Italian identification card, which he possessed because of his origins in Dalmatia. They carefully replaced Fulgosi's picture with Band's, but left the name Ante Fulgosi.[80] Under this false identity, Band lived uneventfully for four years under Italian occupation in Split, while the real Fulgosi ran the risk of being caught without proper documents.

POSTWAR REGISTRATION OF JEWS

When the war ended and the surviving Jews returned to their communities, the authorities requested that they reestablish their organizations for the purpose of collecting data and distributing food and clothing donated by international humanitarian organizations. The questions they asked the survivors were routine: name, surname, date and place of birth, name of parents, profession, and current employment, as well as the names and ages of immediate family members residing in the same household.[81] The survivors were also asked about their whereabouts during the war. Their responses, which are presented in the chart below, provide critical statistical information. The data are, however, seriously incomplete in that they record the locations of survival only for the head of a family, and only the names and ages of surviving family members. This was a grave omission since in most cases family members were separated during the war. As mentioned, men were most often the first to escape and among the first taken to concentration camps. They were also often among those who survived as prisoners of war in Germany; from Sarajevo 127 men survived as prisoners of war. Under these circumstances, women often became heads of families, and, with responsibility for the elderly as well as for young children, they had limited mobility. Nevertheless, the data gathered is extremely valuable in allowing us to understand the many ways Jews survived. It also confirms that the men who escaped Sarajevo early into the war had the highest rates of survival: teenagers and men up to age forty—those groups that the Ustaše, both Croats and Muslims, wanted to exterminate first.[82]

Immediately after the war, the United Nations initiated a process of collecting and processing demographic information, which began in 1945 and ended in 1952. Each family was given one card on which to enter pertinent information. In Yugoslavia, the distribution of questionnaires and the collating of information from the years 1941 to 1952 was the responsibility of the Jevresko Kulturno Prosvejetno Društvo Sloboda (The Jewish Historical and Cultural Society). The agency in charge of this project, the United Nations Relief and Rehabilitation Administration

Jewish survivors who lived in Sarajevo before the war and returned to the city during the years 1945 to 1952.[84]

Survival Locations 1941–1945	Heads of family	Family members identified by family heads	Total # of survivors
Concentration Camps, both German-administered and Croatian	86	55	141
Dalmatia: Korčula, Split, Dubrovnik, and other locations	139	33	172
POWs in Germany	127	123	250
NOB & NOV (Partisans groups), from 1941	114	27	141
Rab (island on Adriatic Coast)1943, Partisans 1943-1945.	667	274	941
Italy (before September 8, 1943)	82	78	160
In Sarajevo	138	129	267
Rescue in other or unspecified Locations within NDH	222	161	393
Total	1,575	880	2,455

(UNRRA), required accountability; thus, every survivor's family, before receiving its weekly rations, had to register with the local Jewish Community. Despite the acute need for rations, some 200 survivors' families in Sarajevo refused to register with the Jewish Community, remembering that the administrators of the Jewish Communities had given lists of their members to the Ustaše and the Gestapo.[83]

In expectation that peace would come, the United States, Great Britain, the Soviet Union, and representatives of the Nazi-occupied nations of Europe, in agreement on the need for a postwar United Nations assistance, gave their support to an effort to reconstruct what had happened during the war, in part as a basis for what they hoped would be a just and lasting peace. Consequently, they encouraged each of the occupied nations to create its own commission to investigate crimes by the occupation forces and their collaborators. In the territories of the former Yugoslavian Kingdom, this led in 1944 to the establishment of a separate *Croatian National Commission and the Yugoslav Commission for the Ascertainment of Crimes Committed against the Jews by the Occupiers and their Collaborators.*[85] Yugoslavia engaged in every republic hundreds of historians, lawyers, and accountants with the skills to establish what had happened, how it happened and why, as well as the identity of the perpetrators. The investigating task force had the right to subpoena witnesses and survivors with first-hand information to testify about atrocities committed against the Jews. An additional task confronting the commissions was to determine not only the number of casualties but also the financial loss, injuries, and deaths extrapolated from the number of those who survived. In this regard the authorities encountered several major problems.

As mentioned earlier, historian Gerald Reitlinger has observed that: "In no country of Axis-occupied Europe is the fate of Jewry more difficult to trace than in Yugoslavia."[86] The lack of accurate data begins with the way in which Jewish Communities historically collected internal data; for example, they rarely reported the death of a young child or a Jewish visitor who came from another country and decided to stay, not to mention the many transient refugees that passed through Yugoslavia, some of whom decided to stay without a visa or other legal documents. The

Jewish Communities, like other ethnic groups, were responsible for collecting their own demographic data, as parishes had long been throughout Europe. Three different statisticians and historians have made notable efforts to assess Yugoslavia's prewar Jewish population: David Levi-Dale estimated approximately 75,000 Jews in 1941 Yugoslavia;[87] Albert Vajs, a leader of the Jewish Communities of Yugoslavia, approximated the number at 71,000;[88] and Jaša Romano, who spent an inordinate number of days working with a wide cross-section of documents and records, came up with the largest and certainly the most precise number: 82,242.[89] Given the major numerical discrepancies and the disagreements among experts, it seems unwise to invest too many words on an issue that ultimately does not affect the purpose of this book.

The inability to establish the exact number of Jews in prewar Yugoslavia does of course prevent any accurate assessment of how many survived and how many perished during the war. Unfortunately, counting the number of survivors was not an option. Disregarding such problems as the chaos and destruction that followed world war and civil war, any such count would have missed the many Jews who crossed the borders of Yugoslavia and never returned. And some Jews who did return to their former cities and villages refused to register with the local Jewish Communities. Some refused because of the consequences of their previous self-identification as Jews and out of continuing fear of government authorities. Others had joined the Partisans or Marshal Tito's government. In line with communist ideology, they no longer defined themselves by their ancestral faith.

My interviewees provided a few stories that have helped me understand how easily errors could be introduced into the records. Dr. Teodor Gruner, for example, recalled an incident that he had previously considered private. In May 1941, his fiancée, Matilda Berger, was sent to a detention center in Zagreb, pending deportation. As a physician on government assignment in Bosnia, he had the privilege of asking his immediate family—wife, children, and parents—to join him. By marrying Matilda before his departure for Bosnia, he could rescue her from nearly certain death. However, his immediate superiors had a bureaucratic problem, namely, how to release his fiancée from detention without causing procedural and legal chaos. Their ingenious solution was to declare Matilda Berger dead and release Matilda Gruner, a name that did not appear on the center's records. As a result of this deception, one still finds Matilda Berger on the list of Yugoslavian Jews who perished, and Matilda Gruner among the survivors. Thus, one individual appeared in both columns—once accurately, but once in error.

After the war, both government agencies and the Jewish Communities compared their lists of survivors with registers from the prewar period. While working in the Croatian National Archives during the academic year 2002–2003, I found in the *Dotrščina* files [90] a list compiled by archivists in the 1990s of Jews from Zagreb who were believed to have perished during the war. Yet in other documents in the same archive I found indications that some of the Jews who allegedly died in 1941 were still alive in 1943, and even in 1945. The archive's director, Dr. Josip Kolanović, explained that when the lists were compiled it was assumed that any Jew deported to a concentration camp in 1941 would be dead. Yet some individuals, however improbably, did survive even long incarceration in the camps. And while the case of the "two Mathildas" involved obsessive record-keeping, in other cases, it was sloppy, and no record was made of an inmate who was released. For example, Djuro Schwarz, who himself conducted research in this area, arrived in the Jasenovac camp in August 1941. Accordingly, the archive's researchers listed him as dead. Yet he was released in April 1942 as a spouse in a mixed marriage. [91] As discussed in Chapter 3, the NDH government released from the camps a number of Jews with valuable professional skills, without always correcting the records. Individuals whose names did not appear after the war in either the Dotrščina file or the Jewish Community records were identified as: fate unknown, missing in action, or place and date of death unknown.

One frequent reason for "losing" returned Jews was the sizable number who at some point Croatized their names. Most of these changes involved straightforward translations. For examples: Stein became Kamenić, and Gudmann became Dobrić. Aware of this issue, I looked for some of these Croat names in the Zagreb telephone books of the 1950s. As a result of this hunch, I uncovered several individuals whose origin was Jewish, but who had chosen not to register with the Jewish Community.

Indeed, this was not just a postwar phenomenon. Although the Ustaše demanded that Jews register in their respective Jewish Communities under their given names and not under the Croatized version, some flouted this rule. During my conversation with Nada Schterk—married name Grgeć—she told me that for many years she had never mentioned that her mother Netika Klein was Jewish and her father was born into a mixed marriage. A priest who before the war had officiated in the marriages of her two older sisters helped them leave Zagreb and settle in a small village on the city's outskirts. After the war, they let no one know of their survival and continued to live among Croatian villagers. Nada first contacted the Jewish Community in Zagreb in the 1990s, and did so then only because it was required in order to apply for and receive the German government's restitution payments for Jewish Holocaust survivors.

It is clear that, with the passing on of the generation that lived under German occupation, it will be ever more difficult to fill the gaps in the record of who—and how many—survived. Still more difficult will be the task of identifying the hundreds who risked their lives to rescue Jews, yet never received recognition and acknowledgement for their actions. This is the primary reason why it is so important to document and examine in detail as many stories of rescue as possible.[92]

While this chapter recounts the measures taken by Nazi Germany and the Ustaše to dispossess and annihilate Yugoslavia's Jews, it also shows the will of these Jews to survive and provides numerous examples of the help they received from ordinary citizens in Croatia and Bosnia-Herzegovina. Hitler's obsession with the idea of a Yugoslavia free of Jews failed. He and the Ustaše's are responsible for the demise of 70-75 percent of the prewar Jewish population; nonetheless, 9,500 Jews prevailed and survived.

3

NDH Officials Approve "Exceptions"

THE RESCUE OF JEWISH PROFESSIONAL AND INDISPENSIBLE WORKERS

Even as the Ustaše officially embraced the Nazi goal of a genocidal Final Solution and threatened NDH citizens who aided Jews, elements in its hierarchy, from Ante Pavelić on down, shielded selected categories of Jews. Selectively following Nazi proclamations that Jews were the national enemy, they worked to protect those individuals whose education, skills, or family ties they deemed vital to Croatia's national interest.[1]

The NDH regime first exempted from persecution those Jews whom they designated "Honorary Aryans,"[2] that is, persons who had excelled in some area and whose endeavors had contributed to Croatia's economy or culture. This category encompassed approximately 100 Jews and their immediate family members, totaling some 500 persons. The second group consisted of Jews in mixed marriages, if solemnized by the Catholic Church, and their offspring.[3] Several high-ranking NDH officials, including Pavelić, the Poglavnik himself, and Slavko Kvaternik, the head of the Croatian armed forces, had Jewish wives. As will be discussed in Chapter 4, Archbishop Alojzije Stepinac of Zagreb recognized, as did other prelates, that the clergy must try to protect Jews living in mixed marriages or accept the nullification of the sacrament of marriage. More than one thousand Jews married to gentiles survived in the NDH.

The third group of protected Jews included a few thousand individuals who applied for, and received, "Aryan rights," without formal recognition as "Aryans" per se.[4] This category consisted of Jewish professionals such as engineers, businessmen, physicians, and lawyers, and their immediate family members, who were shielded until 1943.[5] Finally, the Ustaše exempted from deportation some Jewish Community leaders and their employees, since they depended on them for information and to perform such services as collecting and enforcing "contributions," and providing food and health services for Jews in detention and in the concentration camps.[6]

Historians of the Holocaust have paid scant attention to the procedures whereby NDH officials arrested and subsequently released at least 521 managers or employees or former owners of nationalized firms, 169 Jewish physicians, an undetermined number of lawyers, and even some former government employees. The few published discussions contain serious factual errors, leading to erroneous judgments. The episode remains virtually absent in literature intended for the general public. But since reliable documentation exists, and because these rescues involved sustained and organized actions, they are worth examining in some detail. The officials who approved exemptions acted out of motives that included personal friendships, professional or business connections, religious or humanitarian beliefs, pragmatic self-interest, and outright greed.

ARYANIZED BUSINESSES IN NEED OF JEWISH PROFESSIONALS

The expropriation and Aryanization of Jewish commercial enterprises began in earnest in June 1941, two months after the Ustaše came to power. Jews in most sectors of the economy were dismissed from their employment,[7] and Ustaše party loyalists were assigned as trustees (*povjerenici*) to fill the vacancies created when Jews and Serbs were dismissed. However, since most of these new workers lacked professional credentials and experience, the sudden removal of the Jews led to chaos, massive business failures, and unemployment. The regime confronted the intractable problem that approximately 44.6 percent of the population was illiterate and 76.3 percent comprised of subsistence farmers.[8] Most Ustaše came from the rural and mountainous regions of Croatia and Bosnia-Herzegovina, where at best some had elementary school education; it was inconceivable that they could be quickly transformed into trained professionals.[9]

Despite the already evident shortcomings of the trustees, in November 1941, the NDH Office of the Treasury declared "the notion of Jewish assets" legally null and void. Thus Aryanized Jewish-owned businesses were nationalized and turned over to loyal Ustaše trustees who lacked prior experience in managing any businesses, let alone national and international companies. In addition to its incompetence, crony management brought pervasive looting and private profiteering. Because the regime's haphazard implementation of the Racial Laws largely ignored the likely adverse consequences for the economy, Croatia soon began to suffer from acute unemployment and bankruptcies.

Pavelić's government recognized that they had to provide jobs and feed the masses if they were to avoid discontent, rebellion, and a possible coup d'état.[10] As a result, the Treasury and the Department of State Property dismissed most of the party loyalists from their trustee positions and created a new department known as *Ponova* (renewal of the economy). This new entity was ordered to devise a plan that would assist companies to improve their productivity and balance sheets.[11] Because it was clear that the local labor force lacked the qualifications to keep the economy going, some prewar Treasury employees, Jewish and otherwise, were brought back to devise a plan to boost the hiring of Croatian workers and keep the formerly Jewish-owned businesses solvent. Under these circumstances, the regime decided to recall some of the Jewish professionals from the labor gangs and concentration camps to which they had initially been sent. The Ustaše also suspended the deportation of those who were still employed.

To avoid problems from the German authorities, the Ustaše emphasized that the recall of Jews was temporary and conditional upon finding suitable local replacements. Of course, neither the appointed trustees nor the government officials truly believed that the local Croats would be able to replace the highly skilled and trained Jewish professionals under any reasonable scenario. But they wanted to reassure the Germans that releasing a few Jews from concentration camps did not imply any weakening of the Ustaše commitment to the Final Solution.

Many of the new trustees understood that they needed a professional labor force in order to revive their companies. Thus they began spontaneously petitioning *Ponova* and the Ministry of the Interior for the release from concentration camps of their indispensible former Jewish employees, as well as an unconditional stay for those still employed until qualified replacements could be found.[12] Such concepts as "indispensible" or "irreplaceable" employee, "business need," or "interest of the state" were key to a successful petition and to obtaining at least some of the employees needed. The trustees often attached to their own petition letters written and signed by their employees who separately requested the release of their former employers and managers. In some cases, they named individuals who might not be the most necessary for the business, but whom they liked and respected, doing so at some risk to themselves.[13] In parallel the trustees pressured *Ponova* officials to attach their own letters of recommendation on behalf of their company and send it to the Ministry of the Interior.[14] The archival records of this process demonstrate that the regime's efforts to create a rational process fell somewhat short.

On July 1, 1941, trustee (*povjerenik*) Dr. Kulović of the Našička factory in Zagreb petitioned the Interior Ministry for the return of forty-one of the eighty-nine prewar Jewish employees. The success of his business lay in the hands of these forty-one indispensable individuals:

> Because of the deportation of employees undertaken by the various Law and Order entities, soon we will be forced to stop all production in many sections of our plant. ... From all that was mentioned above, this cessation of work would be neither in the interests of the State, nor would it benefit our 10,000 Croatian Aryan employees. Therefore we request that the Jewish workers listed above remain employed....[15]

When no reply arrived, Kulović wrote an updated letter to *Ponova*, requesting that twenty-nine of his Jewish employees be assigned permanently to the Našička Company.[16] Nearly six months after the trustee's first letter, on December 29, 1941, the Jewish section of the Office for Law and Order wrote to the Minister of Industry, inquiring whether the Našička firm still needed all twenty-nine Jewish employees. By that time, Kulović had left or been replaced, and on December 30, a new Našička trustee, Ing. [Engineer] Rajko Hvala, replied that, in fact, thirty Jewish employees were now deemed irreplaceable to the company's proper functioning.

The HIGIEA Cork and Plug Factory, Ltd., in Zagreb, also experienced major difficulties due to the government's request to dismiss some of their key Jewish employees. The firm's trustee, on June 1, 1941, thus requested that deportation orders for their Jewish employees be rescinded. Attached to his petition, and with his agreement, a petition letter signed by sixty-six HIGIEA employees requested the immediate release from a concentration camp of their manager, Mr. Vilim Berger, who—they said—would find a way to keep HIGIEA's eighty Croatian employees working and producing. The Chamber of Industry in Zagreb attached its own letter to confirm the description of Berger as irreplaceable.

Since no reply was forthcoming, on June 25, 1941, the HIGIEA factory sent a second letter, this time signed by fifty-two employees:

> Once more we urge the authorities to release without delay Mr. Vilim Berger, and place him at the disposal of our company. He is a technical specialist and irreplaceable; therefore we would request his immediate release from concentration camp and safe return to work; he is essential for our company.... Attached please find a letter from "The Chamber of Industry" in Zagreb that confirms the truthfulness of our request.[17]

It appears that as these letters were making their way through the bureaucratic maze, Vilim Berger perished in one of the Croatian concentration camps. Next to his name in the lists of the Jewish Community in

Zagreb is the information: "Died in the summer of 1941, place and date of execution unknown."

The Intercontinental International Caro and Jelinek Transport Corporation used its financial strength to pressure the *Ponova* officials to ensure that eight of their most valuable Jewish employees were released from concentration camps. In a letter of May, 30, 1941, the company's trustee stressed that, should the authorities continue to deprive their company of its most capable employees by sending them to forced labor camps, the consequence would adversely affect their company and the Croatian people:

> Our company is in business since 1919, with capital of 5,000,000 Dinar and 1,200,000 Dinar in reserve funds. Our head office is in Zagreb. We are an Aryan firm, registered with the Ministry of National Economics, Department for Manufacture, Industry and Trade, on the 16th of April 1941, under no. 19783. We employ 69 workers. Redundant Jewish employees were dismissed; those named below are indispensible to our company as well as to the restoration of Croatian industry.[18]

The names of the critical employees were Slavko Neumann, Kosser Jakob, Altstadter Pavao, Berger Geza, Schaffer Aleksander, Salzberger Branko, and Frolich Fritzi. It is known that four of the eight survived; the fate of the other four is unknown.

In addition to the trustee's letter, thirty-two Caro and Jelinek employees signed and sent their own letter, dated May 30, 1941:

> We the employees of The Intercontinental International Cargo and Jelinek, Co. Ltd., testify and sign with our own names that Mr. Slavko Neumann worked with many of us for 19 years, in a very friendly atmosphere. He has always been a loyal, friendly and honest employee. As we all know, he was a distinguished Croatian patriot. He suffered unjust persecution and imprisonment by the Belgrade regime. At a time when others were afraid to stand up for their national feelings, he stood up for Croatian rights. He always and everywhere emphasized his Croatian nationality, and suffered hardship because of it.

Considering all of the above, our company has decided to engage his services not as a regular employee, but as a sales representative. For 20 years, he cultivated excellent business relations with customers and he will continue do so for the benefit of our firm and Croatian Industry.[19]

The testimonies of support for Slavko Neumann from his former company saved his life. After returning to Zagreb, he had opportunities to consider other options for survival. Thus, he was one among the four survivors from this company.

It took great courage on the part of both trustees and employees to put themselves on record with officials commending Jewish employees and former owners. Attributes such as honesty, integrity, and Croatian patriotism were usually assigned to Aryan Croats, not to Jews. Indeed, the petition letters directly countered the portrayal of Jews disseminated in the official media as "greedy industrialists who feed on the blood of the Croatian people." Thirty-four Caro and Jelinek employees expressed dismay upon hearing that their own government would send their capable and loyal colleagues to concentration camps at a time of great economic hardship.[20] The NDH Office for Law and Order, after consultation with the Ministry of the Treasury, approved most of the requests made by the trustees and the employees.

Although it would not be feasible to describe in detail each of the 521 cases of petition letters I examined, a few additional examples demonstrate the scope of the requests and the variety of industries that spoke up about their need for Jewish manpower against the daily assaults of antisemitic propaganda. One of the most important revelations to come from examining these petitions is the number of entities that had the authority to release Jews from concentration camps and detention centers. The confusion and overlapping of authority reflects the arbitrary and capricious nature of Ustaše rule.

For example, on July 31, 1941, Krešimir Meštrović, the trustee of a conglomerate of five companies, petitioned the Ministry of the Treasury and *Ponova:*

As a trustee of the companies Papieros, Jadran, Koncentra, Zora d.d. and the Paper and Glue Factory, I confirm that the individuals listed below are indispensible for the proper functioning of our companies. Would you please lend support to our request by appealing to the Ministry of the Interior to issue work permits for the below-listed non-Aryans:

Zora Factory: Isak Hochberger and Franjo Fischer;

Koncentra: Slavko Rosenberger;

Papieros: Adolf Waltuch, Miško Beck, and Gjuro Strauss;

Jadran: Pavao Schrenger and Ernest Fried, Paper & Glue: Eugen Pichler and Dušan Ungar.

On August 28, 1941, the trustee Meštrović received a short two-word reply from the Ustaše Supervisory Management: "Confirmed" and "Approved." Their request for the employees listed above was accepted.[21]

On January 17, 1942, the Office of Government Assets in the Ministry of the Treasury, made a request to UNS on behalf of its own business, the Wagons, Engines and Bridges Co., to obtain a work permits for the following "essential and irreplaceable" individuals: "Julije Goldberger, Ing. Josip Vendra, Dr. Friedrich Oppenheimer, Stjepan Čapo."[22]

As in the previous case, on July 8, 1941, the Treasury Ministry requested that the UNS issue work permits for four current workers of the Schreiber & Mayer firm, nationalized on April 16, 1941. They also requested information on the whereabouts of their only bookkeeper, Fanika Baum, who had disappeared.[23-]

On March 23, 1942, the Office for Law and Order, Jewish Division, petitioned UNS as per the request of the Italian Military Legation in Croatia:

The Legation currently employs four Jewish merchants that are greatly needed. The Italian military had requested that the NDH police refrain from taking measures against their merchants such as are commonly taken against non-Aryans. They requested uninterrupted work permits for the following merchants:

Mirko Pichler, Felix Brichta, Aleksander Weiss, Milan Lichtenberger.[24]

As we have seen, after requesting the release of employees from concentration camps and detention centers, the trustees and employees had to wait for replies. Some arrived promptly; others took several months. Most enterprises hoped to receive a short memo with a caption reading *Dozvola* (permit). The format in most cases was similar, although the permits came from various ministries and police offices. The following four examples of permits convey an idea of the bureaucratic processes involved in releasing Jews:

From: the Directorate of the Ustaše Police Surveillance, NDH, Jewish Division:

Dozvola

From: NDH, Ministry of the Interior

To: Main Supervisory Directorate for Public Order and Security, Jewish Division

This permit gives Ing. Armin Friedman, a surveyor from Zagreb, 68/a Vlaška Street, the freedom of movement throughout the city in his supervisory role, and as such he is also absolved from wearing the Jewish identification Z. His request for Aryan rights has not yet been approved by the Ministry of the Interior. Zagreb, May 3, 1942.[25]

Signed: Kuhnel. Zagreb, December 18, 1942.

Dozvola

With this memorandum we give permission to Ing. Milan Spietzer, employee of the government electrical enterprise Elektroproizvod [electrical manufacturing], Zagreb, to remain in his post as an indispensible expert in his field. His wife Dr. Serena Marija née Friedman and his daughter Blanka Spitzer gain automatic protection and are permitted to remain in their apartment at 30/I Tratinska Street. It is in effect until new orders are issued.[26]

Dozvola

From: Headquarters of Ustaše Police, Jewish Division, June 17, 1942.

To: The Ministry of the Treasury:

With this, Arpad Weiller from Zagreb, Krajiška Street 13, an employee of the NDH Ministry of the Treasury, Office for the Maintenance of Assets, Zagreb, [it is ordered that] until new orders are issued, no punitive action should be taken against him, such as are taken against non-Aryans. He is also excused from wearing the Jewish identification sign.[27]

Dozvola

From: Headquarters of Ustaše Police, Jewish Division, June 19, 1942.

To: Magnezit Factory:

Since it was verified that Ing. Rudolf Steiner, Zagreb, employee of the Magnezit Factory, Zagreb, is an expert in his field, and as such he is authorized to continue working for your company; punitive action should not be taken against him and against members of his family without consulting the above office; registration number 50397, as of June 1, 1942. This order is in effect unless other orders are issued.[28]

Despite the need for Jewish employees and talent, on May 5, 1943, Heinrich Himmler visited Ante Pavelić in Zagreb and insisted that all Croatian Jews be handed over to the SS in exchange for financial and economic assistance. Pavelić accepted Himmler's offer, which meant that all remaining Jews, excluding those in mixed marriages, would be deported to German camps, in most cases to Auschwitz.

THE FATE OF BOSNIAN BUSINESSES

In Germany itself, the National Socialists' expropriation and Aryanization of Jewish businesses was meant to benefit the Third Reich, not individual looters.[29] The Nazis closed failing businesses, and consolidated and merged others so as to maximize revenues and profits. Since the German plan for Southeastern Europe was to eliminate all production of finished products and exploit the territory for agriculture and raw materials, the Nazis encouraged the plunder and looting of businesses in the NDH, promoting irregularities they had banned in Germany.

Although the Ustaše initially turned a blind eye to plunder and looting by their loyalists as a way of rewarding them, they were not ready to turn over their manufacturing to Germany. The Ustaše never considered liquidating former Jewish businesses; they recognized the need to keep the population employed. Therefore, immediately upon the creation of the NDH, the Ustaše insisted that Germany fulfill its promise to turn over all Jewish businesses and confiscated assets to the Croatian government once the owners had been deported to concentration camps. On April 17, 1941, Germany approved this arrangement. Like most other agreements with Germany, this one involved exceptions, with the NDH the loser, which is demonstrated later on in this chapter. The Germans' violation of NDH rights to control Aryanized businesses was most prevalent in areas with large Volksdeutsche and Muslim populations, in particular Bosnia-Herzegovina, where the German presence was augmented by the occupation's headquarters in Sarajevo. After confiscating the Jewish businesses, the Germans typically took over and liquidated the businesses themselves or turned them over to loyal Volksdeutsche for liquidation. The proceeds went into Nazi-controlled banks.

The fate of the formerly Jewish Šik factory in Sarajevo demonstrates the extent to which Pavelić was a puppet in German hands. He promised to give the factory to a Muslim welfare society, Merhamet. But when the society's administrator attempted to collect the documents of ownership, he was informed that the Germans had assumed control of the factory as their "property of war," and that it was essential for the support of the war effort.[30] In this way the Germans achieved two objectives: First, they demonstrated that they, not the Ustaše, were in control; Second, they aimed to belittle Pavelić himself in the eyes of the Muslims.

In testimony to the postwar National Commission, Judge Srećko Bujas, the NDH-appointed trustee of the Sephardic Jewish Community in Sarajevo, revealed that only 171 of 340 prewar Jewish businesses had been listed with the Treasury. The others had been looted by the Nazi occupiers and by the local Muslim elite. Larger and more prosperous businesses did not appear on the lists, either because they had been merged with international German enterprises or because their inventories had been channeled to existing German businesses in the city.[31] Bujas stressed repeatedly that only when the businesses had been completely plundered and nothing was left, particularly in the case of retail stores, would a sign be posted stating: "Nationalized Property, NDH."[32]

The NDH Ministry of the Treasury hired professionals whose task was to identify why, unlike in Croatia, Aryans in Sarajevo were not requesting the release of their Jewish employees from concentration camps. Still more important, they wanted to know why funds from Aryanized businesses were not being transferred to the NDH Treasury. The information that reached the Treasury from several different sources indicated that various individuals of Volksdeutsche heritage had received written orders from the local Wehrmacht command to sell the assets of the listed businesses and deposit the proceeds, less 10 percent commission, in the account of a "Hitlerhaus, Njemačka Narodna Skupina"[33] [German Provisional National Bank], an entity set up by the German Army in which the Nazis collected the money before sending it to Germany. In HDA, Zagreb, I found records of the Hitlerhaus bank in Bijeljina, but similar entities existed in other Bosnian cities.[34] It took the NDH Ministry of the Treasury two years of thorough investigation in small communities to discover what had gone on with the former Jewish businesses in Bosnia.

Because of the efforts of NDH Treasury officials, archival documents now available from the *Ponova* files help answer the mystery of the missing petitions for the release of Jews from concentration camps.[35] After pocketing what they wanted from the liquidated Jewish businesses, the Germans channeled some of the proceeds to the Volksdeutsche and to the Muslim elite "to keep them happy and willing collaborators in future activities."[36] Since most of the confiscated businesses were liquidated, there was no need to recall Jewish employees. The Germans had full and absolute control over affairs in Sarajevo and in Bosnia-Herzegovina.

In general, the fate of Yugoslav Jews during World War II, while catastrophic everywhere, depended in large measure on the occupation regime or collaborationist government in power. In Bosnia-Herzegovina, due to the support Germany received from local Volksdeutsche and the Muslim elite, their control was absolute. Because the Nazis had the power to impose anti-Jewish measures earlier and more consistently, the destruction of Bosnian Jews initially was far greater than in Croatia itself.

JEWISH PHYSICIANS SENT ON A MISSION TO ERADICATE ENDEMIC SYPHILIS IN BOSNIA

The story of NDH efforts to address endemic syphilis in Bosnia-Herzegovina reveals that, despite the regime's thwarted efforts to gain economic control in that territory, the Zagreb authorities demonstrated remarkable solicitude for Bosnia-Herzegovina. This becomes more explicable considering that a large number of the Ustaše leaders came from Herzegovina. Ante Pavelić, the Poglavnik himself, was born there, as were Vice-President Dzafer Kulenović, a Muslim, and Interior Minister Andrija Artuković. A high percentage of the rank and file had similar origins. Since these NDH leaders were not themselves from Croatia, they had to find ways to gain support of the Croatian elite, while also integrating Bosnia-Herzegovina into the expanded NDH.

To achieve this objective they attempted to merge the ideology of Racial Laws with the ideals of Ante Starčević, a nineteenth-century Croatian politician and writer who was considered the father of modern Croatia. Like Starčević, the Ustaše considered the Bosnian Muslims to be the purest form of the Croatian race. Pavelić regarded them as an integral part of the Croatian nation, seeing their origins in the Bogomils, a medieval offshoot of Christianity. Indeed, he went so far as to call them the "flower" of Croatia. One of the most ardent Ustaše, Jozo Dumandižić, described this affinity metaphorically: "The Poglavnik kisses the Muslims in the manner, and with same passion, that Starčević did."[37] Thus personal connections, regional geopolitics, and a romantic nationalism steered the Ustaše leadership to reach out to Bosnia. A crusade to heal the Muslim population from endemic syphilis satisfied this goal.[38]

Dr. Ivan Raguz, head of Bosnian health services, had high expectations of the Ustaše regime when he asked for assistance in supplying medical personnel who would be eager to heal the Muslim population.[39] Because of the Croatian Ministry of Health's own shortage of physicians after the purge of Jewish and Serbian medical staff, Raguz's request was shelved; but it was not forgotten.[40]

As early as May 1941, one month after the NDH assumed power, a sizable number of Jewish physicians had been deported to concentration camps. It was obvious to the remaining physicians that if something drastic were not done to prevent further deportations, within a few months the remaining Jewish physicians would suffer a similar fate. Based on testimony by Major General Dr. Stjepan Steiner, most Jewish physicians—both in government service and in private practice—were out of work by June 1941. Moreover, Ankica Budak, a Ministry of Health official, made rounds of the doctors' private practices and confiscated their instruments and supplies.

In an interview, Dr. Teodor Gruner, a participant in the Bosnian mission, indicated that the scheme to engage Jewish doctors, specifically, for this initiative was the brainchild of Dr. Miroslav Schlesinger, a Jewish physician from Zagreb who saw it as a feasible way to spare the Jewish physicians.[41] Gruner described Schlesinger's "miraculous" ability to devise a plan for keeping the Jewish physicians out of sight while also addressing the overall shortage of physicians in the NDH and the government's urgent obligation to cope with the endemic presence in Bosnia-Herzegovina of a highly contagious disease that had systemic implications for the victim's health.[42]

Supporting Gruner's account, Major General Steiner explained in an interview Schlesinger's confidence that the Minister of Health would be inclined to participate in a "conspiracy" to rescue the remaining Jewish physicians: "The Minister of Health, Dr. Ivan Petrić, held the Jewish physicians, including his former professor Dr. Izidor Steinhardt, in high regard. He fought vigorously to obtain for him the prestigious title of 'Honorary Aryan,' and succeeded."[43] Consequently, colleagues believed that Dr. Petrić did not harbor antisemitic beliefs and thus might be willing to assist in the rescue of other Jewish physicians.[44]

Acting in concert with concerned Croat colleagues, the group of Jewish doctors began to develop plans to broach the idea of a mission of Jewish physicians to Bosnia to the NDH regime—specifically to the Minister of Health. Success depended on finding the right individual from among the Croats, someone who was respected and trusted by both the Jewish practitioners and the NDH hierarchy.[45] Dr. Schlesinger, probably in consultation with other Jewish physicians, selected Dr. Ante Vuletić, a noted specialist in venereal diseases and epidemiology, to present the plan to Dr. Petrić.[46] Vuletić explained that sending the Jewish doctors to Bosnia would at the same time benefit his ministry, improve the health of the Muslims, and ease the pressure on gentile doctors in the NDH, who were caring for both the civilian population and the army.

Although the plan appealed to Dr. Petrić, he had to find a way to most effectively present the idea to his ministerial colleagues as well as to Ante Pavelić. Petrić won the support of three out of the seven NDH ministers. His strongest opponent was a powerful antisemite, Minister of Religion and Education Dr. Mile Budak. Nevertheless, Dr. Petrić prevailed, especially with the backing of Pavelić, who accorded a higher priority to healing the Bosnian population than to "eliminating" Jewish physicians.[47] Or at least the Jews could be eliminated after the public health mission to the Muslims had succeeded.

At the request of the Ministry of Health, sometime in June 1941, the Jewish Community in Zagreb counseled all the Jewish physicians whose names were on a list assembled by the community to attend a special meeting to be held at the community's new premises at Strossmayer

Square 4.[48] At the meeting, officials from the Ministry of Health informed the doctors that an excellent chance of survival existed for those who volunteered for a mission to treat endemic syphilis among the Muslim population in Bosnia-Herzegovina. No prior medical experience in treating venereal diseases was required, although the doctors took a mandatory two-week preparatory course prior to leaving for Bosnia. Upon its completion, two groups of physicians would go as a mission under NDH Health Ministry auspices. This amounted to an existential choice.[49] Most physicians saw merit in the offer considering that their families and assets would be protected, although some declined for personal reasons, or stated that they preferred to remain in Zagreb and work with inmates in the concentration camps.[50]

Those who joined the Bosnian medical team would become contract employees of the NDH.[51] Their duration of employment was not specified; the contract stated only that it would be honored as long as both parties adhered to its conditions. Each physician was compensated according to previous medical work experience and family status. For example, Dr. Alfred Neufeld (Najfeld), under contract # Z.36.249/1941, received a monthly income of 4,000 kuna (Croatian currency) per month.[52] Dr. Hinko Marić, from Varaždin, under contract # 60127-Z-1941, was offered 5,000 kuna.[53] Dr. Teodor Gruner, under contract CDXXXVII-2115-Z-1941, initially received a salary of 4,900 kuna per month. When he signed another contract (# 21062-0-1) after one year of service, his compensation was raised to 7,000 kuna, possibly due to the high rate of inflation.[54] Married physicians received a supplement of 300 kuna for their wives and 206 Kuna per month for each child. As any other employee, these physicians had to pay taxes on their income. One of the contract's most important provisions was immunity from deportation to the camps for the physician's immediate family—parents, wife, and children.[55]

Once preparations were completed, sometimes in June, the first group of physicians departed for Bosnia. Some of the physicians received their assignments before leaving Zagreb, while others went first to the offices of the Institute for Combating Endemic Syphilis (henceforth the

Institute) either in Mostar or in Banja Luka in Herzegovina, where they were assigned to posts based upon specific regional needs.

The Jewish medical team was divided into four groups: Group I comprised 23 physicians, of whom three were women; Group II numbered 52 physicians, including 10 women. These two groups were initially to have included a total of 81 physicians, all from Zagreb. However, before orders for their mobilization reached them, six of the selected physicians had been deported to concentration camps. The physicians in Group III were recruited individually from all over the NDH; five of its 55 physicians were women. Group IV included only 12 physicians, all released from internment in August 1942. Eleven of them had been interned in June before the invitation to join the syphilis mission reached them; the twelfth was a physician from the Home Guard (*Domobranstvo*). Their release was facilitated by the intervention of Drs. Ante Vuletić and Stanko Sielski, the Croatian physicians who managed the Institute.[56] The physicians immediately joined their colleagues in Bosnia. Thus the total number of physicians in Bosnia was 142, of whom 21 were women. In addition, twenty-seven Jewish physicians served in the Home Guard in late 1941 and early 1942.[57]

Table: (1) Rescue of Jewish physicians in a Medical Expedition to Bosnia-Herzegovina and Jewish Physicians in the Home Guard, (M-male; F-female)[58]

Groups	Total sent to Bosnia M+F	Total Survived M+F	Total Killed M+F	Total Unknown M+F
Group I	20+3	11+0	9+3	0
Group II	42+10	25+6	12+3	5+1
Group III	49+6	36+5	13+1	1+0
Group IV Release CC	10+2	5 (gender unknown)	1+0	5
Sub Total	142	88 (62%)	42 (29%)	12 (8.2%)
NDH Home Guard	27+0	10	3	14
Total, M, F	169 148M+21F	98 87M+11F	45 38M+7F	26 24M+3F

The Institute's journal, *Vjesnik* (Journal), of which six issues appeared from the end of 1941 through 1942, reported on some of the success stories and challenges encountered during the medical campaign.[59] Issue 4, published in Banja Luka in 1942, indicates that the physicians selected for groups I and II did not all arrive at the same time; some reached Bosnia in July 1941, others not until August 1942, after the Institute had negotiated their release from internment. The same issue provides some vital statistics on the two groups from Zagreb. For example, seven of the doctors left in the first year: two were transferred to hospitals, one physician retired, another left voluntarily, one was dismissed (reason not given), and two died from typhus—the only fatalities among physicians while in NDH service. In addition, 51 of these physicians were married, and they had 43 children. Most of their family members preferred to remain in Zagreb in their prewar homes.[60] Little else is known about their lives, unless they also were members of the medical mission, or they were arrested and then released from concentration camps. From an interview with the author, we know that Dr. Gruner was a newlywed whose wife joined him in Bosnia, where she stayed until 1943, when she left Bosnia for Zagreb to deliver their first child.

The articles and information in *Vjesnik* make clear that Dr. Petrić, as minister of health, paid special attention to the first group of 23 physicians. He had a great deal to lose if they performed poorly, or if the operation was sabotaged, but he also had much to gain. Petrić pleaded with the group not to disappoint him, to work hard, and to demonstrate good progress in the treatment of syphilis. The primary rationale for the Bosnia project, for those who initially conceived it and for some who implemented it, was to save as many Jewish physicians as possible. However, if some Bosnians could be treated for syphilis and the level of suffering reduced, then the project could claim success, and other groups might be sent.

In an interview Dr. Gruner recalled the first few months of the project, stating:

> We worked extremely hard and under difficult conditions. We knew
> what was at stake both for them, and also for the others that might

follow should the first group be successful against syphilis. Our first task as physicians was to go to the most remote regions of Bosnia and convince the local population that we were there to help. Once word about the quality of our treatment went out and confidence was gained, the success of the physicians was guaranteed. Due to our accomplishments within a few weeks of our arrival, a second group of 52 physicians joined the project in September 1941.[61]

From 1942 onward, however, some doctors defected to the Partisans fighting against the Nazis and NDH forces. From the first and second groups recruited in Zagreb, 46 men died in combat, while eight of the female physicians died either in combat or from typhus. Others, like Dr. Draga Weinberg, left Bosnia but was captured by the Ustaše in 1944 and sent to Auschwitz.[62] The fate of 26 physicians has not been confirmed; they are still unaccounted for, neither registered as deceased in the Croatian Dotrščina file (which lists all the victims of war in the Zagreb area), nor in the listings of the Jewish Community of Zagreb.

PROTECTION OF PHYSICIANS' FAMILIES

Ustaše commanders periodically sent circulars ordering regional and local police units to refrain from sending family members of physicians in the NDH service to concentration camps.[63] The government Office for Law and Order (UNS) issued each family member a special identification card stating that the holder was protected at the request of the minister of health and with the approval of UNS, under supervision of the minister of the interior.

Yet, despite such measures to prevent their eviction and deportation, some family members were detained and deported.[64] Among 51 letters examined between the UNS and the physicians, more than 80 percent dealt with requests to release family members from concentration camps.[65] Rejections of these requests usually stated that the relatives did not strictly fall into the category of "immediate family"—defined as parents, spouses, and children.

In the case of Dr. Gruner, his request for the release of his parents was immediately approved, and they were rescued.[66] However, his request for the release of his sister, Edit Gruner, and his mother-in-law, Greta Berger, was denied.[67] On the other hand, Dr. Alfred Neufeld's request for the release of his mother-in-law, Helen Rudolf Spitzer, was granted, since she was also the mother of his wife, Eta Neufeld, who had been a medical student before the war and herself worked as a member of the mission.[68]

The Institute, as the officially responsible entity, handled the release of family members from camps and other special requests. Occasionally, the authorities approved the rescue of children even if they were not an immediate family.[69] In an interview, Dr. Darko Fišer, the current president of the Osijek Jewish Community, reported that, since both his father's brother and his wife were physicians and part of the mission to Bosnia, they were granted permission to bring his brother's wife and two children along to their assigned post.[70] Dr. Fišer, his mother, and sister spent more than a year in Bosnia before escaping to Hungary.

Other requests to release children were also considered. Dr. Margite Heimer-Cegledi obtained the release of her eleven-year-old orphaned niece, Vera Heimer.[71] In addition, the Ustaše Law and Order Office sent a letter to seven physicians informing them that twelve of their family members had been released from concentration camps.[72] While some mistakes occurred, and family members were improperly deported, the Institute made attempts to obtain their return. The Institute personnel who supervised the program apparently made sincere efforts to honor the terms of the contracts with the physicians.[73]

The Institute's support made the physicians sent to Bosnia a privileged group, as illustrated by the survival of Dr. Gruner, Bela Hochstader, and others. When Institute officials became aware of fierce fighting near his post between German and Ustaše forces and the Partisans, they urged Gruner to collect his belongings, hire a car at the Institute's expense, and return without delay to Banja Luka. Dr. Stanko Sielski, who managed the program, personally signed the telegram warning Gruner.[74]

Most of the physicians seem to have maintained regular correspondence with their families. But during the turmoil caused by his relocation,

Dr. Gruner failed to contact his parents for a period of several weeks, causing them concern. Thus his father, Cantor Bernard Gruner, wrote to the minister of health, asking about the whereabouts of his son and describing the excellent work he was doing to curb endemic syphilis, as well as to provide care for local children. The ministry's response assured the father that his son was working in the service of the Institute.[75]

DEFECTIONS TO THE PARTISANS

Archival documents record a gradual decline in the number of Jewish physicians serving in the anti-syphilis mission after early 1942, as some of them deserted their posts in Bosnia to join the Partisans. A larger number followed their lead after the capitulation of Italy on September 8, 1943.[76] Other doctors elected to remain in NDH service almost until 1944. The Partisans desperately needed medical personnel, and urged the Jewish physicians to join. Many doctors, while inclined to accept the offer, were also deeply concerned for the well-being of their families at home. They had reason to believe that their families would be in danger should the news of their defection reach the NDH authorities, since their protection depended on the physicians' service to the government. In one known case, two physicians used a cover story to cloak the defection. In my interview with Dr. Stjepan Steiner, he described how, in mid-1942, he and his wife, Dr. Zora Goldsmith, joined the Partisans after a staged kidnapping. The incident took place in broad daylight, allowing witnesses to observe their struggles to escape from the Partisans' grip.[77]

Regardless of when the physicians deserted their posts, both Drs. Gruner and Steiner related that Drs. Vuletić and Sielski had shielded the family members left behind. Dr. Steiner reported that, although the physicians in charge of the mission were aware of the defections to the Partisans, they did not inform the Ustaše authorities. On the contrary, they kept these doctors' names on their lists, thus risking their own professional careers, their own lives, and those of their families.

As noted earlier, on May 5, 1943, SS chief Heinrich Himmler personally visited Croatia, in part to let Pavelić know of his dissatisfaction with the pace of deportations in the NDH. Following Pavelić's promise to do better in return for Germany's financial support, the Institute was ordered to deliver all the physicians and their families to the authorities.[78] Again, the courage of Dr. Sielski and Dr. Vuletić was put to the test. They responded by saying that all the doctors were needed to treat a new epidemic of "spotted typhus." Moreover, removal of the Jewish physicians would create such a shortage of physicians that they would be unable to provide medical assistance to German soldiers in case they contracted the disease.

By disobeying orders to report deserting physicians, and by their firm stand against deportations, these two physicians saved a number of Jewish lives. Drs. Vuletić and Sielski nurtured and protected the physicians and their families as long as they remained in the service of NDH, and after. For his courage, generosity of spirit, and humanity during World War II, Yad Vashem posthumously awarded Dr. Ante Vuletić the title of "Righteous among the Nations."[79] Dr. Stanko Sielski, who was responsible for the mission's daily operations, and who worked for the release of personnel and families sent to concentration camps, also merits recognition for his courage in rescuing many Jews.

AFTERMATH

In 1945, after the war ended and continuing through the years of the Yugoslav Communist regime, the Jewish physicians who had practiced their profession in the "syphilis mission" and in the Croatian Home Guard experienced political disadvantage, having to explain and justify their voluntary service to the NDH regime. Political realities made it risky to admit outright that they had consented to join the Bosnian Medical Expedition because they wished to live and because by joining they shielded their immediate families from deportation. Politics also slanted the way some historians dealt with the episode.

During the 1960s, Dr. Zdenko Lowenthal[80] and Dr. Samuel Dajć,[81] who had remained in Yugoslavia, published articles on their experiences in the Bosnian mission. By this time each had a vested interest in describing Jewish participation in the project in the context of Communist Party ideology. In both men's accounts Dr. Miroslav Schlesinger, who had first had the idea of an mission, was acting as a communist on the instructions of, and in the interest of the party, to rescue the Jewish physicians. Their versions then alleged that many of the Jewish physicians were encouraged by this news and thus decided to join the mission to Bosnia.

In response to this outrageous revision of history, in the mid-1970s, Dr. Jaša Romano pointed out that as of June 1941, when the idea of sending Jewish physicians to Bosnia first developed, there was not yet any concrete plan to establish the People's Liberation group from which the Partisans arose. Romano thus notes that it was highly unlikely that the Communist Party would at that time have either considered or supported a plan to send Jewish physicians to Bosnia in the service of the NDH regime, some of whom only later joined the Partisans.[82]

Five years after his earlier article, at a 1968 conference in Jerusalem organized by Yad Vashem on the subject of Jewish resistance during the Holocaust, Dr. Lowenthal offered a revised version of the mission story. In this account, during the summer of 1941—Croatia was occupied in April—a group of eighty Jewish physicians decided to form a special organization for the control of infectious diseases in Bosnian villages. Sixty of those Jewish physicians joined the Partisan Army and played an important role in its health services.[83]

Although this version was even more far-fetched than the earlier one, it went unchallenged. Yet it totally failed to explain why, when the NDH regime was deporting Jewish physicians to concentration camps, the Ustaše would suddenly organize some eighty Jewish doctors and allow them to move about in remote rural areas of Bosnia. Nor did it explain why—given Muslim adherence to the Ustaše—any Jew would, on his own accord, choose to roam about in Muslim territories in wartime. It is reasonable to assume that Lowenthal's version had been formulated with the help of Yugoslav communist authorities. Worthy of note here is the fact that Dr. (and Major General) Stjepan Steiner served as personal physician to Marshal Josip Broz Tito, president of the Socialist Federal

Republic of Yugoslavia. Other veterans of the Bosnian mission occupied important posts in various hospitals in postwar Yugoslavia.

While Jaša Romano rejected the accounts given by Drs. Lowenthal and Dajć, he reported a figure of only eighty physicians who served on the mission to Bosnia: sixty-eight doctors from Croatia and twelve from Bosnia. Other historians have uncritically accepted his figure, despite the existence of contrary archival data. In fact, as noted, a total of 142 physicians were sent to Bosnia; of those, sixty-four survived, as did most of their family members. [84]

However, Romano may have unintentionally introduced another misconception into the historiographic literature by claiming that the regime sent the Jewish physicians to Bosnia in order to eliminate professional competition with Aryan physicians. In an interview with the author, Dr. Stjepan Steiner clarified this issue. He recalled that the private practices of Jewish doctors in Zagreb had been plundered sometime in May and June 1941, before the idea of sending Jewish doctors to Bosnia was broached.[85] Since the Jewish practices were already closed, the issue of competition with Aryan physicians was moot. Furthermore, the Ministry of Health did not have to send the doctors to Bosnia in order to remove them as competitors, since they could easily have been sent to Jasenovac, as indeed some were.

Romano also claimed, without providing any evidence, that the mission to Bosnia should be considered forced labor (*prisilan rad*). But the well-documented circumstances under which the doctors worked make this characterization inappropriate. Jews in forced labor did not receive daily meals, nor were they compensated for their professional services. The inmates in labor camps were in fact slaves. Unlike the physicians in Bosnia, they were denied the privilege of being with their families; nor could they request the release of their loved ones from concentration camps, or the safekeeping of their apartments. Although at least one participant in the syphilis mission, Dr. Eta Nafield, has referred to the service in lectures as "forced labor," such loose usage is at variance with the archival record and with all accepted definitions of compulsory labor service for Jews in Axis-occupied Europe. While the physicians in

Bosnia toiled under difficult conditions and lacked urban conveniences, their living conditions remained far superior to those in the actual labor camps.

4

Archbishop Stepinac of Zagreb Confronts Antisemitism and Totalitarianism, 1941–1945

Love toward one's own nation cannot turn a man into a wild animal, which destroys everything and calls for reprisal, but it must ennoble him, so that his own nation secures respect and love of other nations.[1]

THE TRIAL

Sixty years after the end of World War II, Alojzije Stepinac, the archbishop of Zagreb, remains one of the most elusive and controversial religious leaders to emerge from that era. This chapter will describe the archbishop's outspoken sermons against Ustaše and Nazi brutality and terror and his effort to aid and rescue Croatia's Jews. Yet today, as in Tito's Yugoslavia, Stepinac is viewed from two different perspectives: the Croats and the Roman Catholic Church have one version; the Serbs, the Serbian Orthodox Church, and old-guard communists have another. To begin to understand these two diametrically opposed accounts of Stepinac's conduct during the years 1941–1945, one must look backwards to the worldviews of the two key protagonists as they emerged in the years before the war.[2]

Josip Broz Tito became general secretary of the Communist Party of Yugoslavia (CPY) in December 1937, the same year in which Alojzije Stepinac, at the age of 37, though below the prescribed canonical age of 40, became one of the youngest archbishops in the church's history. Tito's motto was "brotherhood and unity" (*bratsvo jedinstvo*) of all Yugoslav citizens, regardless of religion, ethnicity, or class.[3] In the name of this goal, the CPY promoted the rejection of all religious authorities: "If the South Slavs would abandon religion and embrace socialism, then the scourge of religion would wither away together with the bourgeois national states."[4] For Stepinac, however, as he declared on August 15, 1940: "Communism is the greatest modern enemy of the Catholic Church, there can be no cooperation with the communists until they give up their teaching and their crimes and thus cease to be what they are."[5] Yet despite Stepinac's identification of communism as the mortal enemy of the Roman Catholic Church, he was soon faced with a more immediate threat to his beliefs, to the physical and spiritual well-being of his parishioners, and to the autonomy of his church—the brutal Nazi-Ustaše rule over Croatia.

In 1944, as the war in Europe was winding down, Tito and his Partisans, with the help of western anti-Nazi forces and their Soviet allies, gained the leadership of what would be a new, again united, Yugoslavia. Tito's most urgent task was to unite the many warring ethnic and religious groups.[6] Acting in the name of "brotherhood and unity," he simultaneously identified divisive individuals and entities that posed ideological threats to his regime. Tito first targeted Draža Mihajlović and his Četniks, the remnant of the Serbian Royal Army. Its members were imprisoned, and after an ad hoc trial, Mihajlović was charged with treason and executed.

Despite his view of the Roman Catholic Church as the enemy of a communist Yugoslavia, Tito initially avoided confrontation. Indeed, he repeatedly declared, "I would have liked to see in Croatia an independent Catholic Church."[7] His understanding of "independent" became clear when, in June 1945, Tito met with a Catholic delegation in order to "convince them" to disassociate the Catholic Church from Rome. Stepinac, who vehemently opposed all suggestions of separating the

Croatian Catholics from the universal church in Rome, was noticeably absent from these discussions. Not surprisingly, the talks failed.

Stepinac continued to publically object to the new Yugoslavian state's confiscation of church lands, the closing of Catholic schools and youth clubs, and to the civil marriage requirement for Catholics. Tito recognized that the Ustaše had not been primarily a Catholic movement; rather they had viewed the church as a *differentia specifica* from Serbian Orthodoxy.[8] Nevertheless, he linked the Ustaše with the church and used allegations of Stepinac's collaboration with the Ustaše to make him a target of attack. But those who recognized that the Ustaše violated every precept of the church, like Milovan Djilas, Tito's former secretary for propaganda and the media, observed that: "the problem Stepinac had with Tito was not his politics vis-à-vis the Ustaše, but his politics vis-à-vis the communists and mostly his fidelity to Rome."[9] In Tito's own words: "It is not true that we persecute the church. We simply do not tolerate that certain people serve with impunity foreign interests instead of the interests of their own people."[10]

On September 30, 1946, the Federal People's Republic of Yugoslavia arrested Stepinac. Dr. Ivo Politeo served as attorney for the defense of Archbishop Dr. Alojzije Stepinac before the Special Council of the People's Supreme Court at the proceeding on October 8, 1946 in Zagreb. Stepinac was tried on six counts, including treason and assisting the Ustaše in wartime, and on October 11 he was found guilty on all charges and sentenced to sixteen years imprisonment and hard labor. In Miroslav Akmadža's view, the communists used their criminal justice system as a "tool for solving political problems, such as Stepinac."[11]

Dispatch No. 536 November 9, 1946, from American Embassy, Belgrade, notified the U.S. State Department: "Everybody in Yugoslavia knows that Archbishop Stepinac was arrested and condemned by the Communist Party, and that his sentence was fixed outside the Court and long before the trial itself took place. While the trial was still in progress, a highly placed Communist in the Executive branch of the Government said: 'We can't shoot him as we should like to do, because he is an Archbishop; he will get a term in prison.'"[12]

In 1950, a group of American senators made freedom for Archbishop Stepinac a condition for American aid to Yugoslavia. Tito, eager to improve his relationship with the West, agreed to the deal with one stipulation: Stepinac must leave Yugoslavia. The Vatican, in consultation with the archbishop, quashed any such agreement, citing Stepinac's declaration: "They will never make me leave unless they put me on a plane by force and take me over the frontier. It is my duty in these difficult times to stay with the people."[13] Finally, in December 1951, Tito ordered Stepinac's release, but sentenced him to house arrest in his native village of Krašić, where he remained until his death in 1960. Tito's acts against Stepinac made him both a Croatian martyr and a Catholic icon; in January 1953, Pope Pius XII elevated Stepinac to cardinal and on October 3, 1998, Pope John Paul II beatified him.

I became acquainted with Stepinac's stories of assistance and rescue to Jews during the war from my interviews with survivors in 2002 and 2003 in Zagreb and Israel, and in 2007 in the United States. The second invaluable source on Stepinac's wartime role was U.S. diplomatic correspondence during the trial, which reported in detail on Dr. Ivo Politeo's defense and on the prosecution by Jakob Blažević.[14] I gained particular insights from daily dispatches to the U.S. State Department from American, French, and British diplomats who had been posted to the NDH, or from diplomats stationed in Turkey who had access to various agents. Most of this information became available after the dismemberment of a second Yugoslavian state in the 1990s and the declassification of U.S. intelligence records under the Nazi War Crimes Disclosure Act of 1998, after which many one-sided perspectives on the war and occupation are being revisited and corrected.

DIPLOMATIC MAIL

Both Nazi reports to Berlin and western diplomatic dispatches provide crucial perspectives for understanding Archbishop Stepinac's role during World War II. They also throw light on the connection between his personal fate and views of the church's actions during wartime. On

December 29, 1941, Hans Helm, the German police attaché in Zagreb, informed the office of SS-Sturmbannfuehrer Hanke, Einsatzgruppen Sipo and SD (Security Police and Security Service) in Berlin, about the troublesome archbishop:

> We were informed all along about the political meddling of the cleric [Stepinac] in the internal affairs of the country. He has connections in every department; most churches in Croatia have contacts with London and the government-in-exile. This approach undertaken by the Church could be viewed as contrary to the interests of the Third Reich and of the NDH. Our objective is to eliminate the influence of the cleric.[15]

Nine months later, on August 28, 1942, Helm informed Berlin of Stepinac's hostility toward National Socialism and specifically emphasized his motto "*Mir*" (peace), which the Nazis saw as undermining the war effort and demoralizing the Ustaše troops.[16]

In October 1942, an informer revealed to Glaise von Horstenau, German plenipotentiary in Zagreb, that "Archbishop Stepinac of Croatia and his entourage are "judenfreundlich" [friendly to Jews], and therefore enemies of National Socialism. The same archbishop had been the protector of Jewish émigrés under the Yugoslav regime, although he paid no attention to the misery of his own people."[17] Although Stepinac did in fact assist the fleeing Jews, it was never at the expense of his own people. The point of this remark was that the Germans should pay attention to Stepinac's activities and perhaps to imply his lack of popular support should the Germans take action against him.

As evidence that most Croatians were not likely to reject Stepinac, the first secretary of the Italian embassy in Zagreb reported in 1942 that most of the people in Croatia could not trust the government in power and found themselves to be at the mercy of the ongoing activities of the Ustase. He indicated that the majority of the people in Croatia were opposed to the policies of the Ustase that unfairly targeted the Jews and that the Croatians had grown suspicious about the future. Even those who had originally been supportive became cynical.[18]

Stepinac's sermons were inspirational and resistance came from all strata of society, from members of the regular army and the *Domobranstvo* (Home Guard), from the Catholic Church, and from ordinary citizens, who began flocking by the thousands to the Croatian Partisans.

Diplomats from the U.S. and its allies also took a great interest in the outspoken archbishop's fiery sermons. For example, on November 23, 1943, the U.S. consulate in Bern, Switzerland, sent a telegram to the secretary of state quoting a Zagreb headline of November 20: "Controversy between the Roman Catholic Primate and the State Authorities." The same consulate also sent Washington a summary of an editorial in the daily *Hrvatski narod* (Croatian People), in which Julija Makanec, NDH minister of education, mounted an attack on Stepinac based on sermons in which he had stated: "The Catholic Church only knows races and peoples as God's creatures and values the one with the noblest heart more than the one with the strongest fist; all men are alike in God's eyes whether European or colored men from Central Africa."[19] Makanec explicitly stated that Catholic ecclesiasts are God's servants with religious tasks not of this world; for secular tasks Croats have secular leaders. It is wrong when men, lacking knowledge in secular problems, inexperienced in hardships, and mercilessness of this world, spread political misunderstanding and defeatism among the fighters who assure with their lives not only the foundations of the Croat state but also those of the Catholic Church. The worst political error is to saw off the branch upon which you sit. This applied even to a high church dignitary who had recently used a sermon to overstep the limits of his office and interfere in affairs of no concern to him. NDH authorities subjected Stepinac to a short house arrest, as well as to public mockery, and warned him to expect heavy penalties should he dabble in politics.[20]

The Allies in 1943 were eager to use Stepinac and his church for their own purposes, when they broadcast parts of Stepinac's sermon on "Races" to German-occupied Europe. The broadcasts further aggravated Stepinac's relationship with the Nazis and the Ustaše regime, and put him in harm's way.

For example, on August 5, 1944, the American Embassy in Cairo sent to the State Department a confidential airmail dispatch, "On the Policy of the Catholic Church in Yugoslavia." It read:

> Enough information is available to enable one to conjure up, first of all, the reign of terror which must have existed under the German plan for Yugoslav self-destruction with the advent of the Pavelich [sic] regime. . . . It fell on the Catholic Church in Croatia frequently to be inculpated, in outside opinion, in Croat crimes against Serbs. The Church was accused of collaborating with the enemy, forcing conversions of Serbs to Catholicism in the manner of the Inquisition, of being passive about helping the victims of the terror, and not sounding its clarion cry in the protest against the outrages.[21]

THE YUGOSLAV STATE AGAINST STEPINAC AS REFLECTED IN DIPLOMATIC DISPATCHES

The U.S. State Department received daily reports and summaries from diplomats who observed Stepinac's trial and assessed the evidence and summaries of the archbishop's defense lawyer, Dr. Ivo Politeo, as well as the trial proceedings themselves. These documents helped change historians' views of the archbishop when they became available in the 1990s. In particular, they revealed the key role for the defense played by the testimony of Stanislav Rapotetz (Rapotec in Slovenian), a Slovene and a former captain in the Yugoslav Army.

Rapotetz testified that six lengthy meetings with Stepinac during the war persuaded him that the archbishop was being truthful and that the charges leveled against him and the church were baseless.[22] This, in turn, raises the issue of the credibility of Rapotetz's testimony in the face of evidence citing Stepinac's support for the Ustaše, such as a circular published on April 29, 1941, in the weekly *Katolički list* in which Stepinac expressed his elation over the freedom Croatia had gained after the collapse of what he termed the "Kingdom of Serbia":

There is no one among you who has not been a recent witness to the
momentous events in the life of the Croat nation. . . . No reasonable
person can condemn and no honest one can cast blame, because the
love toward one's own people is inscribed in the human heart by God
and is His commandment.[23]

In fact, Stepinac was initially overjoyed that his people had been
freed from what he viewed as bondage to Serbia. By the following
month, however, Stepinac had already distanced himself from the Ustaše
regime, on the grounds that actions by the German occupiers and the
Ustaše harmed the aspirations of the Croatian people.[24]

Rapotetz himself had no motive for shielding Stepinac. After leaving
the military and escaping from Yugoslavia, he had met the archbishop
in mid-1942 on a secret mission to the occupied territories on behalf of
the Yugoslav government–in–exile. His mission was assisted by British
military authorities and a secret network of specialists in underground
espionage. First, Rapotetz was to ask the archbishop to intervene with
Pavelić on behalf of the starving Serbian population and to inquire
whether he knew of a financial mechanism through which London
could transfer money to help them. Apparently the government-in-exile
was convinced that, if there was a way, Stepinac would help. Rapotetz
was also asked to explore Stepinac's views on the future of Yugoslavia.[25]

Having arranged another meeting, Rapotetz informed the archbishop that world opinion of the Catholic hierarchy's conduct in Croatia
was negative: "The clergy had been remiss in its moral leadership in
the midst of the German-inspired bloodletting in Bosnia, Croatia, and
Herzegovina."[26] Although grieved by the news, Stepinac cited his own
sermons and those of other clergy directed against the Nazi occupiers
and the Quisling Ustaše regime. Moreover, he had barred a number of
priests who committed heinous crimes, among them Ivo Guberina and
Zvonko Brekalo, from performing such priestly duties as preaching and
administering the sacraments.[27] But he had been unable to prevent all
Croatian priests from joining the Ustaše, despite invoking the words
of the Apostle Paul: "No one who fights for God involves himself in
the affairs of this life so that he may gratify Christ." In the same spirit,

Stepinac denied the Ustaše's accusations that the church, under his influence, was turning spiritually communist. Stepinac never sanctioned expropriating land from peasants, factories from industrialists, or their souls from workers, nor would he approve of any political system that destroyed families by taking children from their parents and desecrating marriages.[28] Reflecting on changes wrought by the war, during his conversations with Rapotez, Stepinac lamented with pain the damage the Germans and the Ustaše had done to his people:

> The Germans and Ustaše destroyed our people's souls and bodies. Their gory work was made easier by those in our midst who are false of heart. Among the false, to our shame, were Catholic priests in isolated localities, who as individuals used their holy robes for treacherous political purposes. They were no longer men of God acting under the authority of the Church. They represented nothing, no one, but their own warped desires, whetted by what they saw with their diseased eyes of German power and glory.[29]

In one of his meetings with Rapotez, the archbishop revealed his own personal dilemma in the face of the calamity that had befallen his country. Namely, the Vatican had offered him a haven within its territory, from which he could issue radio protests and appeals to audiences worldwide. Stepinac recognized that by leaving the NDH, he would spare himself grief and gain the world's approval, but this would come at the price of betraying his people. He had a choice. He could remain in Croatia and speak out against the Ustaše, who—he predicted—would either banish him to a monastery or imprison, or even execute, him. Stepinac did not fear for his own life, but either of these punishments would remove him from public life. Instead, he chose the third course: "Of staying and humbling myself daily in order to help my people practically. My voice was not stilled; rather, I raised it at every opportunity."[30]

Unwittingly, the Nazis' initial tolerance actually made it easier for Stepinac to raise his voice in outrage against them and the Ustaše. Since Stepinac no longer controlled the Catholic media, specifically the *Katolički list,* and thus he could reach people only in the confines of his cathedral, they believed he posed no danger to the German cause.[31] During the trial, Stepinac's defense lawyer, Ivo Politeo, described the power of Stepinac's sermons in denouncing the racial laws and atrocities and in defending human rights:

> [the sermons] were attended in masses not only by the Catholics but even by those who otherwise did not go to Church. Those sermons were spread, recounted, copied and propagated in thousands and thousands of copies among the people and even penetrated to the liberated territory. ...They became an underground press, a means of successful propaganda against the Ustaši, a partial substitute for an opposition press.[32]

In his testimony, Rapotetz reported that his own travels among the Serbs and Croats had established that Stepinac was truthful about his good works; indeed the archbishop had saved thousands of lives, including those of a great many Jews. He had secured food and medical aid for the persecuted, hidden them and otherwise protected them."[33] On the occasion of a feast day in Zagreb's main square, Rapotetz personally heard the archbishop deliver a "stinging tirade" against the atrocities committed by the Ustaše.

Despite his rejection of the Vatican's offer of a refuge, Stepinac nonetheless attempted to spread the word about the atrocities in Croatia and his efforts to alleviate the plight of the oppressed. Thus, at the archbishop's urging, Monsignor Augustine Juretić left the NDH for Switzerland in September 1942. In June 1943, he provided copies of a fifteen-page exposé in French, "The Catholic Episcopate in Croatia," to the coordinator of information in the U.S. Office of Strategic Services (OSS), as well as to other Allies. Juretić's report stressed that the *Katolički list* had become an organ of the Ustaše government, and was no longer a voice of the church. The new editors frequently distorted Stepinac's words and even criticized papal encyclicals and pronouncements when it was to their advantage.[34] That December, Juretić forwarded other material to the OSS, with the objective of reaching Allen Dulles, then head of operations.[35] The priest apparently believed that Dulles would be aware of the situation in the NDH and protect Archbishop Stepinac's reputation for his high moral standing, despite the malicious and erroneous accusations leveled against him. It is not clear whether Juretić's information was of any interest to the OSS. In any case, it would take Stepinac's trial to persuade people around the world that Stepinac was innocent of collaboration.

The fact that Juretić's mission was at least in part a public relations project for Stepinac was due to the picture of the Croatian church that was reaching the outside world. For example, on August 5, 1944, the American Embassy in Cairo sent to the State Department a confidential airmail dispatch, "On the Policy of the Catholic Church in Yugoslavia." It read: "The Church was accused of collaborating with the enemy, forcing conversions of Serbs to Catholicism in the manner of the Inquisition, of being passive about helping the victims of the terror, and not sounding its clarion cry in the protest against the outrages.[36] Thus, the power of Juretić's message was also undercut by the reality that—despite their best efforts to alleviate suffering—Stepinac and other clergy could claim only limited success. Thus Stepinac's experience illustrates the observation of Holocaust historian Raul Hilberg that the churches, once a powerful presence in Europe, reached the nadir of their influence during World War II, unable as they were to maintain independence against the political order.[37] This disparity in power is reflected in Stepinac's letters to Pavelić, such as this one cited by Juretić:

Poglavnik:

I am sure that such unjust measures do not come from you, but rather from irresponsible persons who have been guided by passion and personal greed. But if there is here the interference of a foreign power [Nazis] in our internal and political life, I am not afraid if my voice and my protest carry even to the leaders of that power, whatever it may be, when it is a question of defending the most basic rights of men. ... But this happiness and prosperity depend on our respect for the natural and positive law of God, on the respect for this law by the government of the state as well as by the people...[38]

ARCHBISHOP STEPINAC RAISES HIS VOICE AGAINST NAZI AND USTAŠE BRUTALITIES

In a circular letter on February 12, 1935, repeated on August 10, 1938, and again on October 26, 1941, Stepinac warned all priests under him against siding with any political party.[39] This did not keep him from addressing political philosophies when he used his sermons to clarify his position regarding both fascism and communism:

> We should shed light on those questions which trouble the world today, and on the chaos of war, a war that would not be if the voice of the Teacher had been heeded. The questions are these: (a) the freedom and worth of the individual as an independent entity; (b) the freedom and respect for religion; (c) the freedom and respect for every race and nationality; (d) the freedom and respect for private property as the basis of the personal freedom of the individual and independence of the family; and, finally (e) the freedom and respect for the right of every nation to its full development and to independence in its national life.[40]

On the day the Germans entered Zagreb, one of Stepinac's priests informed him that the Germans were approaching the *Ban Jelačić trg* (Zagreb's main square). He responded: *"Ne viruj Nimcu, ko ni suncu zimsku"* (Distrust the Germans as you would distrust the winter sun).[41] Stepinac acknowledged that the Ustaše would destroy the humanitarian fabric of Croatian society for years to come. He detested the Nazis and the communists equally.

The Ustaše considered Stepinac "an embarrassment to the regime," not only because of his activities on behalf of Jewish refugees but even more because of his sermons. Anthony O'Brien, who knew Stepinac from his prolonged stay in Zagreb, described the crowds that packed the Zagreb Cathedral when Stepinac said mass: "The people yearned to hear the only voice, which even the dreaded Gestapo could not silence. His voice was raised time and again against the pagan doctrines of totalitarianism."[42]

From both a historical and a moral perspective, Stepinac opposed Hitler's and Pavelić's aspirations to divide the world into races and then annihilate those they considered superfluous and unworthy of life. As early as 1936, he provided assistance to Jewish refugees who were fleeing Nazi Germany and Austria, and in 1938 he founded Caritas, a charitable foundation that provided help to refugees. On behalf of this predominantly Jewish population, Stepinac sent fundraising requests to 298 eminent Croats.[43] Stepinac was supported by the papal nuncio to Croatia, Monsignor Marcone, who had secured a large number of visas for South American countries, with which he succeeded in smuggling hundreds of Jews out of German-occupied territories. In 1940, in the *Hrvatica*, Stepinac summarized his thoughts regarding the outcome of totalitarian philosophies: "We are retreating to old desecrations. And with desecration there is a return to brutality and slavery. Concentration camps, like the forced labor that in the old system encompassed millions, all these are new names for a very old principle, totalitarianism."[44]

On October 26, 1941, during the Feast of Christ the King, from his pulpit in Zagreb Cathedral, Stepinac appealed to his parishioners to avoid fighting in the name of the Catholic Church. He explained that atheistic ideologies infected much of the world with hate: "The danger in such ideology is that many, in the name of Catholicism, may become victims of passion and of hatred, thus forgetting the most beautiful characteristic trait of Christianity, the law of love."[45]

Amiel Shomrony, the personal secretary of Chief Rabbi Miroslav Šalom Freiberger, recollected a memorable sermon delivered by Stepinac in October 1941, shortly after the destruction of the main synagogue in Zagreb. The archbishop had proclaimed that: "A House of God, of whatever religion, is a holy place. Whoever touches such a place will pay with his life. An attack on a House of God of any religion constitutes an attack on all religious communities."[46]

In a sermon in late May 1942, Stepinac informed his congregation that it would be absurd to speak of a new world order, as the communists and the Nazis did, if in that order the human personality were not valued: "Each soul has its inalienable rights which no human power can or ought to limit."[47] He also declared that it would be absurd to suggest that the Catholic Church feared any human force when defending the elemental rights of human beings and freedom of conscience.

On October 25, 1942, Archbishop Stepinac asked his parishioners a laconic question: "How then must we judge individuals who arrogantly behave as if God no longer exists on the earth?" He answered his own question:

> Only one race really exists and that is the Divine race. Its birth cer-tificate is found in the Book of Genesis. . . . All of them without one exception, whether they belong to the race of Gypsies or to another, whether they are Negroes or civilized Europeans, whether they are detested Jews or proud Aryans, have the same right to say "Our Father who Art in Heaven!"[48]

It is not surprising that Ante Pavelić visited the Zagreb Cathedral only once during the war years.[49] He would have found no words of com-fort there. Stepinac's sermons reached an increasingly wide audience, a fact that angered the Nazis and the Ustaše. As time went on, rumors cir-culated in the country and abroad that he was dead. His followers feared for his life; many, in fact, predicted that Stepinac's days of freedom were numbered, as was seen when he was under house arrest.[50]

In another sermon, delivered on March 3, 1943, Stepinac argued that no one had the right to dissolve a marriage consecrated by the Roman Catholic Church.[51] Because of its belief that marriage and bap-tism were holy sacraments, the Catholic Church recognized, at least in principle, that they must shield baptized Jews and Jews involved in sanctified mixed marriages. Thus they could not remain silent about the dissolution of such a union because one of the partners was unable to demonstrate that all four of his or her grandparents were Christians.[52]

On July 9, 1943, Radio Vatican, in its program "Free Yugoslavia," portrayed the archbishop as "a resolute soldier advocating moral justice and freedom." In response, Stepinac received words of thanks and grati-tude from throughout the free world. Around this time, Stepinac gave several sermons in which he denounced the barbarism of the Ustaše, and when they declared that all Jews, including those in mixed marriages, had to register with the police, Stepinac again declared his opposition. The NDH media responded to this challenge with silence. They had no intention of publicizing Stepinac's attacks on separating couples in mixed marriages.[53]

As important as were Stepinac's philosophical and theological pronouncements about the nature of humanity and the individual's proper relationship with God, he had to confront daily and directly the atrocities perpetrated by the Ustaše regime. Stepinac's behavior toward the Ustaše would become a subject of controversy during his trial, especially the apparent initial support for the regime. Already by the second month of occupation, however, Stepinac realized that Pavelić was no more than a power-hungry puppet of Nazi Germany and, to a lesser extent, Fascist Italy. From this point forward, Stepinac distanced himself from the NDH authorities. He began in earnest to protest against the mass deportation and extermination of Jews in concentration camps. In 1941, when two of his priests and six nuns who were Jewish converts were excused from wearing the yellow Star of David, Stepinac solemnly declared: "I have requested that these priests and nuns continue wearing this sign of belonging to the people from which Our Savior was born as long as others will have to do so."[54]

Pavelić knew that he needed the Vatican's recognition in order to consolidate the support of the Croatian people.[55] On May 17, 1941, he was slated to visit Italy's King Victor Emmanuel III, the Duke of Spoleto—the king's designee to rule an eventual Italian Croatia—and other members of the Italian hierarchy.[56] Hoping at the same time to receive recognition from the Holy See, he insisted that Stepinac arrange a meeting for him with the pope. He did so, but refused Pavelić's request to join the delegation to Rome. The pope agreed to see Pavelić, but as a private individual, not as a head of state. When asked to clarify the reasons for the animosity between Pavelić and Stepinac, Bishop Salis-Seewis, a Croatian cleric who was part of the delegation, explained that he had objected to "being mixed up in this business … [knowing] that the people from the Peasant Party were against it, and seeing the people already in sympathy with the

English and French. Stepinac, however, just said: 'that's the way it's got to be' (*Kaj je, je*)…at that moment we couldn't all withdraw and someone had to go as a matter of form."[57]

It was curiously surprising that Stepinac's first reaction to the Nazi appearance at the gates of Zagreb was so negative. But one has to remember that already in the *Mein Kampf* Hitler attacked both Christian Churches in Germany for their failure to recognize the racial laws. And then for political gain on July 20, 1933, Hitler concluded a concordant with the Vatican in which he guaranteed freedom of the Catholic religion. On July 25, five days after the concordant, the German government began to violate the tenants of the agreement. On March 14, 1937, Pope Pius XI issued an encyclical "Mit Brennender Sorge" (With Burning Sorrow) charging the Nazi government with "evasion" and "violation" of the concordant and accusing it of sowing the "tares of suspicion, discord, hatred, calumny of secret and open fundamental hostility to Christ and His Church." The Pope recognized that on "the horizons of Germany" the threatening storm clouds of destructive religious wars…which had no other aim than… destruction."[58]

Stepinac was aware that the Serbs accused him of atrocities committed by the Ustaše and held him responsible for the forced conversions of Orthodox Serbs to Catholicism.[59] Yet the Catholic Church in Croatia had stated its position in the "Resolution on Conversions," reached during the Episcopal Conference in Zagreb on November 17 and 18, 1941: "Only those may be received into the Catholic Church who are converted by Church appointees and without any constraints, completely free, led by an interior conviction of the truth of the Catholic faith, and who have entirely fulfilled ecclesiastical regulations...."[60] In time, however, Stepinac realized that the rate of exterminations at the hands of the Ustaše was greater for Orthodox Serbs than for converts. Accordingly, he encouraged his clergy to comply with those who sought conversion in order to save their lives:

> When you are visited by people of the Jewish or Eastern Orthodox faith, whose lives are in danger and who express the wish to convert to Catholicism, accept them in order to save human lives. Do not require

any special religious knowledge from them, because the Eastern Orthodox are Christians like us, and the Jewish faith is the faith from which Christianity draws its roots. The role and duty of Christians is in the first place to save people. When this time of madness and savagery passes, those who would convert out of conviction will remain in our church, while others, after the danger passes, will return to their church.[61]

Stepinac was correct that formal conversion saved the lives of a number of Orthodox Serbs. In the 1970s, Reverend Dušan Kašić, an Orthodox Serb, attested that it was difficult to ascertain the number of converts, since all forced conversions had been deemed acts of political violence and annulled by the postwar civilian authorities. Of the converts from that time, only a few Orthodox Serbs who had married Catholics chose to remain Catholic.[62] In retrospect, Stepinac's directives for voluntary conversions saved the lives of many Serbs, who later were able to return to their own Orthodox churches.[63] Unfortunately, conversions to Catholicism meant little for Jews; the Third Reich was determined to annihilate all those who had three Jewish grandparents, regardless of religious affiliation. Nevertheless—as discussed further below—Stepinac managed to rescue most of the Jews who were in mixed marriages consecrated by the Catholic Church prior to April 10, 1941, as well as the offspring of these marriages. In 1948, many of these survivors chose Israel over Yugoslavia.

STEPINAC'S NATIONAL AND INTERNATIONAL CORRESPONDENCE

In addition to his public sermons, Stepinac used private correspondence to press his cause with Croatian officials, the Yugoslavian government-in-exile, and Catholics around the world. Reports from foreign diplomats provide evidence that Stepinac reacted forcefully when the news of atrocities reached him.[64] As early as May 22, 1941, the archbishop wrote to Andrija Artuković, NDH minister of the interior, objecting to implementation of antisemitic legislation:

But to take away all possibility of existence from members of other nations or races and to mark them with the stamp of shame is already a question of humanity and of morals. And moral laws have application not only to the lives of individuals but also to those who rule the states. . . . Why treat in this way those who are members of another race through no fault of their own? . . . Do we have the right to commit this outrage to the human personality. . . . I ask you, Mr. Minister, to give appropriate orders so that the Jewish laws and others similar to them are executed in such a way that the human dignity and personality of every man is respected.[65]

On March 7, 1942, Stepinac wrote a second letter to Artuković: "I do not think that it can bring us any glory if it is said of us that we have solved the Jewish problem in the most radical way, that is to say, the cruelest."[66] He went on to remind Artuković that capital punishment inflicted on innocent people was contrary to Catholic teachings; penalties should be inflicted only on those who have committed a crime. "The system of shooting hundreds of hostages for a crime, when the person guilty of the crime cannot be found, is a pagan system which only results in evil."[67]

News of Ustaše persecution of Serbs, Jews, Gypsies, and Croat dissidents spread throughout Yugoslavia and beyond, to Europe and the United States. In late June 1941, Stepinac forwarded Pavelić a letter from the Catholic archbishop of Belgrade, Monsignor Dr. Josip Ujčić, in which he appealed to the Ustaše head to cease the persecution of Orthodox Serbs. He also demanded a more humane treatment of prisoners held for political or racial reasons.[68]

The atrocities also became an embarrassment to Croat citizens abroad. On July 19, 1941, Stepinac received a letter from Dominik Mandić, a prominent Franciscan friar who resided in the Vatican.[69] Mandić, obviously oblivious to Stepinac's constant condemnation of the regime, wrote that the Ustaše's policies were harmful and gave Croatians throughout the world a bad name. He thus asked Stepinac to intervene with Pavelić's regime. On November 16, 1942, in a broadcast from London, Juraj Krnjević, the former secretary general of the Croatian

Peasant Party, now in the Yugoslav government-in-exile, appealed to Stepinac and his countrymen:

> I am not appealing to Dr. Sarić [archbishop of Sarajevo], who is behaving like those who have lost their soul and conscience, but to you and other heads of the Catholic Church in Croatia to search your conscience to see whether you have fulfilled your duty one hundred percent.... What is necessary is your manly word of condemnation in agreement with the feelings of the Croatian people and the teachings of the Church...[70]

Other Croats, at home and abroad, demanded that the Ustaše distance themselves from Nazi ideology. They seemed to agree that Archbishop Stepinac should deliver their urgent request to Pavelić. But even before their pleas reached Stepinac, he and many other clergy had urged their parishioners to do what they could to prevent the moral and ethical damage the Ustaše were inflicting on the Croatian people. As early as September 7, 1941, Stepinac wrote to Pavelić himself, asking that the regime stop treating, non-Aryans, as the Ustaše liked to define them, in an inhuman and cruel manner.[71]

On March 6, 1943, Stepinac practically pleaded with Pavelić, asking for justice and humanity when dealing with Jews. Indeed, even if anti-Jewish policies resulted from "the interference of a foreign power in our internal and political life," Stepinac declared that he was not afraid to take his protest even to the leaders of that power because the Catholic Church knows no fear of any earthly power, whatever it may be, when it is a question of defending the most basic rights of men.[72]

Stepinac knew that the atrocities committed in the name of the Croatian people would have bitter postwar consequences for Croatia. On one occasion he remarked that because of the malicious conduct of the Pavelić regime, the Croatian people would have to bear full responsibility for Ustaše conduct as well as for the growth of communism.[73]

STEPINAC AND MIXED MARRIAGES

Stepinac's defense of Jews in mixed marriages deserves particular attention. From 1938 on, in ever-increasing numbers, Croatian Jews began
converting to Catholicism. In mid-1941, the Jewish Community in
Zagreb, numbering approximately 12,000, was reduced by 3,860 Jews
who declared themselves Catholics, a process facilitated by Stepinac's
instructions to his clergy to issue certificates of baptism on demand to
endangered Jews and Serbs.[74] Acting on these instructions, priests such
as Dr. Mijo Selec of the Church of Saint Blasius (sv. Blaža), recognized
that in time of war they must not only care for their parishoners' souls
but also save the lives of Jews and Serbs by providing them sanctuary in
their churches, or if need be in villages outside Zagreb.[75]

Although by 1942 about 30 percent of the Jews of Zagreb had converted, Stepinac was painfully aware that it would likely be impossible to
rescue everyone. However, because of the many baptized Jews, Vatican
Secretary of State Maglione obtained the Italian government's permission to allow Yugoslav Jewish refugees to remain in the Italian zones.[76]

When the Croatian government instructed all Jews to register
with their local Ustaše authorities, those in mixed marriages turned to
Archbishop Stepinac for help.[77] In 1942, Stepinac was besieged with letters from Catholic women throughout the NDH whose husbands had
been deported to concentration camps, in particular Jasenovac. The
most concentrated effort was made by forty-eight such women from
Osijek. Together with their priests and bishops, the women came to see
Stepinac.[78] Having received hundreds of such letters from Catholic wives,
Stepinac knew that he had to act immediately and forcefully; doing nothing would have been tantamount to violating the sacrament of marriage,
and this he aimed to prevent, even at the risk of his personal safety.[79]
Should action be taken against these men, he threatened to temporarily
close the churches in Croatia and let the bells ring continuously.[80] At the
same time he requested the Vatican's assistance on this matter.

Initially, Pavelić took Stepinac's threats into consideration. Even
Hans Helm, the SS police attaché at the German Embassy in Zagreb,

underscored in his daily briefings to Berlin that Archbishop Stepinac was a great friend of the Jews, and that he would surely involve himself on their behalf.[81] In September 1942, SS officer Franz Abromeit, advisor on Jewish issues for Croatia in Adolf Eichmann's office, was appointed to organize the final deportation of all Croatian Jews, including those in mixed marriages. When Giuseppe Marcone, the Vatican's visitor to Croatia, and Archbishop Stepinac heard about this plan, they sent a letter to Pavelić demanding that Helm and Siegfried Kasche, German ambassador to the NDH, stop the deportation of protected Jews, converts, and partners in mixed marriages.[82] Despite his explicit instructions from Pavelić, Kasche reported to Berlin that the final *Judenaktion* in Croatia would end in March 1943.[83] Stepinac promised that if the NDH regime undertakes action against mixed marriages, which he considered interference in the internal affairs of the church, then in protest all the churches in Croatia would close their doors.[84]

Most Jews in mixed marriages survived the final deportation of Jews to Auschwitz.

STEPINAC'S INTERACTIONS WITH THE JEWISH COMMUNITY

Throughout the war years Stepinac maintained close contact with the Jewish Community in Zagreb and with individuals from other Jewish Communities. His accessibility, and the fact that people turned to him, demonstrate his readiness to act on their behalf. The letters of Croatia's Chief Rabbi, Dr. Miroslav Šalom Freiberger, attest to their close relationship as spiritual leaders who shared the burden of caring for the bodies and souls of their congregants.[85] Most of Freiberger's letters contained requests to address the looming crisis.[86] On December 15, 1942, Rabbi Freiberger, through the apostolic visitor to Croatia, Abbot Giuseppe Ramiro Marcone, asked the Holy See for help in transferring fifty to sixty orphaned children from Zagreb to Florence, Livorno, or Padua, with expenses to be covered by Zagreb's Jewish Community.[87] In another letter the rabbi asked the archbishop to speak on behalf of the evacuation to Italy of two hundred Jewish orphan boys, ages seven to seventeen.[88]

And on January 9, 1942, Stepinac requested Cardinal Maglione's intervention in the transfer of two hundred boys to the Jewish Community in Florence—or to any other community outside the NDH that would care for their upbringing and education.[89]

The Jewish authorities also turned to the archbishop to intercede with Interior Minister Artuković. On one such occasion, Stepinac made a plea on behalf of Jewish orphans:

> At the request of the Jewish Community in Zagreb of April 13, 1942, I personally delivered to the office of the Minster, permit #2550-I-A-1942 on April 15, 1942. This was a request for the relocation of 50 Jewish children to Turkey. But of the 50 children, who obtained permits to relocate, there were only 11 survivors [the others had been killed]. In the current request, I ask of you to activate the 38 unutilized permits and put them to use by assigning them to other Jewish orphans.[90]

On April 8, 1943, Stepinac again wrote to Artuković at Freiberger's behest, this time to request help in obtaining release from detention and work permits for employees of the Jewish Community:

> Mr. Minister: I feel free to present to you a request from the Jewish Community in Zagreb, in which they are asking to free from detention several of their employees so as to resume work for the welfare of those who are still left in Zagreb. Enclosed are the names of their employees. I ask of you, Mr. Minister, please assist them by giving instruction for their release. I am thankful to you for all you have done so that the ethical and Christian character of our people may be saved.[91]

On December 6, 1943, SS authorities in Zagreb entered the Lavoslav Schwarz home for elderly Jews, and ordered the residents to vacate the building within ten days. They were told that anyone remaining on the premises would be deported to Auschwitz. At the request of Zagreb's Jewish Community, Stepinac organized the transfer of fifty-eight of the residents to the archbishopric's building in Brežovica, near Zagreb.[92]

On October 16, 1944, Stepinac was informed that an Ustaše officer and his agents had entered the premises of the Jewish Community and arrested eight of their employees, including Dr. Robert Glucksthal, the Jewish official representative of the Jewish Community in Zagreb, and his assistant, Asher Kisičkog. Although six of those arrested were killed in detention, Glucksthal and Kisičkog were released due to intervention by Stepinac and representatives of the International Red Cross.[93]

As a result of his efforts on their behalf, Stepinac received many letters that acknowledged with gratitude his work on behalf of the Jews.[94] One such letter came from Dr. Meir Tuval Weltmann, representative of the Jewish authorities in Palestine, who, on June 11, 1943, wrote two letters of thanks to Catholic clergy who had helped Jews during the war, one to the apostolic legate Monsignor Angelo Giuseppe Roncalli (later Pope John XXIII) in Istanbul, and the second to Archbishop Stepinac: "With deep gratitude, recognition, and appreciation to the Holy See and to Archbishop of Zagreb Stepinac for his conduct and assistance to the Jews of Croatia and especially for assisting Dr. Hugo Kon and the Chief Rabbi Dr. Freiberger."[95] Weltmann also made a specific request that the archbishop use his influence to persuade the regime to allow Jews to be moved to Hungary and Italy and, from there, to Palestine.

As a result, on May 30, 1943, the Apostolic Legation in Istanbul wrote to Cardinal Maglione in the Vatican, with a copy to Archbishop Stepinac, passing on the request of the Jewish Agency in Palestine for assistance in helping "400 Jewish deportees," including Hugo Kon, the president of Zagreb's Jewish Community, and Chief Rabbi Freiberger and their families. The letter explained that they had previously been under Stepinac's direct protection; once the archbishop's life was in danger, they had become candidates for deportation to concentration camps.[96] The agency expressed its need for information without delay regarding their whereabouts and mostly if they were still in Jasenovac or possibly in Stara Gradiška camp. Immediate reply was requested: "We are prepared to act and transfer them to Palestine."[97] Despite the efforts on their behalf by Stepinac and others, the entire transport of four hundred Jews was taken to Auschwitz; only a few survived.

The files of the postwar National Commission contain further testimonies to Stepinac's actions on behalf of Jews. Hinko Mann, a former board member of Zagreb's Jewish Community, who was mentioned earlier in Chapter 2, lauded Stepinac, while acknowledging the difficulties he faced:

> The archbishop was called to act on behalf of the Jews on many occasions; he always responded favorably, but, very often, his interventions were unsuccessful since he was considered a "Jew lover" by the regime. Obviously, the regime had no interest in assisting him, particularly when the cause involved helping the Jews. . . . There was a major conflict of interest between Stepinac's position toward the Jews and that of the Ustaše and the Gestapo.[98]

Before Stepinac's trial in 1946, twenty Jews still living in Yugoslavia who attributed their rescue and survival to the archbishop approached his defense lawyer, Ivo Politeo, and offered to testify in his behalf, despite the danger to themselves. Survivors living in Palestine also volunteered to testify. Politeo advised them not to take the risk, certain that Stepinac's fate was sealed.[99] Nonetheless, survivors and rescuers one-by-one began speaking out on his behalf, in particular in testimonies to representatives of the Steven Spielberg Shoah Foundation. During my travels through the countries of the former Yugoslavia, Israel, and the United States, the name most frequently mentioned in my seventy-two recorded testimonies was that of Archbishop Stepinac.[100] Among these many interviews, three stand out: Dr. Stjepan Steiner, Dr. Teodor Gruner, and Olga Rajšek-Neumann.

In 1942, Steiner, who was one of the fortunate physicians serving in the Bosnian syphilis mission, escaped from Bosnia and joined the Partisans, soon becoming Tito's personal physician. In his interview, he spoke highly of two extraordinary Croatians who had rescued hundreds of Jews during the war: one was Dr. Ante Vuletić, whose actions were discussed in Chapter 3. The other was Archbishop Stepinac, whom Dr. Steiner credited with saving at least four hundred Jews and hundreds more living in mixed marriages, all under the watchful eyes of the Ustaše and the SS.[101] Steiner also recalled an incident after the war when, out of curiosity, he asked Dr. Miroslav Dujić (Deutsch) why he had waited until 1943 to join the medical mission to Bosnia. Dujić, a convert to Catholicism, replied that at that time Stepinac informed all the Jews under his protection to depart Zagreb without delay, because his own life was in danger. Those who heeded his advice and fled survived.[102]

Dr. Teodor Gruner related how his father, Bernard Gruner, the chief cantor of the Jewish Community in Zagreb, was taken to Savska Street, the city's central detention center. A short time after Stepinac heard about his detention, Cantor Gruner was released.[103] He survived the war.

Olga Rajšek Neumann described how she became a rescuer when her Jewish fiancé, Zlatko Neumann, a Yugoslav Army POW in Germany, asked her in a letter to fetch his nephew, Danko Shtockhammer, from Pakrac, a village in Slavonia, and bring him to live with her in Zagreb. Danko needed special care because, at the tender age of eight, he had already been in two concentration camps. After she brought the boy to her home, a neighbor reported to the Ustaše that Olga Rajšek was shielding a Jewish child. On April 12, 1943, Danko was sent to the detention center on Savska Street. Uncertain what to do, Olga ran to her parish priest, who reassured her that Archbishop Stepinac would come to their aid. After a few hours, Danko was brought back. Although Olga was Danko's guardian, to ensure his safety and again with Stepinac's help, he was placed in a Catholic orphanage until the end of the war.[104]

Olga Rajšek-Newmann was deservedly honored by Yad Vashem when on January 14, 2003, the Commission of Designation of the Righteous decided to award her the title of "Righteous Among the Nations" for help rendered to Jewish persons during the period of the Holocaust.[106] However, it seems peculiar that Archbishop Stepinac, the person responsible for Danko's rescue, was not even mentioned at the ceremony.

Dr. Amiel Shomrony (Emil Schwartz) was a personal secretary to the Chief Rabbi of Zagreb, Dr. Freiberger. Since Emil's father was an "Honorary Aryan," he too was free to move about in Zagreb. In July 1943, on an errand to the archdiocese, he was told about an anticipated wave of roundups of Jews. He was also to tell Rabbi Freiberger that the archbishop would welcome him, his wife Irena, his parents, and his sister Ljubica as guests at the archdiocese. However, when the Freibergers learned that the roundup would include all the Jews of Zagreb, they declined Stepinac's offer, choosing instead to be deported with their congregation. The rabbi did, however, ask if he could move his library to the archdiocese for safekeeping.[105] (After the war, the entire library was returned to the Jewish Community in Zagreb.)

Finally, in the late 1990s and early 2000, sixty Jewish survivors rescued by Stepinac wrote to the Remembrance Authority at Yad Vashem to request that Dr. Alojzije Stepinac be recognized as a Righteous Gentile. Their request was not fulfilled because some survivors maintained that there was no danger to his life and that he could have done more for the Jews. Yad Vashem's decision is, in the end, less important than that these and other survivors acknowledged Archbishop Stepinac's responsibility for their rescue and survival. Despite recognition by those he saved, Stepinac met a harsher fate in postwar Yugoslavia.

THE EVOLUTION OF ATTITUDES TOWARD ARCHBISHOP STEPINAC SINCE 1945

People around the world, from all walks of life and religious affiliations, expressed their surprise and anger upon hearing in October 1946 that Tito's regime had not only arrested Stepinac, but also sentenced him to a sixteen-year prison term.[107] Heads of state, diplomats, journalists, humanitarian organizations, and social and religious leaders published articles and editorials expressing outrage at the treatment of a man whose record during the war years was widely admired. The following examples are characteristic of the hundreds that were published:

> The Yugoslav propaganda against Archbishop of Zagreb has only one purpose, i.e., to prepare the trial of the Archbishop. (Randolph Churchill, son of Winston Churchill, and from 1943 to 1945 a member of the British Military Mission to Tito's Headquarters, writing after his visit to Stepinac. (From *The Daily Telegraph*, January 23, 1946.)

No one in or out of Yugoslavia doubts that the verdict of the four-men court, at once judge and prosecutor, is already signed and sealed. . . . The trial of Archbishop Stepinatz [sic] is the heaviest weapon against the church Tito has yet rolled out. If the lessons of religious history mean anything, he is merely making a martyr, whose spirit and influence he cannot kill. (Editorial, *The New York Times*, October 3, 1946.)

When the Nazis occupied Croatia, Archbishop Stepinac risked his life to aid Jews. With his aid hundreds of Jews were smuggled out of Yugoslavia. He obtained the repeal of an order that all Jews must wear a yellow tag. He denounced the Nazi race laws. He worked with the International Red Cross to rescue Jews in other counties. He concealed Jews under his own roof, and many of his priests did likewise. (Editorial, *The New Leader*, the self-described "Liberal Labor Weekly," October 12, 1946.)

Dignitaries in the United States, among them two governors and scores of other officials, condemned Stepinac's conviction. In New York City, seven U.S. Congressmen and seven council members eulogized Stepinac on February 10, 1980, the day West 41st Street was renamed Cardinal Stepinac Place. Speaking at the event, Representative James M. Hanley (32nd District, New York), noted that the renaming "is to honor this great man for his strength, courage, and ability to stand up for his beliefs in the face of incredible adversity." New Jersey Congressman (and later governor) James J. Florio added: "The greatest tribute we can pay to him today, and in the future, is to unite in our efforts to continue the work for which he laid his life in service for mankind."

Vladko Maček, former head of the popular Croatian Peasant Party, contributed one of the most striking postwar assessments of Stepinac's actions and values. Although he had been sentenced by the Ustaše to the Jasenovac concentration camp, and then to house arrest after he rejected Nazi overtures to lead the NDH, Maček was rarely in agreement with Stepinac's religious stance. Nonetheless, he respected Stepinac's ethical, moral, and humanitarian values.

Archbishop Stepinac was not a man of idle words, but rather, he actively helped every person when he was able, and to the extent he was able. He made no distinctions as to whether a man in need was a Croat or a Serb, whether he was a Catholic or an Orthodox, whether he was Christian or non-Christian. All the attacks on him, whether the products of misinformation or . . . of a clouded mind, cannot change this fact.[108]

Stepinac's reputation in the non-Croatian parts of Yugoslavia and among the country's diehard communists did not improve in the years following his trial and conviction. Outside the counties of former Yugoslavia, however, accounts more sympathetic to the archbishop gradually began to appear, especially in the 1990s after the opening to the public of the Croatia's national archives.[109] The most striking, and diametrically opposed views were expressed, on the one hand, in the book *Holocaust in Zagreb*,[110] co-authored by the Croatian historian Ivo Goldstein and the journalist Slavko Goldstein, and on the other hand in *The Catholic Church and the Holocaust, 1930-1965*, by American historian Michael Phayer.[111]

Ivo Goldstein and Slavko Goldstein—son and father, respectively—described Alojzije Stepinac as a brave man of high moral principle, strong passions, and of narrow political horizons because he was fanatically pious and endlessly loyal to the Vatican even though, until the reforms of the Second Vatican Council in the 1960s, papal policy was basically unsympathetic to Judaism as a religion. In regard to Stepinac, the Goldsteins argued that had he not been sympathetic towards the NDH regime, he would not have on April 12, 1941, rushed to visit Slavko Kvaternik, the head of the Croatia's armed forces, who was awaiting the arrival of Pavelić.[112] They also questioned "how Stepinac thought it possible to reconcile discriminatory laws against an entire people while, at the same time, honoring the 'person and dignity of every member of these people.'"[113] To support their claim they cite Stepinac's letter of March 7, 1942 to the Interior Minister Artuković:

... I take the liberty, Mr. Minister, of asking you to prevent through your power, all unjust proceeding against citizens who individually can be accused of no wrong. I do not think it can bring us any glory if it is said of us that we have solved the Jewish problem in the most radical way, that is to say, the cruelest. The solution to this question should provide only for the punishment of Jews who committed crimes, but not for the persecution of innocent people..."[114]

I argue that even recognizing that the concern for the protection of innocent individuals may be inadequate in a regime that effectively made Jews a criminal class and whose definition of "crimes" was arbitrary in the extreme, it is not at all clear that Stepinac's letter to Artuković supports the Goldsteins' assertion that he somehow accepted the Ustaše regime's antisemitic laws. On the contrary, if he had agreed in principle with the Racial Laws, or even remotely been sympathetic to them, then why he was in such a rush to write to Artuković two letters of protest in less than a month of the regime's rise to power? I cited parts of this letter earlier in this chapter in support of Stepinac's opposition to the Ustaše policies.[115] It is also telling that the Goldsteins' book contends that Stepinac used the weekly *Katolički list* to communicate with his parishioners during the war, although, as noted already, the Ustaše government had taken control over the weekly and appointed new editors who frequently distorted Stepinac's words.[116]

Michael Phayer, who has written widely on the Catholic Church and the Holocaust, points out that Stepinac did indeed take action early on:

Bishop Alojzije Stepinac began to distance himself from the Ustaše in May 1941, just a month after Pavelić came to power. He objected publicly to the fascist's racial laws, complained about converted 'Jews' having to wear the Star of David, and then extended his concern to all Jews. . . . In comparison with other eastern European church leaders, especially those in neighboring Hungary, Bishop Stepinac showed courage and insight in his actions.[117]

Phayer also criticizes Pope Pius XII for failing to let other prelates know of Stepinac's courageous conduct:

> No leader of a national church ever spoke about genocide as pointedly as Stepinac. His words were courageous and principled, because he, a Croat, denounced Croatian nationals. . . . Unfortunately, the Holy See let no one know that Archbishop Stepinac had dared to speak out against racism and genocide or whether it approved of his conduct.[118]

How do we reconcile these two points of view? Although their books came out in 2001, Ivo and Slavko Goldsteins' bibliography indicates that their sources were dated, and that they were influenced by Slavko's experiences during the war, most specifically the murder of his father, and by Tito's propaganda against Stepinac and the church.[119] Phayer came to the issue as an American historian with interests in the Holocaust and the Catholic Church, but with no personal agenda. His book is based on broad research using archival and secondary sources.

The late Jozo Tomasevich, a Yugoslav-American historian and author of three authoritative volumes on Yugoslavia during World War II, like Ivo and Slavko Goldstein, criticized Stepinac for legitimizing the Ustaše regime by rushing to visit Slavko Kvaternik, the army commander-in-chief on April 12, 1941, and Pavelić, on April 16. He had other objections to Stepinac's conduct but none was as acute as the one mentioned above.[120]

The work of Menahem Shelah, an Israeli historian born in Croatia, offers another important perspective on Stepinac. Writing in the early 1980s, he characterized the archbishop as a church functionary, introverted and ascetic by nature and unable to cope with the tragic challenges of the period. Yet, he rejected the accusations made by many Yugoslavs because "there is no doubt that [Stepinac] worked behind the scenes, and toward the middle of 1943 tried in public to save Jews, and he condemned the atrocities perpetrated by the regime." Shelah credits the interventions of both Stepinac and Vatican emissary Abbot Giuseppe Ramiro Marcone with the survival of Jews in mixed marriages and their offspring.[121] At the same time, he argued that Stepinac cannot be absolved, because through procrastination and public expressions he convinced the public that the Ustaše were a lesser evil than the communists. Shelah also accused Stepinac of failing to take action against dozens of Croatian priests who willingly took part in the murder of Jews.

In the late 1980s, American historian Stella Alexander attempted to critically analyze the "Stepinac affair." She theorized that three distinct groups exploited the controversy to create their own myths and propaganda. The Orthodox Serbs, in particular Serbian bishops, persisted in demonizing Stepinac: "The most that they will concede is to reproach him, not for what he did but for what he failed to do to protect the Serbian population." Alexander, like some others who have examined the issue, characterized Stepinac as "a conscientious and brave man, of deep piety and considerable intelligence, but with a blinkered world view. . . . In the end one is left feeling that he was not quite great enough for his role."[122] It is surprising that Alexander would reach this conclusion given the evidence in her book of Stepinac's forceful actions in defiance of the Ustaše. It is possible that through Stepinac she intended to criticize the postwar propaganda advanced by the Croats who idolized him and the Serbs who demonized him.

American historian Jonathan Steinberg agrees with the view that Pius XII might have done more to assist prelates like Stepinac, even while questioning whether the pope's clear and direct statement of support would have altered the course of events. "It would, conceivably, have strengthened the hands of those prelates, such as Stepinac or Cardinal Gerlier of Lyons, in occupied countries where puppet governments still preserved a semblance of independence." But ultimately, he admits: "I doubt if it would have halted the German murder machine."[123]

It is apparent that the defeat of Nazism and Italian and Croatian fascism required much greater power than that available to Stepinac or even the Vatican. Their defeat was in the realm of possibility only when the peoples of the world united in their common goal to free the world from the Third Reich and their collaborators.

In evaluating the frequent characterizations of Stepinac as righteous but weak, one must consider what was required of him in his office as archbishop. As a Roman Catholic prelate, Stepinac was bound by the Church Constitution, "*Solicitude Ecclesiarum*," issued by Pope Gregory XVI in 1831.[124] This document was consistent with provisions of the 1907 Hague and 1929 Geneva conventions, which affirm that, during a state of war, all legal power passes into the hands of the occupier, who is authorized and obligated to maintain public order and public life by demanding obedience of the inhabitants, with specified exceptions. More specifically, the church's constitution commanded that in order to ensure the spiritual welfare and rights of its parishioners, church representatives should enter into a relation with those persons who actually exercise power. These representatives also have a duty to defend the rights of the Roman Catholic Church as they existed prior to the occupation. Under these obligations, Stepinac acted as his vows and the Vatican expected of him. He chastised the regime for daily violations of church ordinances, such as forced conversions of Serbs who had already been baptized, although he approved conversions that were voluntary and undergone in order to save human lives. He also raised his voice against violations of human rights and for human dignity. Historians who questioned his visits to Kvaternik and Pavelić failed to consider the constraints under which he was obliged to act in his official role as archbishop.

The Vatican, moreover, instructed Stepinac to be mindful of his words and conduct in the interest of saving lives. This was especially true after the vigorous efforts to defend Jews by the Catholic hierarchy in the Netherlands were followed in 1942 by a roundup of all Jews, even long-time converts, including priests and nuns. The Dutch bishops demonstrated great courage, but 79 percent of the country's Jews, 110,000 individuals, were murdered. The Nazis were determined to prevent similar attempts elsewhere.[125] On June 2, 1943, as on many previous occasions, Pius XII sent a letter to the Sacred College of Cardinals advising that:

> Every word that We address to the responsible authorities and every one of Our public declarations have to be seriously weighed and considered in the interest of the persecuted themselves in order not to make their situation unwittingly even more difficult and unbearable.[126]

The pope emphasized that one best assisted the oppressed by quietly and persistently performing acts of rescue. Stepinac recognized
the validity of these instructions. He had to act prudently and without
ostentatious protests, especially in order to prevent his replacement by a
fervent Ustaše such as Sarajevo's Archbishop Sarić.[127]

Ernst von Weizsäcker, the German ambassador to the Vatican
from 1943 to 1945, and later the president of the Federal Republic of
Germany, confirms this view in his memoirs, discussing why prelates
like Stepinac did not raise their voices more loudly:

> Not even institutions of worldwide importance, such as the
> International Red Cross or the Roman Catholic Church saw fit to
> appeal to Hitler in a general way on behalf of the Jews or to call openly
> on the sympathies of the world. It was precisely because they wanted
> to help the Jews that these organizations refrained from making any
> general and public appeals; for they were afraid that they would
> thereby injure, rather than help, the Jews.[128]

Why, then, should Stepinac have been expected to act differently?
Historians should also take into account the Vatican's long relationship with
Croatia, extending back to December 1519, when Pope Julius II declared:
"the Head of the Catholic Church will not allow Croatia to fall, for they
are the *Antemurale Christianitatis* (shield and bulwark) of Christianity."[129]
He bestowed this accolade upon the Croats for their tenacity and valor in
resisting the Ottomans, who posed a threat to the Vatican's presence in
the Balkans and throughout central Europe. More recently, the position
of the Roman Catholic Church in Yugoslavia had been under pressure
during the interwar period. Demographically, Croatia was heterogeneous.
Although it had a Catholic majority, it also had a sizable Serbian Orthodox
minority, which held political control in Yugoslavia, thus posing a threat to
Croatia's independence. Whether the Vatican was right or wrong—given
the Ustaše regime's atrocities—to uphold the ancient promise not to let
Croatia fall is beyond the scope of this study.

It is clear, however, that Stepinac found himself between a rock and
a hard place. He acted to the best of his abilities as a loyal servant of

the Roman Catholic Church, while never forgetting his belief in moral law as a guiding principle. This encouraged him to denounce, at every opportunity, the inhumanity of the Ustaše regime's laws and actions. Throughout the war years, Stepinac followed but one rule: Only one race exists and that is the Divine race. Its birth certificate is found in the Book of Genesis.

5

The Rescue of the Jews by the Italians, 1941–1943

On the day Italy capitulated—September 8, 1943—the head of that country's legation in Zagreb ignored explicit directives from the Ustaše to leave all their files and documents behind before leaving Croatia. Carefully and systematically, Roberto Ducci removed hundreds of documents related to the rescue of Jews by the Italians. In 1944, he relied on these documents to publish a short article under the pseudonym Verax, thus revealing the story of the Italian Army's rescue of thousands of NDH Jews.[1] The Italian Foreign Ministry published its own memorandum on the rescue of Jews by the Italian Second Army a few months after the end of World War II.[2]

Initially, neither of these rescue stories was considered reliable, or even credible; after all, Italy was Germany's major ally. Moreover, historians who were familiar with the retributions the Nazis inflicted upon those who betrayed them doubted that Italy would have dared to derail one of Germany's main objectives: resolution of the Jewish Question. In 1951, however, French historian Jacques Sabille substantiated Verax's story in a published article, "The Attitude of the Italians toward the Persecuted Jews of Croatia," based on eleven documents from the period of July 24, 1942, to April 10, 1943, that he had uncovered in the German Foreign Ministry archives. Sabille's findings, published in a book he coauthored with Leon Poliakov, became a watershed in research on the rescue of Jews by Italian non-Jews.[3]

More than six decades later, however, questions remain, such as: Why did generals and administrators in Italy's fascist regime choose to risk their careers to rescue a few Jewish refugees? Italian officials already had evidence that Jews were being slaughtered in 1941; why did they wait until the summer of 1942 to actively participate in their rescue? And why in 1942, despite mounting pressure from the Ustaše and Nazi Germany to extradite the Jews in their zones of occupation, did the Italian officials flex their muscles and refuse to oblige? These are but a few questions addressed in this chapter.

HISTORICAL BACKGROUND

On September 27, 1940, Germany, Italy, and Japan signed the Tripartite Pact, whereby they became known as the Axis Alliance. The pact recognized German hegemony over most of continental Europe, Italian hegemony over the Mediterranean Sea, and Japanese hegemony over East Asia and the Pacific. The partners also had common interests. First, they aimed to obliterate or neutralize Soviet Communism. Second, they sought territorial expansion that would support empires based on military conquest and the overthrow of the post–World War I international order. In April 1941, the major European Axis partners, Germany and Italy, joined by two minor partners, Hungary and Bulgaria, invaded Yugoslavia. The resulting cycle of violence eventually culminated in a civil war that in its brutality rivaled that of Yugoslavia's dissolution in the 1990s.

On April 21 and 22, Italian Foreign Minister Galeazzo Ciano[4] met with his German counterpart, Joachim von Ribbentrop, in Vienna, where they divided the former Yugoslavia's Croatian territory into two spheres of control: the German Army would control the northeastern part, and the Italian Army the southwestern section. Under this agreement, the now Independent State of Croatia (NDH) was to become the domain of Italy's King Victor Emmanuel III. Neighboring Slovenia, between Croatia and Italy, was for the most part under Italian occupation.

Notwithstanding the Vienna agreement, German troops swept into Croatia with sufficient force to let the Croatians know who was in control. Despite Germany's assurances that it regarded Croatia as lying in Italy's sphere, the Italian Foreign Ministry understood that Germany had no intention of surrendering these territories. Hitler soon decided to dismember Yugoslavia, grab the lucrative territories regardless of any previous agreements with Italy, and rid the country of its Jews. Nonetheless, on April 25, 1941, Ciano met in Ljubljana, Slovenia, with Ante Pavelić, recently installed head of the NDH, to discuss possible expansion of Italian administrative control within the NDH. After this meeting, Ciano noted in his diary:

> I saw Pavelić . . . he declares that the solutions proposed by us would get him thrown out of government. He makes a counterproposal . . . that Spalato and Ragusa [Split and Dubrovnik], would remain Croatian.[5]

On April 30, 1941, the Italian General Staff advocated a political solution for Croatian territorial disputes, since any military action related to Dalmatia could backfire and result in local uprisings.[6] But Italy's plans were largely irrelevant. In his diary, Ciano noted, "Maybe I am mistaken in my personal impression, but there is a feeling in the air that Italian domination in Croatia is to be temporary."[7]

Ciano was right; within days Germany had yet another plan for Croatia, one more favorable to Germany's position in the region. The new plan divided the territories in question into several parts. It awarded a sizable section to the new Croatian state; Italy and the NDH would jointly hold a strip of the Adriatic shore, about fifty kilometers wide—which included Mostar, the capital of Herzegovina. This area was designated as Zone B.[8] Italy suffered an enormous setback, receiving only a narrow stretch of land on the Adriatic designated as Zone A. The Italians suddenly recognized that the Third Reich had wooed Mussolini to join the Axis by promising the surrender to Italy of Croatia and the Mediterranean Sea, but that the Nazis now made it impossible for Italy to extend its influence over these territories.

It is likely that Germany had been aware all along of these territories' strategic importance to gain control over the Danube Basin. On June 10,

1941, Germany signed a special agreement of protection and reciprocity with Croatia, thus introducing yet another change to the triangular relationship among Germany, Italy, and the NDH. Mussolini expressed outrage over this act of German perfidy:

> It is of no importance that the Germans recognize our rights in Croatia on paper, when in practice they grab everything and leave us only a little heap of bones. They are scoundrels and act in bad faith, and I tell you that this cannot go on for long. ... I've had my fill of Hitler and the way he acts.[9]

This may well have been the first time that Italy understood that the Germans were masters of deception, even though as late as December 15, 1941, Italy still harbored hopes of controlling Croatia. As Ciano stated:

> It all depends on the Germans. If they keep their obligations according to which Croatia has become a Zone of Italian influence, a great deal can be accomplished by us yet. If, on the contrary, they should again try to force our hand and press their penetration, there is nothing for us to do but to haul down our flag and return home.[10]

Within a few months, Italian authorities became certain that their stake in Croatia would remain insignificant and that the NDH had surrendered its destiny to the Nazi regime, without even attempting to resist Berlin's control.

The final breaking point between Germany and Italy came about incidentally. While the Italians were considering their response to ongoing German requests to hand over Jews in the Italian-occupied territories in Zone B, they once again encountered Nazi duplicity. The story is revealed in an Italian Foreign Ministry document that describes what happened when the Italian Murge Division hosted a group of German officers and engineers assigned to a unit of the Todt Organization that was in charge of mining bauxite ore in the area of Mostar (Zone B). During a friendly conversation at the officers' club, on June 23, 1942, a German officer informed his Italian hosts that his government had signed an agreement with the NDH under which the Jews of Croatia, including those in Italian territory, would be handed over to Germany.

Immediately after this incident, the officers of the Murge Division reported the conversation to Second Army headquarters, which in turn contacted the Foreign Ministry in Rome. In light of Italy's exclusion from the agreement between Germany and the NDH, the Italian General Staff expressed its outrage and stated that removal of the Jews from Zone B should not be carried out. The Italian Army considered the German-Croatian agreement a blow to its status and authority, as well as one more attempt by the Nazis and the Ustaše to disregard Italian control and policies in the occupied territories. An additional concern was that should Nazi Germany prevail in this matter, the international community might consider the Italian Army a mere puppet of Nazi Germany.[11]

On July 24, 1942, the Todt Organization's inspector-general for mining activities reported to Berlin that the Chief of the Italian General Staff had informed him that he would not hand over the Jews, since:

> It is not in keeping with the honor of the Italian army to take such exceptional measures against the Jews as those adopted by the Todt Organization, which is aimed at requisitioning housing accommodations which are urgently needed. …Yet everyone knows the harmful activity of the Jews in Mostar, who constitute the most dangerous source of disturbances.[12]

The news of Italy's betrayal by Nazi Germany reached all the parties involved in the occupied territories: the Second Army, the Italian legation in Zagreb, and the Foreign Ministry in Rome, which resolved not to carry out any agreement reached between Hitler and Pavelić. From June 1942 on, the Italian Foreign Ministry and Supersloda (Italian High Command in Slovenia and Dalmatia, *Commando Superiore di Slovenia e Dalmatzia*) began devising a detailed plan to delay indefinitely the handing over of Jews in their territories. Thus, one can argue that the accidental revelation in Mostar marked a turning point in the relationship between Italy and its so-called allies, as well as between Italian General

Mario Roatta, the commanding officer of the Second Army, and Jewish refugees in Italian-controlled territories.

THE ITALIAN RESPONSE TO THE PERSECUTION OF JEWS IN THE NDH

To expedite the expulsion of Jews from the NDH, the Nazis offered to share looted Jewish assets with the Ustaše, Muslims, Croats, and Volksdeutsche. On February 27, 1945, Judge Srećko Bujas, the Ustaše-appointed trustee over Sarajevo's Sephardic Jewish Community, sent a written testimony from liberated Bosnia to the National Commission that vividly portrayed the lawlessness and brutality that had permeated the NDH and the other occupied territories of the former Yugoslavia: "They [Ustaše] understood that the so-called Racial Laws placed the Jews totally outside the realm of the law, regarding their very existence as worthless and their earthly possessions as belonging to the individual Ustaše."[13]

In the summer of 1941, news of the plight and murder of Jews in the NDH began to reach the Italian Foreign Ministry. First, the Jews of Sarajevo and Split wrote long memoranda informing the authorities of mass killings of Jews and Serbs. The leadership of the Jewish Communities in Croatia and the Union of Jewish Communities of Italy, who had also heard of atrocities from fellow Jews, sent their own accounts to Italian authorities in Dalmatia and also to Italy. Despite these reports and unceasing requests for assistance, the Italian Foreign Ministry initially paid scant attention to the "so-called rumors" of inhumanity against Jews in the NDH.[14]

Jews who had escaped to the Italian zones from Zagreb, Osijek, Sarajevo, and other places were often caught by the police and Italian troops and extradited to the Ustaše. On May 15, 1941, Giuseppe Bastianini, the civilian governor of Dalmatia, sent an official report to Rome in which he stated that thousands of Jewish refugees had already settled in Dalmatia. He asked the Foreign Ministry and the Italian Army in Croatia to find an immediate solution to the Jewish refugee problem.[15]

Rescuers' and survivors' testimonies dramatically recount the consequences of Bastianini's request in conjunction with Ustaše brutalities in
Dubrovnik and other Dalmatian towns. Dr. Emil Freundlich and his parents, for example, were sent to the detention center in Gospić, Croatia.
From there they were sent to the local hospital, from which, during the
night, Dr. Ante Fulgosi and a group of nuns allowed them to escape.[16]
Once outside the compound they hired a taxi and crossed the border
into the Italian zone. When the Freundlichs arrived in Crikvenica, a
small town on the Adriatic, they encountered hundreds of Jewish refugees. Their first instinct was to look for a smaller place with fewer refugees. They decided on Sušak, but as they were about to disembark, the
local Italian police captured them and handed them over to the Ustaše.
Upon arriving back on Croatian soil, they luckily found someone who,
for a substantial fee, transported them to Italy.[17]

The Freundlichs were not alone in being remanded to the Ustaše.
Hundreds of Jews were extradited, and only a few were lucky enough to
get a second chance. Every few days truckloads of captured Jewish refugees arrived at the Jasenovac concentration camp.[18] Dr. Charles Steckel,
the former rabbi of Osijek, wrote that the Italian authorities often made
it impossible for Jewish refugees to save themselves. Whenever they
noticed an unfamiliar face they would question the person, and in most
cases, hand him or her over to the Ustaše.[19] Many refugees who managed to remain on Italian soil experienced extreme poverty; barely able
to scrape together enough money to emigrate, they were left nothing for
their daily sustenance.[20]

Emilio Tolentino, the secretary of the Jewish Community in
Dubrovnik, in his 1945 testimony to the National Commission described
the hardship he and the other 112 Jewish residents of Dubrovnik had to
endure when, in May 1941, the Ustaše assumed administrative control.[21]
Although the Ustaše shared control over the Jews with the Italians, who
had military authority, they unleashed vicious antisemitic propaganda,
followed by swift implementation of the Racial Laws and then deportations. Many of Dubrovnik's residents provided their Jewish neighbors
with food and shelter; nonetheless, only 23 of the city's Jews survived.[22]

Not just in Dubrovnik, but throughout Dalmatia, ordinary Italian citizens who resided in Dalmatia as well as Italian soldiers helped many NDH Jewish refugees. The review of hundreds of documents and testimonies of rescuers and survivors makes it possible to draw a reasonably accurate picture of events in the Italian zones of occupation. For example, Ivo Herzer's testimony to the United States Holocaust Memorial Museum (USHMM) depicts how he and his parents left Zagreb by train in the summer of 1941.[23] Without explanation, the train was halted and the passengers forced to disembark. They knew they were stranded on NDH territory. Luckily, the place where they disembarked, exact location not mentioned, was near a garrison of the Italian Second Army. At a distance they saw three or four solders, and asked them for help. Since they knew little Italian, the conversation was awkward, but one soldier called on their sergeant. Without asking for payment, the sergeant—who, like the Herzers, knew French—took it upon himself to help them board an Italian military train the next morning. Accompanied by the sergeant, they crossed to the Italian side. Herzer emphasized that his experience as a Jew being helped by Italian soldiers was by no means unique.

Obviously there are considerable differences between Freundlich's story and the one told by Herzer. Whereas Freundlich—like Steckel—dealt with Italian officials who followed orders in acting against Jewish refugees, Herzer encountered one officer who exhibited a soft spot for unarmed Jewish refugees appealing for his help.

In August 1941, an incident of Ustaše atrocities committed against Jews and Serbs left several Italian officers stunned and remorseful. "Rumors of atrocities" on the Island of Pag, within the Italian zone of occupation, had been circulating for several months. Finally a commission of Italian officers stationed on the Dalmatian coast was sent to investigate the allegations of murder. When the Italian officers, accompanied by a local guide, Duje Bilić, arrived on Pag, they found a scene of unimaginable carnage: thousands of people heaped one atop another in eighteen ditches, fifty to seventy people to a ditch.[24] In all, the Ustaše had murdered 4,500 Serbs and 2,000 Jews.[25]

Branko Polić, a Jewish refugee in the area, related that his mother, who had daily conversations with the wife of an Italian officer living in the same hotel,[26] one morning found the other woman sobbing. Concerned, Mrs. Polić asked what had happened. The officer's wife confessed that she had seen photographs her husband had taken in the concentration camp, and she could not erase them from her mind. "The pictures," Branko added, "began to kindle in the Italian officials a sense of justice."[27] The documents, the testimonies of survivors and rescuers, and the photographs make clear that, while the Italian occupation authorities, including the military, had initially doubted the rumors, the information gathered by the officers jolted them into the realization that they had to do something concrete to prevent an even larger catastrophe. Reports of the commission's findings were sent to army officials and the Foreign Office. Mussolini himself apparently saw the uncensored photographs.

Historians have by and large praised the Italians for their efforts on behalf of the Jews in Croatian territory. In the first decade after the war, French historians León Poliakov and Jacques Sabille, after examining ten key documents from the German military archives, recognized "the Italian officers and men whose wonderful rescue work calls for recognition and admiration."[28] Similarly, Croatian historian Zdenko Levental argued that only in exceptional instances had the Italians failed to protect the Jews.[29] Over thirty years later, Menahem Shelah, an Israeli historian born in Zagreb, also gave the Italians high marks:

> Italy's behavior toward the Yugoslav Jews represents something unique in the annals of the Holocaust, for it consists of protection and rescue rather than persecution and slaughter. . . . As historians, Jews, and humanists, we have a historical and moral obligation to illuminate those noble and humane deeds that shone through a political firmament blackened by savagery and death camps.[30]

American historian Jonathan Steinberg explained the Italian attitude toward the Jews by referring to national culture: "the totality of Italian experience—to political institutions, social practices, personal habits, language, values and norms." Indeed, he goes so far as to describe the Italians' rescue of Jews as "a moment of light in the darkest night of the human soul, [which] deserves telling for its own sake."[31] In this regard, he was following in the footsteps of Hannah Arendt, whose report on the Eichmann trial includes a comparison of various European countries' treatment of Jews: "What, in Denmark, was the authentically political sense, an inbred comprehension of the requirements and responsibilities of citizenship and independence, was in Italy the outcome of the almost automatic general humanity of an old 'civilized people.'"[32]

It is possible that Steinberg, Arendt, and Shelah correctly assessed an Italian national character. However, it is essential to emphasize again that, until December 1941, the Italian government still entertained the idea of controlling Croatia, and thus they were reluctant to act in any overt way against Germany. From April 1941 to August 1942, the conduct of the Italian government toward Jewish refugees was considerably harsher than was the case between August 1942 and September 1943. Some of the variations in descriptions of Italians' behavior toward the Jews—in particular those from bystanders—surely relate to changes over the course of the war, notably the Italians' growing disillusionment with the good faith of their German ally and the increasingly brutal implementation of Nazi and Ustaše policies.

By the spring of 1943, Axis forces faced defeat in North Africa and Germany's military offensive in Russia had stalled. As soon as the war ended, most Jews who had survived the Holocaust in Croatia—whether citizens or refugees—realized that in one way or another most of them had been rescued in the Italian occupation zones or had reached refuge in mainland Italy. It was also common knowledge that, unlike the Germans, Italians by and large did not murder Jewish refugees, and especially not women, children, and the elderly. In general the Italian Army recognized early on in the war that the Jews were not Italy's enemies; on the contrary, they needed Italy's protection.[33]

ITALY'S TURN FROM AXIS PARTNER TO RESCUER OF JEWS

Italy's military and civil authorities played a central role in the rescue of Jews in the Italian zones of occupation. However, their efforts would have been impossible without the sustained financial support of DELASEM (*Delegazione Assistenza Emigranti Ebrei;* Delegation to Assist Jewish Immigrants) and other national and international humanitarian organizations. In addition, thousands of ordinary NDH citizens did their part, both within Croatia and Bosnia-Herzegovina and on the Dalmatian coast, as did Archbishop Stepinac of Zagreb and the Vatican's emissary in Croatia. The Jewish Community of Zagreb and the Union of Jewish Communities in Italy supported refugees who were without any means of subsistence. The noteworthy assistance given to Jewish refugees by the Italian Army, diplomatic corps and civilian personnel should not be considered independently from the help provided by these other entities.[34]

In June 1942, Siegfried Kasche, the German ambassador in Zagreb, sent a memorandum to von Ribbentrop informing him of the German-NDH agreement on the deportation of all Jews from Croatia, including those in Zone B. Kasche specified that the success of the transport, which was anticipated to include between 4,000 and 5,000 Jews, would require the support and intervention of their Foreign Ministry in dealing with the Italian authorities. While not explicitly stated, the NDH regime was evidently aware that the Italians would oppose deportation.[35] Kasche expressed confidence in German strength and Italian weakness, adding that even without Italian consent, Germany and the NDH would soon take formal steps to deal with the matter of the Jews in Zone B.[36] It is not clear whether the Nazis seriously considered the use of force against their Italian allies. On July 24, 1942, six weeks after officers of the Murge Division heard about the surreptitious Nazi-Ustaše deportation agreement, Italian civilian authorities in Dalmatia decided to shield the Jews seeking refuge in the Italian zones.

On August 21, 1942, Foreign Minister Ciano informed Mussolini that Prince Otto von Bismarck, the counselor in the German Embassy in Rome, had delivered a memorandum from von Ribbentrop, requesting extradition of all Jews currently residing in Italian-occupied territories. Ciano noted that the stated reason for Germany's request was that a labor transport of Jews was about to leave for Russia, and that the Jews in the Italian territories should be included. Ciano also mentioned that von Bismarck had hinted that the Jews were destined for liquidation. Despite the information provided, Mussolini—to the surprise of many—wrote in bold on the memorandum two often-quoted words: *"Nulla Osta"* (no objection). With these two words, Mussolini absolved himself of any responsibility toward the fate of the Jews in Dalmatia.[37]

Disregarding Mussolini's sign-off, Ciano instead recommended the concentration of Jewish refugees in Zone B, a policy based on a memorandum of August 22 by Roberto Ducci (later Verax), the head of the Croatia office in the Foreign Office.[38] It appears that neither Ciano nor Ducci was aware of the overextension of Italian troops, especially in Zone B, where the army faced three enemies at once: the Ustaše, the Četniks, and the Partisans.

As commander of the Second Army, General Mario Roatta was intimately familiar with the military situation in Zone B. He agreed with the idea of consolidating the Jews in one location, but he had long suggested that the only practical and safe solution was to transfer the Jews to the more compact Italian-annexed territories in Zone A. Roatta knew firsthand that the endless skirmishes among the Ustaše, Partisans, and even the Četniks, with whom the Italians at times cooperated, depleted the army's manpower and exhausted its resources. The Italian Army was in no position to protect several thousand Jews in Zone B, should they be attacked.[39]

JEWS DOUBT THE SINCERITY OF THE ITALIAN RESCUE EFFORTS

Although the Italian Foreign Office gave orders not to carry out requests from Germany, Berlin considered the issue still under negotiation. On September 11, 1942, Vittorio Castellani, the liaison officer between the Foreign Ministry and the army high command for Slovenia and

Dalmatia (Supersloda), informed his superiors in the Foreign Ministry of the Second Army's plan. The first step would be to round up the Jews in one location, making it easier to protect them. As a delaying tactic, the army would simultaneously begin conducting a fictitious census in order to determine who among the NDH Jews should be counted as Italian citizens. They also aimed to identity only those Jews who had arrived in Croatia after 1933, since the Germans had requested a deportation list with the names of former Yugoslav citizens. Castellani also informed the ministry that the army would engage in a display of "bureaucratic incompetence," while simultaneously reassuring the Germans of its cooperation. Only a few officials were privy to this correspondence; neither the Jews nor the Italian soldiers knew what was going on regarding the preparations for "deportations."[40]

While the Italians were deciding how best to assure the safety of the Jewish refugees in Zone B, DELASEM assisted by financing their upkeep and cultural activities in the various camps where they were accommodated. Survivors of these camps who later published their life stories in journals such as Ha-kol,[41] Novi-Omanut, and Bilten,[42] described life under the Italian occupation as relatively pleasant, particularly for children and teenagers, who attended school and enjoyed a number of social and cultural activities. However, rumors of Italian cooperation with both the Četniks and the Nazis caused sleepless nights for many refugees. The Jews were understandably terrified of being deported to Ustaše and German camps. When the Italian Army began rounding up the Jews, many panicked, and some even committed suicide.[43] Life in the camps deteriorated especially in psychological terms, since the interned Jews considered any reorganization in their lives as a preparatory stage toward their deportation.[44] Moreover, they had no assurance that Italy was serious about protecting them.[45]

On November 4, 1942, Major-General Giuseppe Pieche, deputy commander of the Royal Carabinieri, notified the Foreign Ministry of the disappearance of a large transport of about 1,500 Jews from Osijek. According to his information, these NDH Jews under German control had been handed over to the SS for transfer to labor camps. However, while still on the train they had all been gassed—men, women, and children. Based on notations on the document, it is apparent that Mussolini saw the letter, but again he took no action to prevent future deportations.

The next day, November 5, the Foreign Ministry received a letter signed by Raffaele Guariglia, the Italian ambassador to the Vatican, which stated that it was now public knowledge that the Italian secretary of state, Marquis Blasco Lanza d'Ajeta, had received a demand from the German government to hand over 2,000 to 3,000 Croatian Jews, including women, children, and the elderly, who were under Italian control. The Vatican asked the Foreign Minister to do whatever was necessary to prevent their deportation.[46]

On November 7, 1942, a letter was sent from the NDH authorities in the region of Mostar in Zone B to the Interior Ministry in Zagreb reporting that the Italian Murge Division had given unequivocal orders to all NDH officials not to remove Jews from the territories under their occupation. The NDH director of the region, who signed Zlatar, wanted to know how he should respond to such a situation.[47]

On November 13, 1942, Archbishop Stepinac and Cardinal Luigi Maglione, the Vatican nuncio, asked Monsignor Borgongini-Duca in Rome to intervene on behalf of the Croatian Jewish refugees who were currently in Italian-occupied territories.[48] It is thus clear that the Italian authorities were well aware of the atrocities committed against the Jews.

The news of the systematic annihilation of Jews strengthened General Roatta's determination to rescue the Jews in the territories under his command. Based on contemporaneous documents and the historiographic literature, it appears that a unique relationship developed between the Jews and the Italian general. Roatta understood that the Jews urgently needed protection and that they also considered the Italians liberators. Under the circumstances, Roatta wanted the Italian Army to be remembered in this light.

Branko Polić vividly recalled November 27, 1942, the day General Roatta visited the Jewish camp in Kraljevica (Porto Re) and reaffirmed his commitment to protect the Jews from the Ustaše, saying: "If I had submarines at my command, I would transport all of you to the safety of

Italy." Asking the detainees not to despair, he promised them safety on the island of Rab.[49]

In early December 1942, General Roatta met Mussolini in Rome and recommended that the Jewish refugees be transferred to camps on the Italian mainland. Organizing such a transport at any time would be an enormous undertaking, let alone in wartime. Italy had to consider the danger and the responsibility it assumed should such a transport be bombed; Italy would then become complicit in the extermination of Jews. The financial cost of such an undertaking was also more than Italy could bear. Another complication was that in August 1939 the Interior Ministry had denied the Jews in zones A and B the right to obtain visas. Roatta also had political concerns, in particular, that handing over the Jews would be the "betrayal of a promise" given to the primarily Serbian Četniks: "My own point of view," declared Roatta, "is that consigning the Jews to Germans or the Croatians would end in practice by harming our prestige because … it would cause grave repercussions among armed volunteer Četniks … who might be induced to believe one day they too might be given over to the Ustaše."[50] In response to Roatta's request the answer was: no, to the Jews' transfer to Italy, but yes, to their transfer to Italian-annexed territories in Zone A.[51]

On December 19, 1942, the Italian military divisional counselor, Dr. Gropuzzo, wrote to the NDH authorities that it would be inadequate if they gave guarantees that they would not deport physicians, engineers, and lawyers; the Italian authorities had to verify the citizenship of all those who might be deported.[52] Obviously, this was part of the Italians' delaying strategy. By December 1942, it was clear the Italians had no intention of handing over Jews to the Germans.

THE CONFLICT BETWEEN THE ITALIAN CIVIL AUTHORITIES AND THE MILITARY

In the early months of 1943, Italy found itself between the proverbial rock and hard place. Even as Germany unrelentingly pressured Italy to hand over all Croatian Jews, the Allies were extending their grip across

Europe. The Italians therefore decided to begin executing their plan to evacuate the Jews from Zone B to Zone A. Some refugees had already been evacuated to the island of Korčula from Split and towns in that vicinity as early as December 1941. The transfers continued throughout the rest of the war, ending abruptly two weeks after Italy's capitulation.[53] On the island the refugees lived in two towns, Korčula and Vela Luka. While there were no fences, the internees could roam only within a two-kilometer perimeter. They also had strict curfews, but the various restrictions did not bother them as long as they were assured of being beyond the Ustaše's reach.[54] In total, 512 Jews were confined on the island of Korčula: 294 in the town of Korčula (22 of whom were children under the age of 12), and 218 in Vela Luka (24 under the age of 12).[55] Over time, the refugee population on Korčula declined, as younger men and women began joining the Partisans in the Army of Liberation (NOV); and other escaped. Eventually, by September 1943, only 81 remained—women, children, and the few men who remained to protect them.[56] DELASEM and other humanitarian organizations provided essential assistance to the refugees for the duration.

Those who experienced the period of several weeks, from March to early April 1943, in Zone B, described it as nerve-racking. The refugees were not fully convinced that the Italians would dare to defy the deportation orders of their more powerful Axis partner, much less to rescue them. Even when the trucks loaded with Jews began the slow and deliberate drive along the coast, the refugees focused their eyes on the road. Their anxiety reached a climax when the trucks reached a particular fork in the road: a right turn would signal that the convoy was about to leave Dalmatia for Croatia and Ustaše territory. If, however, they took the left fork it meant that the Italians intended to fulfill their promise of protection. Branko Polić described the excitement and joy when they realized that they had taken the left turn en route to the island of Rab.[57] The transfer of Jews to Rab was carried out in two stages. The first convoy to reach the island, on May 28, 1943, came from Dubrovnik, with 110 Jews, both residents of the city and refugees. From June 19 to July 21, 1943, a total of eleven additional transports reached the island, carrying

2,353 refugees: 1064 men, 982 women, and 307 children.[58] The island of Rab became a haven for Jewish refugees from Kraljevica and other northeastern areas of the Adriatic.

THE CAMP ON THE ISLAND OF RAB (ARBE)

The official name of the camp on Rab was *Campo di concentramento per internati civili di Guerra–Arbe*. In addition to the Jews, this large facility held approximately 28,000 Slovenes and Croats who escaped to the Italian zone and who were interned under much harsher conditions. The Italian authorities considered these groups to be their enemies, while the Jews were hapless refugees in need of protection.[59] Jaša Romano, a survivor and historian, described in detail the life of the Jewish inmates—the internal organization, social and cultural activities, the educational facilities, and the daily contact between the Jews and the camp's internal management.[60] Despite the Italians' division between groups, immediately upon their arrival on Rab, the Jewish leadership established contact with the camp's Slovenian and Croatian leaders, and through them with the Dalmatian Partisans. During their first few months in confinement they had to adjust—to wire fences, guards, the sea, and to the ever-changing military and political situation in the Italian zones of occupation.

By late July 1943, Italy had suffered major military setbacks. On July 25, Mussolini was removed from office by King Victor Emmanuel III and arrested. Named prime minister of Italy, General Pietro Badoglio faced major government instability and crisis. Consequently, he had no inclination to consider the situation of the Jews in Dalmatia.[61] Nonetheless, on August 19, 1943, Augusto Rosso, the newly appointed secretary general of the Foreign Ministry, sent a cable to the Ministry's Liaison Bureau at army headquarters in Croatia with the instructions that the army was to adopt all necessary measures to secure the safety of the Jewish inmates on Rab.[62] In Rosso's words: "We must avoid abandoning the Croatian Jews or leaving them to the mercy of foreigners, deprived of all protection and exposed to the danger of reprisals, unless they themselves wish to be set free outside our zone of occupation."[63]

The success of the rescue mission depended on timing. Not only had the complexity of transporting thousands of Jewish refugees across enemy lines to the safety of Italy plagued the operation. Internal frictions between the military and the politicians created a logistical nightmare. The army insisted that women, children and the elderly, as well as young professionals who could contribute to the Italian economy should be transferred first. The Foreign Ministry, however, was bogged down by procedural issues with the Ministry of the Interior; the core issue was a quota that disallowed the transfer of thousands of penniless refugees to Italy. A second issue was what Italy should do about the other persecuted minorities under Italian protection.[64] Thus Badoglio government made feeble attempts to rescue the Jews in Dalmatia, while authorizing the army to "examine benevolently" individual cases and give each Jew an opportunity to make his or her own choice. On September 7, 1943, in desperation, the officers of Supersloda decided to send Major Prolo to Rome to convince the Ministry of the Interior to issue, without delay, entrance visas for all the Jewish refugees. He arrived in Rome on the evening of September 8, the day when the Allied Command announced the surrender of the Badoglio government. The Italian Army laid down its arms and the Wehrmacht immediately moved into most of Italy's former territories in Croatia.

With the capitulation of Italy, thousands of Jews remained stranded on Korčula and Rab. It is clear that both the Second Army and the Italian Foreign Ministry had the will and the plans to transfer the Jewish refugees to Italy, but they lacked authorization from the Interior Ministry, which thought the transport of thousands of Jews across enemy lines to be both too dangerous and too costly. Six months after the capitulation of Italy, the island of Rab fell to the Germans and their Ustaše allies.[65]

RESCUE OF JEWS IN ITALIAN CONCENTRATION CAMPS: FERRAMONTI

Well before the Italian Army's effort to evacuate Jews from zones A and B, Jewish refugees from Yugoslavia and elsewhere in Europe were being interned in camps in Italy. *Campo di concentramento Ferramonti de Tarsia* is the only one of several concentration camps in Italy that is well documented. Based on Carlo Spartaco Capogreco's research, we know that the camp opened in 1938, at which time it held approximately 4,000 non-Italian Jews, primarily from Germany, Austria, and Poland. As the war progressed the camp also interned Greek and Yugoslav Jews. On July 31, 1941, the first group of 127 Jewish refugees from Slovenia arrived, followed in time by inmates from other parts of the former Yugoslavia. Dr. Emil Freundlich, from Zagreb, related how Italian authorities and local police frequently sent small groups of Jews from the villages they were hiding to the concentration camps, mostly to Ferramonti, particularly when their safety in the little Italian villages where they had first found shelter could no longer be guaranteed.[66]

Unlike the Nazi death camps, the concentration camps controlled by the Italian police provided temporary confinement. Life in these Italian camps encroached on the inmates' freedom to move and travel; however cultural, religious, and social activities were approved and encouraged. In Capogreco's words:

> The Ferramonti community proceeded with its social and cultural development. The painter Michel Fingesten obtained a shed from the camp director, which he equipped as a studio, organizing shows and teaching the art of painting to some of the young people. Musical life was nurtured with passion by Maestro Lav Mirski, formerly director of the Osijek Opera in Yugoslavia. He directed both the synagogue "choir" and that of the Catholic chapel, which gave concerts of the highest artistic level. Even sport had a big impetus, with soccer in first place.[67]

After being smuggled to Italy across the border near Trieste, members of the Freundlich family decided to give themselves up to the *questuri* (police) as refugees. The friendly Italian officers told them that they would be placed under house arrest in the village of Cocconato in the province of Asti Piemonte, not far from the town of Torino. Twelve Croatian families in the village, totaling sixty persons, had permission to visit local stores while under so-called house arrest. At the beginning of March 1943, after fourteen months in Cocconato, they were transferred to the Ferramonti concentration camp. Dr. Freundlich's recollections of the camp are similar to those related by Miriam Steiner-Aviezer, who as a child spent several months there.[68] They concurred that, despite the harsh environment and overcrowding, the treatment was not cruel, a fact they attributed to Israele Kalk, a wealthy Latvian Jewish engineer residing in Italy, who took a special interest in assisting these refugees. On his visit to Ferramonti in August 1942, he spoke to the internees:

> I don't think anyone will contradict me if I say that fate has been good to you and that your condition as internees in Italy is probably better than that of other brothers of ours who are still free in other European countries.[69]

Kalk explained that the Italian camps differed from German camps because of the "gentleman's agreement" between the refugees and their Italian guards. His message to the internees was: "Do whatever you want as long as appearances are safeguarded."

On September 3, 1943, vehicles of the Herman Goering Panzer Division appeared on the horizon, driving toward the camp. The deputy camp commander opened the gates to allow the internees to flee; two thousand scattered in small groups through the hills to the neighboring villages, where they received help from the local population. Those remaining included some old and sick internees and a group of young people who chose to stay and defend them. Because their only weapons were a few old guns that would have been useless against a Panzer division, they resorted to deception. At the entrance to the camp the remaining internees hung a yellow cloth on which, in bold letters, they had written: "Cholera Epidemic." The Germans, upon seeing it, turned around immediately and left the area.[70]

From survivor testimonies we know that some of the escapees from the Ferramonti camp chose not to return, heading instead for Campo Bari, a large refugee camp in southern Italy already secured by the Allied forces.[71]

Apart from those in organized concentration camps, such as Ferramonti, some refugees were designated as "enemy civilian internees" and placed in somewhat less structured situations. Chapter 2 described the rescue and escape from Sarajevo of Regina (Gina), her mother Ella and her brother Isak (Ivo) Perera. After crossing the Adriatic from Split, together with other family members, in December 1941, they began a new life as Giovanni and "Ginetta" Ferraro. Under guard, with the men in chains, they were sent by train to Montechiaro D'Asti, Piemonte, in Northern Italy. The men had to report to the police twice a day, the women and children only once a day, but enforcement was lax. The Italian government subsidized the internees' living expenses. They got to know the local population; in particular, they remembered a farm that raised silkworms and whose owner gave them vegetables and fruits in season.

One night in September 1943 the local Carabinieri chief informed them that they must leave immediately because he had orders to arrest all the internees the next day. The local authorities provided false documents to assist them in their escape. They never found out who had arranged for the documents or their transportation that night. One member of the family, Simha Perera Eškenazi, spent the rest of the war in Torino, under the alias Olga Coffano. Other members escaped into Switzerland. Regina, together with her mother and brother and two other relatives, an uncle and his mother, reached Brusson, a suburb of Arcesa, in Aosta province. They lived there clandestinely for a few days in the house of a tailor, Serafino Berguet.

On December 13, 1943, there was a sweep by German and fascist troops in the area. During this time they hid in a cow shed, where the farm family brought them food and water. An old man then guided them in knee-deep snow, carrying Regina on his back, to his house in the mountains. Eventually they reached the village of Challant St. Anselme, and were taken in by the parish priest, Don Giuseppe Péaquin. They lived in the rectory together with his elderly housekeeper for a year and a half. Their mother became the priest's secretary, and the children attended the parish school, which was run by nuns, who were also hiding three elderly Yugoslav Jewish women in the school building. The women were supposedly under the nuns' care as "mentally infirm."[72] The children played with the village children and made many friends. Isak recalled that while they stayed with Don Giuseppe, many other guests came, stayed a while, and then disappeared.

Isak recalled a close call when, during one of the German sweeps, his mother and the two children stepped outside their room onto the rectory's balcony, where they were spotted by a German soldier with a sub-machine gun slung across his chest. He started talking to Isak's mother in German, and she replied, telling him that they were bombed-out refugees from the South. Years later, she told Isak that the soldier had said that he was an Austrian and a Catholic, and didn't like what was going on. Isak and his mother thought that he suspected that something was amiss—why would a Southern Italian woman know German?—but let it slide, perhaps telling her what he did to reassure her. They also received help from several of the priests' friends, Dr. Paolo Todros, and Rina and Edoardo Billeri. Regina concluded her story by saying:

> We do not know, and probably will never know, all the people who protected, helped and assisted us during World War II. They were kind and generous people, who risked their lives and the lives of their families by taking us in, sharing their meager food with us, and saving (literally) our lives. We know that we owe them an eternal debt, which we will never be able to repay.

DELASEM AND OTHER HUMANITARIAN ORGANIZATIONS

Among the many contradictions of Fascist Italy's treatment of Jews was its toleration of the activities of Jewish humanitarian organizations, which operated almost without interruption until Italy's occupation by Nazi Germany on September 12, 1943. These Italian and international organizations' ability to provide a wide range of services was directly responsible for the survival of thousands of Jewish refugees in Italy, North Africa, and Yugoslavia. The most important of these agencies were: DELASEM (Delegazione Assistenza Emigranti Ebrei; Delegation to Assist Jewish Emigrants), the JOINT Distribution Committee (JDC or the Joint), HICEM (an acronym of the Hebrew Immigrant Aid Society [HIAS], the Jewish Colonization Society [ICA], and Emigdirect), the International Red Cross (IRC), and UNRRA (United Nations Relief and Rehabilitation Administration).[73] These organizations' success in providing assistance to Jews was possible because of their collaboration with each other and with local religious and humanitarian organizations.

The Union of the Jewish Communities in Italy (hereafter Union) was one of the most critical of these religious organizations. After a period of inactivity, in response to the growing crisis the Union met in Rome on November 13, 1939, for a dramatic board meeting that resulted in the complete overhaul of its leadership structure. As the Union's new head, Dante Almansi, former councilor to the Courts of Accounts, named Genoese attorney Lelio Vittorio Valobra as vice-president. Together they selected four board members.[74] The Union's new leadership was able to move the bureaucracy. All of a sudden passports were issued to Italian Jews who wished to emigrate. Almansi worked with the U.S. embassy in Rome, obtaining assurances from the Italian government that German Jews would not be "repatriated" and that the flow of refugees would not be blocked at the Italian border.[75]

The most notable success of the Almansi-Valobra partnership was to replace the defunct humanitarian organization Comasebit with DELASEM. With government approval, this organization managed to extend its humanitarian work beyond the Italian peninsula to care for Jews in the Italian zones of occupation in Yugoslavia. Moreover, DELASEM's effective leadership made it possible for refugees to count on the help of several important international Jewish organizations such as HICEM and the JDC, which were in a position to attract large sums of foreign currency to Italy. Working through Sally Mayer, president of the United Jewish Communities in Switzerland, and the U.S. Chargé d'Affaires to the Holy See, Harold Tittmann, the American Joint Distribution Committee continued to provide financial assistance for Yugoslav Jews even after the United States entered the war.[76]

In addition to such material help as food, clothing, blankets, and medicine, these groups provided DELASEM with essential religious items as prayer books and matzoth for Passover. DELASEM took also a leadership role in searching for and communicating with relatives of refugees. Altogether, DELASEM contributed generously to the material and spiritual welfare, as well as to the morale of Jewish refugees in Italy and the Italian-occupied NDH. In September 1939, the Union spread the DELASEM offices to 27 different locations with its headquarters in Genoa.

From mid-April 1941 to mid-August 1943, Valobra visited DELASEM's agent in Dalmatia and Slovenia three times before the Nazi occupation of Italy. He established close contacts with Italian military and political authorities in these Italian-occupied territories, in particular with General Emilio Grazioli, high commissioner for the region of Ljubljana, Slovenia. Valobra's contacts were also helpful in assisting and rescuing about 6,700 Jewish refugees, at least 4,500 of whom were living in Slovenia and Dalmatia. During the summer of 1942, through the Slovenian Red Cross, Valobra obtained permission for the transfer into Italy of more than fifty Jewish orphans who had been hiding in Lesno Brdo, on the border of Slovenia and Austria (their rescue is discussed in detail in this chapter).[77] Valobra's contacts with the military commanders and the Carabinieri, Chief of Police, Carmine Senise, as well as with local DELASEM workers, and his correspondence with several local and international agencies, assured that the conditions of refugees in these regions were brought to the attention of Italian military authorities in Croatia and in Rome.[78]

After Italy's capitulation on September 8, 1943, and the occupation of Genoa by Nazi Germany four days later, DELASEM was forced to conduct its operations underground. The organization entrusted its treasury of five million lire to Father Giuseppe Reppetto, secretary to Cardinal Boetto, the archbishop of Genoa. A fifth of this sum was put in the hands of a Catholic priest, Father Benedetto, the newly appointed president of DELASEM, who took the money to Rome on April 20, 1944. Valobra had a wide network of supporters who were not Jews. He managed to establish close relationships with the Holy See through the archbishop of Genoa, who assisted in the transfer of six hundred Jewish children to Turkey. The cooperation and the trust established among the Union, DELASEM and the Catholic Church, made the joint operation a success. Despite the Nazi occupation of Italy, DELASEM continued operations from its new headquarters in Father Benedetto's residence in Rome. With the help of the International College of Capuchins in Rome, the IRC, the Pontifical Relief Commission, and the Italian police, DELASEM coordinated various rescue activities. Its operations included the manufacture of false documents and establishing contacts with sympathetic Italian, Swiss, Hungarian, French, and Romanian officials.[79]

The Jewish refugees who reached the Italian zones were unaware that DELASEM's financial assistance made possible their daily upkeep, as illustrated in the autobiographical novella by Danko Samokovlija published in 1956 as *Dollar per Day*. The main character, Albert, is portrayed as a typical internee in the Rab island camp, oblivious to the fact that a humanitarian organization is assisting him and his fellow refugees, who take for granted that they have three daily meals, albeit meager, as well as shelter and medical care, during wartime. In the novel, Danko discovers the truth by accident when he visits the infirmary and asks to see a physician. Whereupon he is politely told: "I think all that we provide costs exactly one dollar per day."[80] Suddenly, it dawns on him that someone other than the Italian Army must be responsible for the daily upkeep— at a rate of one dollar per day for each individual. This entity was DELASEM, working with international organizations and the Catholic Church. DELASEM was practically the only humanitarian organization that assisted the Jews of former Yugoslavia throughout the war.

THE CHILDREN OF VILLA EMMA

The project of rescuing European Jewish children began in 1937. Thousands of children, often accompanied by a German guide, were brought from Poland, through Germany, to Zagreb, en route to Eretz

Israel.[81] For over three years, Josef Indig-Ithai, a Croatian Jew, awaited their arrival at a pre-arranged site in a Zagreb suburb, and then took charge of the children while on Yugoslav soil. Toward the end of 1940 it was clear that Yugoslavia would join its neighbors Hungary and Bulgaria in the Tripartite Pact and enter into an agreement with Germany, making such rescue ventures dangerous and more difficult.

The last children whom Indig-Ithai expected before the outbreak of war were a group of sixteen girls who were due to arrive at the end of January 1940. When they failed to show up, the team in Zagreb panicked since this was the worst possible time for a group of girls without proper documents to be lost somewhere in Central Europe. After searching all their projected border crossings and routes, Indig-Ithai discovered that the Yugoslav police had imprisoned them in the town of Maribor on the Slovenian-German-Austrian border. The police insisted that the group be turned over to the German police.

The citizens of Maribor and one border policeman, Uroš Zun, in particular, defiantly refused to obey the orders from Belgrade. When the story of the orphaned girls appeared in the local newspapers, the entire community of Maribor came to their defense. The following day, newspaper headlines declared: "We will not give up our little girls." Eventually, the girls obtained the necessary papers to stay in Yugoslavia until arrangements were made for their travel to Palestine. From that point on, Indig-Ithai came to believe that: "We owe our lives to both good luck and to the many Gentiles who helped us and strengthened our thoroughly shaken faith in mankind."[82]

On March 27, 1941, two weeks before the Axis powers occupied Yugoslavia, Indig-Ithai received a new group of undocumented orphans. A week after the occupation, he decided to transfer the children to Slovenia, which was by then under Italian occupation. Ljubljana, its capital, was the seat of the Italian High Commissioner, Emilio Grazioli. Indig-Ithai traveled to Ljubljana, where he explained the situation to Eugenio Bolaffio, DELASEM's representative in the Ljubljana office. Bolaffio, in turn, told the commissioner about the children's plight, and Grazioli immediately agreed to issue travel papers for the group. Before returning to Zagreb, Indig-Ithai telephoned the DELASEM offices in Italy and also spoke with Nathan Schwalb in Geneva, who represented the Histadrut (Jewish Labor Federation) in Europe.[83] In addition, he telephoned Joseph Schwartz of the American JOINT in Lisbon to inform him of the atrocities being committed in Yugoslavia, and to tell him about his group of children. By informing all these entities about the children he created a support network and secured the children's future.

While in Ljubljana, Indig-Ithai also established contact with another local DELASEM representative, Dr. Enrico Luzzatto, who arranged for him and the children to stay in a four-hundred-year-old Hapsburg hunting lodge on the mountaintop of Lesno Brdo. After obtaining the papers and assuring a safe shelter, he returned to Zagreb for the children. When they reached the border between Croatia and Slovenia, a surprise awaited them: an Italian border patrol, which—once the truck came to a full halt—showered the children with candies and sweets. This small gesture was a welcome change from their customary experiences with people in authority.[84]

In June 1941, the children began their long journey up Lesno Brdo with the understanding that they had to be quiet no matter how hard the climb became. They remained in the lodge from July 1941 until April 1942. While their security situation improved and they received assistance from DELASEM and the Italian authorities, for a time they still experienced serious food shortages. This situation improved considerably after they established contact with the local peasants, who taught them how to survive on berries and other foodstuffs that grew in the forest. During their stay on Lesno Brdo the children were accompanied by six adults from the Jewish Community in Zagreb. Italian officers frequently came for a visit, on one occasion bringing them a radio. The local Partisans protected the group, and they in turn provided the Partisans with a warm place to sleep and medications supplied by DELASEM. In April 1942, fighting in the mountainous area became intense, and Indig-Ithai received orders from Italian headquarters that the children should be relocated to Italy. They walked through the mountains until they reached a road passable by car.[85]

In a letter to Ilva Vaccari of the Instituto Storico della Resistenza, Lelio Vittorio Valobra, the director of DELASEM, described in detail the fate of the children over a period of four years. Vaccari later recounted some of these details in her own account of the children's ordeals.[86] One life-and-death experience took place in Mestre, near Venice, on their way to Modena, when the Germans demanded that the car carrying the children be directed to Verona. The director of the Carabinieri, Major-General Giuseppe Pieche, whom DELASEM had informed of their plight, resolutely intervened and ordered the car to proceed to Modena. By defying the Germans, Pieche prevented a disastrous outcome for the children and the adults who accompanied them.[87]

Before the children arrived, the local Jewish Community, with the help of DELASEM and the Red Cross, had acquired a 46-room villa surrounded by seven-and-a-half hectares of farm-land, in the town of Nonantola, near Modena. When the children reached the town, on April 14, 1942, they were surprised to find Villa Emma locked up. While they were sitting outside, exhausted from the long trip, the local Carabinieri commander ordered all the locks smashed, promising "all necessary permits and orders will come later." The entire community was eager to help the orphaned Jewish children.[88] During this period, the community at Villa Emma formed a relationship with a local farmer, Ernesto Leonardo, who taught the children how to grow crops. They also formed a very close relationship with local church authorities, particularly with priests at the local abbey, notably Monsignor Arrigo Beccari, as well as with Don Rossi from Modena. These priests would later play a crucial role in the children's rescue.

The teachers and guides made sure the children had a regular structure to their lives, and the children stayed busy studying and working. From conversations with Eliezer Kaveson-Hadas, it is clear that the children were responsible for all the tasks necessary for their daily subsistence.[89] They also had academic classes and learned a few trades in preparation for their future in Eretz Israel.[90]

The Children of Villa Emma were told to expect a new group to join their safe haven. On April 14, 1943, thirty-two orphans, nineteen boys, and thirteen girls, most from Sarajevo, and a few from Zagreb and Osijek, joined the original Lesno Brdo group; they arrived from Split with the assistance of DELASEM and that city's Jewish Community.[91] I heard this part of the story from a survivor whom I visited in Israel. Eliezer Kaveson-Hadas was one of the new arrivals. His birthplace had been Sarajevo. Because the deportation of that city's Jews began almost immediately after its occupation by Nazi forces, the Jews of Osijek, who were themselves largely unscathed by the war, invited seven hundred children from Sarajevo to come and live with Jewish families who volunteered to care for them. In addition, on a daily basis, the Jews of Osijek rescued the older children who were incarcerated with their mothers and sisters in the Djakovo concentration camp. Among those children was Eliezer's twin brother. The twins were housed with two separate families, but they had opportunities to meet daily. One night in August 1942, without warning, the Ustaše assisted the Germans in organizing a large transport of Osijek Jews. Their fate remains unknown. In this large transport was Eliezer's twin brother, his last surviving family member.[92]

Fearing future deportations, the remnants of Osijek's Jewish Community decided to send the remaining Sarajevo children, including Eliezer, to Split. That city's Jewish Community, with DELASEM's help, then transferred all the surviving orphans to Italy. Eliezer's own harrowing experiences meant that he was not at Villa Emma during its earliest days. Nonetheless, he soon learned a great deal about the children from Lesno Brdo and their arduous flight across multiple borders.

For security reasons, before the capitulation of Italy, DELASEM transferred its offices from Genoa to Nonantola. The children and their teachers welcomed the move, which meant they were the first to receive information on what was happening in the world, as well as to receive financial assistance. The life to which the children had become accustomed in Nonantola came to an abrupt halt when Marshal Badoglio signed Italy's surrender to the Allies on September 8, 1943. Both adults and children braced themselves for major change; it was clear that the Nazis would not stand by and watch Italy fall into the Allies' hands. Some 120 children and adults had to be evacuated from the premises of

Villa Emma. In a group meeting, it was decided that the older children should be dispersed among the local population, while the younger ones would be sheltered in the local abbey.

Indig-Ithai recalled the morning when he approached the abbot, Monsignor Pelati, with a request to open the abbey's gates to the children. The abbot replied: "Well, actually our archbishop forbids us to help you, but we are Christians so let the boys come." Indig-Ithai continued, "Monsignor, our little girls, they too want to live!" The abbot replied: "Indig, this is difficult, for almost one thousand years there were no girls here; but, so be it . . . in the name of God, the Son and the Holy Spirit . . . Let the children come."[93]

Villa Emma's allies, among them the clergy, then discussed strategy for rescuing the children. One idea was to dress them as orphaned Italian children and bring them to the border with Switzerland. Attempts were made to obtain legal documents via the Swiss border patrol. The Swiss agreed to issue visas, but required a payment of 120,000 lire per child. Initially, getting the money was an issue since the telephone lines with Switzerland, had been cut. Indig-Ithai reported that they immediately appealed to the Swiss authorities in Italy, guaranteeing that maintenance for the children would be provided throughout their stay and that they would leave after the war. Richard Lichteim, the Zionist delegate to the League of Nations in Geneva, provided additional guarantees required by Switzerland.

On October 6, 1943, thirty-three children and seven adults boarded the train to Modena. When the train reached a check point in Milan, the refugees encountered German military police (Feldgendarmerie), but all went well due to identity cards issued to them by the municipal office in Nonantola. Before the train reached Switzerland, they disembarked and continued on foot. The following day, at dusk, the first of three groups crossed the border near Ponte Tresa. On October 15, the last group crossed the Italian border into Swiss territory.[94]

Eliezer recalled that it was Yom Kippur (the Jewish Day of Atonement) of 1943 when his group set out on their dangerous trek. Indig-Ithai decided that they should form a human chain, with the younger children flanked between older ones and the adults. After several arduous hours of hiking through mountainous terrain, they reached the border. They then had to climb through a little window of a bathroom in the Italian border patrol station that had been left open for them. After they crossed the Swiss border, the children were scattered in various quarantine camps. In an effort to reunite the children from Villa Emma, Histadrut and the Zionist organization bought a large building surrounded by farmland in Bex-les-Bains. When most of the children were finally united, they stayed there until the war was over. On May 8, 1945, they left for Barcelona, their final stop before arriving in Eretz Israel. These children owed their rescue to individuals, armies, and humanitarian and religious institutions from several countries.[95] Indig-Ithai concluded his story with thanks to all those who helped them:

> There were many Gentiles—Slovene and especially Italians—who not only helped us, but also gave us spiritual strength to await the final day of war, May 8, 1945. And then we got ready to go to Barcelona through France, to board the ship *Non Plus Ultra*—the first ship after the war, which was to take us to Eretz Israel....And I thought, "How did we actually succeed? Did it really depend on us?"[96]

THE AFTERMATH

Following the liberation of Italy, the care of Jewish survivors fell to the Partisans and to the Allied military administration, as well as to the Displaced Persons Organization and other agencies. In May 1944, a new and permanent entity was formed, a representative of the Intergovernmental Committee on Refugees, under the aegis of the American Jewish JOINT, the Quakers, and the Friends' Ambulance Unit, which had great practical experience in providing aid to refugees, and in assisting those who wanted to return to their homes.

6

Partisan Rescuers Confront Anglo-American Diplomacy

News that the government of General Pietro Badoglio had surrendered to the Allied forces on September 8, 1943, came as a big surprise to the Italian Army stationed in the occupied territories of Yugoslavia. The news spread swiftly, and officers and soldiers soon abandoned their posts in Croatia, Dalmatia, and Slovenia and rushed to cross the borders into Italy.[1] The disappearance of the Italian Army from the Dalmatian coast exposed some 5,000 Jews who had found shelter there to imminent danger. Their rescue and survival was made possible by the swift action undertaken on their behalf by Croatian Partisans fighting to liberate territory along the Dalmatian coast.

The Partisans' steadfast protection of a group of Jewish refugees from the island of Rab who were too young, too old, or too ill to join in the struggle to liberate Yugoslavia is a remarkable story of heroism. Their repeatedly frustrated efforts to secure a safe haven in southern Italy for these most vulnerable refugees reveals the complications of rescue at a time when the two nations with the greatest resources for rescue had other concerns—in addition to the urgent mission of defeating Nazi Germany, the politics of Great Britain's mandate over Palestine and hostility to immigration in the United States. This chapter thus moves from the Partisans' role as rescuers to the stage of Great Powers diplomacy during the last year of the war.

The Partisans arose swiftly from among the people when the

occupation forces and their collaborators inflicted on ordinary citizens severe physical and material hardship. In certain instances, Axis forces and local collaborators, like the Ustaše, would hand or shoot indiscriminately, men, women, and children. Sometimes in reprisal actions that killed up to one hundred local inhabitants for every German soldier killed. Moreover, the country experiences a breakdown of law and order, as Collaborationist Volksdeutsche militia and Ustaše troops roamed the countryside terrorizing the population by looting and plundering food, livestock and weapons.

Chart 1: In April 1945, 800,000 Partisans made up the Yugoslav army.[2]

States	Late 1941	Late 1942	Late 1943	Late 1944	[April 1945]
BiH	20,000	60,000	108,000	100,000	
Croatia	7,000	48,000	122,000	150,000	
Kosovo	5,000	6,000	6,000	20,000	
Macedonia	1,000	2,000	7,000	66,000	
Montenegro	22,000	6,000	24,000	30,000	
Serbia proper	23,000	8,000	22,000	204,000	
Slovenia	1,000	19,000	25,000	40,000	
Vojvodina	1,000	1,000	5,000	40,000	
Total	80,000	150,000	319000	650,000	780,000

Ante Nazor and Zoran Ladić provide reliable information on the ethnic composition of Partisan forces from the NDH territories[3]. Of the 121,351 soldiers in Partisan units in Croatia by November 1944: 60.4 percent were ethnic Croatians; 28.64 percent Serbs, 2.75 percent Muslims, .25 percent Jews, and 7.96 percent other ethnic and religious groups. The main command had 658 Croats, 633 Serbs, 6 Muslims, 14 Jews and 62 members of other nationalities. In Bosnia-Herzegovina there were about 100,000 Partisans.

The Partisans were initially run by people's committees, which were organized to act as civilian governments in territories under their control. During their early formation, the Partisan forces were small, ill equipped, and lacked infrastructure. However, they had two advantages over other local fighting forces in the area. Their most important advantage was a small but experienced core of veterans who had fought under similar circumstances in the Spanish Civil War. The second advantage, which became apparent immediately, was a structure and ideology that encompassed all ethnic and religious groups. The ability to draw some level of support from throughout the territories of dismembered Yugoslavia filled their ranks with recruits and provided their units with mobility and an ability to obtain supplies. Although the Partisans initially suffered major losses in forces and territory, their success was due to their single-minded goal of liberating Yugoslavia from foreign occupation, mainly the Axis powers, and to the discipline imposed by strong and determined commanders. In addition, the Ustaše's war of terror against the Serbs and other ethnic groups continued to drive young men and women into the Partisans' ranks.[4] Notably, they were also the only fighting group that shielded and rescued the Jews. Indeed, to protect their forces' identities and to avoid discrimination, the Partisans used *noms de guerre* and kept silent as to their religious affiliation.

EVACUATION OF KORČULA

On September 9, 1943, the day after Italy's capitulation, Dado Maestro, a Jewish refugee in Vela Luka, Korčula, described his mixed emotions in a diary entry:

> We were euphoric over the news that Italy had capitulated, but this did not last for long as we were aware that Nazi and Ustaše invasion of the Island was imminent. A few hours after Italy's capitulation, a few Partisans arrived in Vela Luka. We had one question for them: What would happen to us? They had neither plans nor orders other than to search for their comrades. The following day, the roar of German planes burst into our ears and minutes later the planes were

seen followed by heavy bombardments. From our experience we knew that these planes would reappear. In the chaos of the moment, the Partisans appropriated one of the Italian vessels with which they intended to escape the area. The Jews were eager to leave with them, but they were told that only a small number could join. It was not until September 30, 1943, that real preparations for our departure were made. At dawn, two Italian ships appeared in Vela Luka; these also were not ready to rescue Jews, as their objective was to rescue the remnant of the Italian soldiers who remain stranded in the area. The 250 Jews that were on this part of Korčula were told should they have excess capacity they would be picked up, despite the explicit instructions they received not to allow civilians on board. The following day 250 refugees from Vela Luka reached Bari, in southern Italy.[5]

Another group of 280 Jews was stranded in the town of Korčula on the island of Korčula, and on several islands in the same region. Zlata Romano recalled how little time for deliberations those who remained had. In the last days of September 1943, the Partisans, with the help of local residents, began to use small boats to search for their own missing comrades as well as for Jewish refugees.[6]

In hundreds of small boats of all kinds, some 250 Jews were taken to a "rendezvous" with a large Allied ship that transported them on the short crossing to Bari, Italy. The rescue and survival of the Jews who were stranded on Korčula depended on cooperation among local Partisans, the Allies, the Italian Navy, and the continuous support of humanitarian organizations. Although each of these entities had its own agenda, together they facilitated Jews' escape from NDH, their security and sustenance over a period of two years, and the safe return to their homes.[7]

At the time the refugees from Korčula arrived to Bari the city already had over 15,000 refugees. Since Bari was being bombarded by German planes, the Partisans, assisted by the Allies and several humanitarian organizations, began dispersing the refugees throughout Southern Italy, mostly in the areas of Santa Croce and Santa Maria di Bagni.

Santa Maria—the largest DP (displaced persons) camp in Southern Italy—housed around 2,300 Jewish refugees from 1944 to1946. They were dispersed over three sites in requisitioned villas in the fishing village of di Bagni. Erna Gaon related that she and her son Dori[8] were accommodated with forty other Yugoslav Jewish refugees in one large villa. They shared a room with Zlata Romano and her son Miro.[9]

The humanitarian organization UNRRA (United Nations Relief and Rehabilitation Association) created an environment based on structure and civic responsibility.[10] Everybody had to work and contribute, and the 258 children aged 10-18 attended school. In addition, ZAVNOH (*Zemaljsko antifasištičko vijeće narodnog oslobođenja Hrvatske*, The National Anti-fascist Council of the People's Liberation of Croatia) organized adult education courses in preparation for assuming an active role in rebuilding the country both in Italy and in freed territories. An American airbase in di Bagni gave the Jewish refugees opportunities to meet Jewish servicemen who came to visit them, always bringing presents and treats for the children as well as for the adults: chocolate, canned goods, coffee, and other delicacies.

The refugees found it revitalizing to have the young Jewish men come to see them and their children; indeed, the airmen also longed for the warmth of friendship and family. As a result, most refugees had excess food, which they bartered with local peasants for fresh produce or sold and sent the proceeds to family members and friends in Partisan-controlled areas of Croatia, such as Lika, Kordun, Topusko, and Barnja.[11] Their remittances made a considerable difference in the lives of these penniless refugees, enabling some to buy fresh produce for the first time since the beginning of the war.[12]

The cooperation between Partisans and Allied military lasted until March 1944, when two British troopships began transporting thousands of refugees across the Adriatic, among them a few hundred Jews from various hiding places. The Jews as well as other ethnic groups that were targeted by the Ustaše and the Germans were eager to leave the NDH territories. After a brief stay in Bari, most of the refugees, excluding the Jews, were transported on British ships to two British-run camps in Egypt, El Shatt, and Khatatba,[13] which officially, in agreement with the Egyptians, denied entry to Jews.

Nonetheless, a number of Jews ended up in the Egyptian camps. They included Mihajlo Tolnauer, whose immediate family's lives were saved by conversion to Catholicism in 1942. He and an older brother, from the Maksimir area of Zagreb, survived the period until the capitulation of Italy in a Dominican school, and were then evacuated with other refugees to Bari. Tolnauer described how the 122 Jews in the El Shatt camp kept their identities to themselves; even those who had known each other before the war, merely acknowledging one another with a brief nod. Despite the prohibition on Jewish refugees, the camps had a few Jewish physicians from British Mandate in Palestine who had volunteered to serve in refugee camps. Tolnauer described the mutual elation of Jewish refugees and physicians at finding one another. The Jewish refugees requested they be treated by these physicians. At every opportunity they exchanged information and experiences about both the war front and progress in the Jewish homeland. After the war ended, in August 1945, British ships returned Tolnauer, along with thousands of other refugees, to Croatian soil.[14]

THE JEWS FROM RAB REACHED A COLLECTIVE DECISION IN FREEDOM

For the larger group of Jews on the island of Rab, Italy's capitulation brought a more challenging period than for those on Korčula. As elsewhere along the Dalmatian coast, most of the Italian guards on Rab abandoned their posts. The inmates—Jews, Croats, and Slovenians—disarmed the remaining guards and used their weapons for self-defense. But they faced several hurdles: first, the distance from the Allies' ships; second, the sheer number of refugees on Rab, including women, children, and elderly—estimates range from 3,300 to 4,000—complicated any evacuation scheme.

Historian Menahem Shelah has used the story of the refugees from Rab to harshly criticize the local British military authorities for their "lack of perception, insensibility and deliberate sabotage" of a comprehensive evacuation plan. "The bureaucratic obstacles heaped upon the route of redemption finally prevented the transportation of the refugees to liberated Southern Italy, and many were left to the mercy of the Germans." Shelah acknowledges that Tito and the Partisan High Command knew about the Jews' plight, but lacked the means for evacuation. [15]

Early on in their internment on Rab, the Jewish refugees had established a form of communal government, with an elected board and meetings. On September 9, 1943, the day after Italy's capitulation, the refugees met to deal with the changed situation. The original board insisted that new members should be selected to devise a strategy for gaining freedom. Thus the meeting selected six new members to represent the internees in negotiations with the outside world. Given their dire situation, in particular the refusal of the British to assist them, it was clear that all hope lay with the Croatian Partisans, with whom they had been in contact for some time.[16] When a Partisan contingent appeared at the camp's gate within days, the Jews gladly put their fate in their hands, given their intimate knowledge of the territory, as well as their experience with the earlier evacuation of thousands of refugees from Korčula and nearby coastal areas.

The Rab camp council sent two of the six board members, Dr. Gustav Jungwirth and an engineer, Andrija Mate, to Otočać, a small island on the Adriatic, where the ZAVNOH (*Zemaljsko antifašističko vjeće narodnog oslobođenja Hrvatske;* National Antifascist People's Board for the Liberation of Croatia) had its headquarters, in order to decide the best course of action.[17] ZAVNOH in essence was the highest governing organ of the anti-fascist movement in Croatia during World War II. It was developed to be the bearer of Croatian statehood when the local Partisans government was an alternative government, controlling a large swath of territory, running its own schools, ministries, and newspapers *Vjesnik* and *Naprjed.*[18] It was clear after the meeting with the representatives of ZAVNOH that the Jews could not remain on Rab, since the Partisans in that area had neither the military capability nor sufficient troops to withstand a German attack. Once the decision to abandon the island was reached, the ZAVNOH issued an order to its marine contingent to prepare vessels and organized a number of trucks to transfer the refugees to Split, a city on the Adriatic coast. From there the refugees could march toward the mainland.[19] Most of the younger people interned on Rab joined the Partisans.

Aware that the German and Ustaše armies could easily conquer the former Italian-controlled territories, the Partisan command determined to undertake the evacuation of the 1,500 non-combat Jewish refugees on their own. To carry out this action, ZAVNOH created a new Committee for the Evacuation and Welfare of Jews. They would first evacuate those Jews who wanted to leave the island of Rab immediately. This group, as well as those who were either uncertain what to do but did not want to stay on Rab or who hoped Allied forces would transfer them to Italy, were evacuated by sea to Split by October 1943.[20] A severe shortage of trucks and fuel complicated their transfer to liberated Croatian territories further inland, causing some refugees to set out on foot over mountainous terrain.

Once the evacuation had succeeded, the Partisans had to find suitable accommodations for the Jewish refugees among the local peasant population, and then to supply them with basic necessities. The Partisans soon recognized that these Jews were unlike any other group of refugees they had helped. Not only had they suffered enormous hardships, loss of family members, fear, and anxiety, they were not accustomed to living like peasants, for example, without elementary facilities for hygiene. The Partisan high command was in constant contact over refugee issues with the eight-member committee, composed of six prominent Jewish evacuees from Rab and two representatives from ZAVNOH, and headed by Dr. Hinko Gottlieb.[21]

Those refugees who, like Ivo Herzer and his parents, still had money or valuables could hire a boat to cross the Adriatic.[22] Of the approximately 3,500 inmates on Rab, 211 Jews chose immediate passage to Italy. Another group of 180 to 205 individuals, mainly the elderly and sick, decided to remain on the island, hoping to evade discovery by mingling with the local population.[23] Edit Armuth was one of those who remained on Rab with her family. Six months after the camp's liberation, on March 19, 1944, a contingent of German troops conquered the island. They captured most of the remaining Jews, whom they put on ships to Rijeka, and from there to Trieste, where, together with 330 Jews from Zagreb, they were loaded on trains, 75 to 80 people per car, headed for Auschwitz. At the time of her postwar testimony to the National Commission, Edit believed that she was the only Auschwitz survivor of the Rab group. However, according to my interview with Branko Polić, editor of the Jewish periodical *Novi Omanut*, four other women from that group survived Auschwitz.[24] The few survivors among those who remained on Rab after the German invasion included the Atias family, who were sheltered by local nuns. Once the troops left, the nuns obtained identification papers that allowed the family to return to already liberated Sarajevo.[25]

The Rab survivors whom I interviewed, as well as histories of events on the island, have attributed the overall success of the rescue to pure luck insofar as Italy's capitulation caught the Nazis off-guard and lacking the necessary manpower to reach and attack the Dalmatian coast. In any case, this brief period free of any German presence gave the Partisans time to organize and formulate a rescue plan before the arrival of the German soldiers and the winter.

Approximately one thousand of the Rab Jews who followed the Partisans joined the fighting forces of the Liberation Army; another 648 joined the auxiliary units, serving as physicians, nurses, teachers, journalists, photographers, administrators, and cooks. Those Jews who could not directly join the Partisans—the sick, the elderly, women with children—followed the troops into the liberated territories of Croatia, where they joined other refugees under the designation "Zbjeg, a name the people of ZAVNOH assigned to all the refugees of Yugoslavia."[26]

The Partisans' own survey determined that of the group from Rab were 38 percent were men, 47 percent women, and 15 percent children under age 15. The combat units included a group of 243 former internees who formed a separate Rab Jewish Brigade (Rabska Brigada), thus expressing their indefatigable determination to fight for their personal freedom and that of their country.[27] By the end of the war, the number of Jewish fighters from the Rab camp reached 1,339, of whom 119 died in combat and another 17 succumbed to various diseases. Most survived the war.[28] The large number of elderly and ill refugees under the protection of the Partisans clearly presented a problem for what was in essence a guerilla army in the midst of a brutal war. As later described in an internal Yugoslav Jewish Circular Newsletter published in Lausanne, Switzerland:

> In December 1943, Dr. Hinko Gottlieb, the renowned Zionist publicist and poet from Zagreb, suggested to officials of Marshal Tito that the refugees from the Croat-freed territories should be transferred to Italy, since they were in no position to assist in the war of liberation. Most of them were elderly and sick and they needed hospitalization and rehabilitation centers. But the debate how to resolve the problem was prolonged and the conclusion reached came too late; by then the German Navy controlled the Adriatic seacoast.[29]

Three individuals—the head of the Croatian Partisan Army in Otočać, Vladimir Bakarić, the British Army representative to the Partisans, Major Anthony Hunter, and Vladimir Lošić, the non-Jewish representative of the Jewish board selected in Rab—proposed using British ships to transfer the vulnerable Jewish refugees to southern Italy. However, the British command rejected the idea on the grounds that German vessels in the region and around the islands of the Adriatic would pose a danger.[30]

The British, according to Menahem Shelah, initially opposed the idea of providing food and clothing for the refugees, arguing that they might then be obliged to provide assistance to all the struggling peoples of Europe. Nevertheless, toward the end of 1943 they sent a request to the Allied forces Headquarters (AFHQ) in Algiers to parachute food and clothing supplies to the refugees from Rab.[31]

Once it was no longer safe to transport the Jews by sea, the only feasible means of evacuating those needing special care would have been by plane. However, the British had placed a halt on the transfer by air of Jews to southern Italy, claiming that they had no room on their planes. Moreover, they were adamant that no information should be passed on to the Americans, out of concern that their allies might reverse mutual agreements regarding the refugees. In particular, the British may have feared that Jewish humanitarian organizations in the United States would exert pressure on them to allow the refugees to immigrate to Palestine.

ASSISTANCE AND MATERIAL SUPPORT ON THE WAY

From January to June 1943, the Partisans withstood major Axis attacks. Because of their unyielding stand, the Allies switched their support from the Četniks, remnants of the Royal Serbian Army, to the Partisans. President Roosevelt, Prime Minister Churchill, and Marshal Stalin officially recognized the Partisans at the Tehran Conference in November 1943. Consequently, a moderate amount of Allied aid was parachuted behind Axis lines to assist the Partisans. ZAVNOH used the period between Italy's capitulation and the Allied recognition of Tito's Partisans to meet every British request without relinquishing their humanitarian work on behalf of the Jews and other refugees. Tito's conduct in this regard was probably responsible for changing the Allies' attitude toward his leadership. For example, in June 1944, the Jewish refugees from Rab sent a letter to the Emigration Board in Jerusalem, to the Jewish International Congress, and to the Union of the Jews of Yugoslavia in Tel-Aviv, noting that:

> The Partisans' authorities are making supreme efforts to assist us... but it has produced no positive results under the current circumstances. The Partisans are fighting a battle for their lives and for the country, and they are in no position to assist us more than they have been doing. Because of the nature of guerrilla warfare, we are under constant attack and we are forced to escape from one location to another; we are in life-threatening situations everywhere.... Our strength is diminishing. We are no longer able to stand the physical and emotional anxiety. More than 1,000 people stand to lose their lives at the threshold of liberation. We are urging you to bring our plight to the attention of the appropriate authorities. Do all you can for our survival![32]

The recipients of this letter had no recourse but to wait, even while knowing that the situation—especially following the harsh winter of 1944—was not on the side of the survivors. During that winter, in fact, the Ustaše captured and killed some two hundred Jews.[33] In addition, ZAVNOH became aware of a serious increase in the number of Jewish suicides. Responding to accusations of British inaction from the Jewish refugees, the military delegation in Topusko wrote a formal, detailed, and somewhat annoyed response:

> The Jews of Topusko: a) were never discriminated against, they in fact received a preferential treatment in comparison to other refugees in Yugoslavia; b) the communication officers spared no efforts to assist this group; c) the planes parachuted supplies in the midst of military activities; d) this group was the only one in Yugoslavia to receive supplies; e) no effort was spared when instructions for assistance were ordered from the headquarters; f) the conduct of the Partisans throughout this period was fair and decent; they approved the evacuation at the expense of their own soldiers that were in dire need for supplies. Even today, they are assisting the Jews who are in lesser danger and difficulty than their own military and civilian population.... It is disappointing to see that all our efforts to alleviate their plight resulted in such accusations.[34]

From this letter, we can deduce that there was considerable miscommunication and possibly misunderstanding by the British personnel in the field concerning the urgent needs of the Jewish refugees. Obviously there was much suffering amongst other ethnic groups, but the Jews were traumatized beyond words.

As late as October 1944, Tito allowed a Jewish delegation to leave for Bari to consult with other Jewish leaders regarding an appropriate resolution of the issue of sick and elderly refugees. In November, the Partisans agreed that supplies should be parachuted exclusively to the Jewish refugees in the Topusko region of Croatia. In January 1945, on the suggestion of Randolph Churchill, who was part of the British military mission to aid the Partisans, the Jews would be transferred by British ships from

Split to southern Italy. Once more and for the last time, the possibility of leaving was held out to the Jews; this time their hopes were especially high since the suggestion came from the son of Winston Churchill. Yet, despite mounting international criticism over their discriminatory policies toward the Jews, the British government aborted the plan that had been conceived by their own representatives in the field.

The Partisans—in recognition that work was the best medicine—had engaged many refugees in projects aimed at rebuilding Yugoslavia and elevating their morale. Thus, despite disappointments and fears caused by the Allies' inability or refusal to organize an evacuation to southern Italy, the able-bodied Jewish refugees found comfort in staying alive and being useful. Through the ZAVNOH work programs, many Jewish refugees found new interests in life. The hard physical and mental labor of erecting schools and kitchens and rebuilding infrastructure signified renewal. The supplies and monies sent to them, especially by friends and relatives from southern Italy and Palestine, boosted their spirits and strengthened their hopes. In my conversations with Ella Finci Koen, Erna Kaveson Debenić, and Erna Gaon Latinović,[35] I began to understand for the first time the difficulties they had endured after Italy's capitulation. But I also noticed, even after sixty years, their enthusiasm when describing their luck and the opportunity they had to live another day as free human beings. Their eyes shone when they described how privileged they had felt, being able to return to school as teenagers and being encouraged to make up for the lost years. They were grateful to the ZAVNOH authorities and to the humanitarian organizations that had cared for them. After all, they had not been forgotten and abandoned. One of these invaluable humanitarian organizations that assisted the Jewish refugees throughout the war was the Red Cross.

INTERNATIONAL AND NATIONAL HUMANITARIAN ORGANIZATIONS

Until the beginning of 1944, the IRC in Geneva opposed any planned activities by its representatives on behalf of the Jews of Yugoslavia on the grounds that the agency lacked the international standing that permitted it to act on behalf of civilian territories. Nevertheless, the representative of the Red Cross in Croatia, Mr. Schmitlin, took it upon himself to provide food rations to the former residents of the Lavoslav Schwartz home for the elderly, who, under Archbishop Stepinac's protection, had been transferred in 1943 to church property in Brežovica, where the archbishop was a frequent visitor.[36]

In 1943, the representative from DELASEM in Switzerland worked out an arrangement with the IRC to send parcels to Zagreb under its supervision. The food was to be delivered to concentration camp inmates and the few remaining members of the Jewish Communities. On June 9, 1945, Josipa Shulhof, one of the last employees of Zagreb's Jewish Community, testified before the National Commission that as early as mid-1942 the IRC in Geneva, via Hungary, sent to the community "three large and magnificent shipments," that contained not just medical supplies, but, most importantly, special prescriptions that were not available in Zagreb. She also reported that the IRC had sent 1,200 containers with medicine and such food products as sardines, sugar, pasta, and canned foods to the concentration camps.[37] In addition, the camps received parcels from the Portuguese Red Cross in Lisbon, which sent over 300 kilograms of vegetables as well as 370 cartons of canned food.[38] It is not clear whether this was a single shipment or ongoing assistance.

During the summer of 1944, the IRC requested that the Croatian government permit Schmitlin, from the Croatian Red Cross, to visit Jasenovac. Although the government granted the request, it notified the Jasenovac authorities of the impending inspection. Thus, when Schmitlin made his brief visit he found a cleaned-up camp and was given a special presentation on the inmates' situation. Unable to verify the true condition of the inmates, Schmitlin's report to the IRC led to no improvements in the conditions of the inmates.[39] The scarcity of provisions in Yugoslavia was a result of the Allies' economic embargo of all territories that were still at war with Germany. Although Jewish emigration was halted, the Red Cross was able to deliver food and clothing. From June 12, 1944, onward, as word of the dire situation of refugees became widespread, the first of a regular flow of food parcels from various international humanitarian and religious organizations began to reach the Jewish refugees who remained in free Partisan territories; first small quantities, and later large amounts, of food and clothing arrived. On August 1, 1944, Dr. Hinko Gottlieb, whom Tito sent to Italy, initiated a campaign to solicit financial donations from organizations throughout Europe and the United States, as well as from Yugoslav Jews living in Italy. Monies arrived at the offices of the Red Cross in Bari from private individuals and from the "Jewish Distribution Committee." The Red Cross forwarded all monies and packages to the offices of ZAVNOH. The instructions from the donors were nearly always the same: "Please distribute the money and the packages wisely; first provide for those who most urgently need assistance and those who cannot fend for themselves."[40]

The "Society for Yugoslav Jewry" in London also offered financial assistance, especially after members learned from Partisan General Vladimir Velebit of the misery Jews had experienced in his country. This humanitarian organization sent a letter to Dr. Gottlieb asking what was needed, and how they could help; however, I did not find further evidence that aid was forthcoming.

A RESCUE MISSION TO ITALY: HOPE AND DISAPPOINTMENT

Although the Allied invasion of Italy in September 1943 would seem to have opened new opportunities for the rescue of Jews, there has been a widespread perception—as discussed above—that the Allies refused to assist the Jewish refugees from Rab. For its part, the U.S. State Department—aware of the continuing danger to Jewish refugees in the former Italian-occupied areas—responded to a plea from the World Jewish Congress by requesting military help to transfer the Rab refugees to Italy. However, the Joint Chiefs of Staff replied that the Allied forces in Italy were already overwhelmed by refugees, and that there was no way to aid the refugees from Rab. As historian David Wyman describes the situation:

Even the State Department was taken aback. Under Secretary Edward Stettinius warned Secretary of State Cordell Hull that if the response to the Rab situation accurately reflected military policy, the United States might as well "shut up shop" on the effort to rescue more people from Axis Europe. Stettinius thought that the President should inform the military that rescue was extremely important . . . in fact sufficiently important to require unusual effort on their part and to be set aside only for important military operational reasons.[41]

On July 11, 1944, Gottlieb sent a letter from Bari to ZAVNOH head-quarters in which he described the situation of the Jewish refugees in the camps of Bari and Santa Maria di Bagni. Jewish refugees in those camps had developed their own communal living, sharing work and resources. Other documents, as well as my interviews, support his report of a situation far removed from the privations faced by the Rab refugees. In Italy, the refugees were free to leave their camps for work, medical care, or leisure activities. Rations were plentiful, and each group of refugees cooked for its own members. Those who spoke English could earn an income as translators. Each camp had some recreational facilities, as well as many educational courses, from basic reading and writing skills to nursing, trades, and languages.

Approximately 1,500 of the Rab Jews were dispersed among local peasants and other refugees in the liberated territories of Lika and Kordun in central Croatia, where—over an unusually harsh winter—they encountered severe hardships because of the lack of food and clothing.[42] Not only had efforts to supply them from outside failed, but the battle for survival among tens of thousands of refugees such as Serbs, Slovenes, Roma and others was keen and merciless. And, once again, the Jews faced antisemitic abuses from peasant populations with a traditional fear of strangers. The Jews also became a target for attack by other refugee populations, as well as from low-ranking Partisan soldiers.[43]

The ZAVNOH authorities responsible for the welfare of the Jewish refugees felt intensely the hardship of having to cope with such a large and helpless population in the midst of a combat zone. Skirmishes with the Germans occurred daily, and there was constant pressure to evacuate the refugees to another location.[44] For example, an effort to evacuate them to Slavonia, the breadbasket of Croatia, was foiled by the harsh winter and German activities in the region.[45] To reduce the level of animosity toward the Jews, ZAVNOH had to exert its authority by issuing successive decrees warning the peasants and other refugee groups that harassment of the Jews must stop immediately.

Moreover, the Partisans' combat effectiveness suffered from the constant need to find shelter and provisions to feed a large number of refugees, who had neither the strength to work nor the means to purchase food from the peasants.[46] The situation began to improve during the summer of 1944 when assistance began to arrive from international Jewish agencies, although this created resentment among other refugee groups who did not enjoy such sources of food. Despite these hardships, the Partisans—for political and humanitarian reasons—kept to their part of the bargain until the end of the war in May 1945.[47]

With no possibility of relief from outside, the Partisans resigned themselves to making the best of their circumstances. Correspondence between ZAVNOH headquarters and local Partisan social workers describe the effort to provide the Jewish refugees with a sense of stability. ZAVNOH requested that all able-bodied refugees work in hospitals, schools and soup kitchens; those with relevant skills were assigned to projects at schools, childcare centers, and dining areas. Teachers and other intellectuals were asked to step forward to fill the sorely needed positions for professionals.

The ZAVNOH authorities insisted on providing structure for the refugee children's lives, as well as on encouraging the adults to move toward self-motivated and productive survival.[48] The slogan was: "All able bodies mobilize for work." For many survivors, the schools offered a miraculous renewal of hope: seeing their children attend regular school under such harsh circumstances allowed them to glimpse a better future. Nonetheless, internal Partisan correspondence reveals the constant frustrations. Thus, in October 1944, the ZAVNOH board asked the planning board to introduce, without delay, improvements in refugee living conditions, in particular the construction of public kitchens.[49]

Since transfers to Italy were unlikely, many more such public facilities would be needed, particularly in the Glina region. This being the case, ZAVNOH demanded that work on the kitchens begin immediately.

Judging by many letters written by the Jewish refugees to ZAVNOH and the Union of Jewish Communities in Italy, the Partisans were truly concerned about the psychological well-being of the Jews. Even before war broke out they had promised not to discriminate between religious and ethnic groups. The Jewish refugees appreciated the conduct of the ZAVNOH administration, even though the level of bureaucratic control could be overwhelming. For example, a special request had to be submitted to ZAVNOH headquarters in order to obtain a truck to transfer the elderly for medical treatment or to take wheat to the mill. ZAVNOH would then instruct local staff in the office of transportation in Topusko to provide the Jewish collective with a truck.[50] The extensive bureaucracy, which assured full employment, might have been a function of the relative shortage of supplies and basic commodities compared to the supply of manpower.

Despite the large number of sick and elderly refugees who were unable to work, the Partisans valued the Jewish refugees for their education and their contributions in a wide range of areas. From my interview with the former head of the first Partisan military task force to London, General Dr. Vladimir Velebit, I learned that in December 1943 he had met with Jewish representatives from Palestine in Cairo. At the meeting, the Jewish delegation offered to send a group of Jewish paratroopers to aid the Partisans in their war against the Nazis and also to provide the Partisans with medical supplies. Tito responded by declaring his favorable attitude toward the Zionist movement.[51]

In the final push for the liberation of their country the Partisans expressed a great need for military supplies and the resupply of food and clothing. The Jewish refugees in the liberated territories believed that if some of their delegates were sent to Italy they could exert pressure on the Jewish Communities in Western Europe to provide needed help to the Partisans. In his capacity as head of ZAVNO's Jewish Board, Dr. Hinko Gottlieb sent many letters and requests to Tito asking for a meeting in which he hoped to explain the predicament of the Jewish refugees in the liberated territories. In particular, he requested that Tito send him to Italy to mobilize support for the evacuation of the sick, elderly, and children to southern Italy. To Gottlieb's surprise, in March 1944, ZAVNOH received a telegram with the message: "Inform Gottlieb that we approve evacuation of the Jews to Italy the minute it becomes feasible." It was signed: "The President of the National Board, Marshal of Yugoslavia, Tito.[52]

On July 3, 1944, Gottlieb, accompanied by his wife, traveled to Italy as the representative of the Croatian Red Cross, with instructions to accomplish two tasks:

> First, to find ways to aid Jews still remaining in the former territories of Yugoslavia; and second, to find a way to evacuate all Jews who wished to leave Yugoslavia for Palestine. Gottlieb carried both a generic letter of introduction from the Croatian Red Cross and a general request for assistance in accomplishing his urgent tasks.[53] In addition, ZAVNOH provided 10,000 kunas (Croatian currency) to cover his initial expenses. Immediately after his departure, the ZAVNOH authorities informed Tito that the evacuation project was in the hands of Dr. Gottlieb, the president of all the Jewish refugees, who was on his way to Bari.[54]

Expectations were high back in the liberated territories. The non-combatant Jews hoped that Gottlieb would find ways to relocate them to Italy, and the ZAVNOH board hoped for contacts that would improve the relationship between the Allied forces and the Partisans. The opening of a British military airport in Topusko in early June 1944 gave Partisans a reason for optimism regarding an evacuation. On their return to bases in Europe after unloading supplies, the planes transferred wounded Partisans to the Allies' medical facilities in Italy. If there was additional space, they also transferred Yugoslav non-Jewish refugees. But by September, 1,500 Jewish refugees remained in Topusko, waiting for a chance to reach Italy. It would be reasonable to assume under the circumstances that the Partisans had self-interest, as well as humanitarian, reasons to evacuate the Jewish refugees from the battle-torn territories.

Namely, they could expect that planes arriving to airlift stranded Jews would bring provisions for their troops. Tito also figured that a large number of emaciated Jewish refugees might arouse the sentiments of Jews in Great Britain and the United States, resulting in pressure on these governments to provide robust assistance to the Partisans.[55]

In July 1944, British Captain Edholm from the Allied Military Liaison (AML) office in Italy asked Tito's representatives, no names given, to provide him with a list of the most urgently needed supplies. He added, however, that these items would not be shipped while the fighting in Yugoslavia continued. The AML would only send food, medicine, technical supplies, clothing, and possibly medical personnel after the enemy had retreated, since they feared that supplies provided to the Partisans might reach the enemy, thus prolonging the war.[56]

Although it cannot be documented, Gottlieb's mission may have had some initial success, since one group of Jewish refugees from Croatia departed for Palestine shortly after his arrival in southern Italy. This first transport, which reached Palestine on November 11, 1944, consisted of 175 Jewish refugees who had escaped from Korčula and Vela Luka.[57] It also proved to be the last Palestine-bound transport from southern Italy. Despite the efforts of many Jewish activists in Palestine and in southern Italy, the British refused to issue entry visas for Palestine to Jews, while issuing thousands of such visas to non-Jewish refugees from Poland and Greece. Historian David Wyman described this paradoxical situation:

> By 1944, 25,000 Greeks had been evacuated. The largest numbers, reported at between 9,000 and 12,000, were taken to Palestine, mostly to a former army installation at Nuseirat, near Gaza. Palestine also sheltered 1,800 non-Jewish Polish refugees. While the British, intent on keeping the small White Paper quota from being filled, turned back endangered Jews, they generously welcomed these other victims of the storm.[58]

The ZAVNOH leadership knew that transports from throughout the Balkans were being sent to Palestine; however, they were oblivious to the details of the British government's 1939 White Paper, which reversed an earlier plan for partitioning its Mandate territory in favor of creating an independent Palestine governed by Palestinian Arabs and Jews in proportion to their population by 1949.[59] Command 6019 of the White Paper contained three elements: the first limited Jewish immigration to 15,000 persons a year (including 5,000 refugees) for a period of five years. A supplementary quota of 25,000 Jews over the five years covered refugee emergencies; any further immigration required Arab approval. Since this was unlikely to be met, the White Paper guaranteed Jews a permanent minority status, at one-third of the population.

The second provision severely restricted the acquisition of land in areas where the Jews constituted a minority. Finally, the White Paper's "Constitutional Clause" promised the creation of an Arab-majority Palestinian state—with vague guarantees for some form of shared representation and Jewish minority rights.[60] Jews throughout the world who were familiar with the British policy saw the White Paper as a repudiation of the Balfour Declaration of 1917, which had pledged British support for "the establishment in Palestine of a national home for the Jewish people," and its League of Nations Mandate. In short, the White Paper seemed to end any possibility of a large-scale rescue of European Jews.

Comrade Gregorić, who was Gottlieb's connection with ZAVNOH, was not only unaware of the problems caused by British concerns regarding Palestine, but he needed some concrete answers for his superiors regarding the evacuation of Jewish refugees. Thus he wrote an angry letter to Gottlieb, accusing him of dragging his heels:

> Dear Comrade: We have exhausted all the avenues in our attempts to transfer the Jewish elderly, women and children to Italy. As you know, we can only organize their evacuation, but the rest depends on the Allies. Most of the Jews here are exhausted and represent the poorest element. Despite our efforts to alleviate their plight, we are being criticized from all sides for not doing enough. It does not seem right that all the blame falls on us because of a very small Jewish minority.
> …The only hope we have is that this war will not last much longer and that, with freedom, all these issues will be resolved. Nevertheless, I hope that you will somehow manage to arrange something for the 670

Jews who urgently need rehabilitation and are impatiently waiting to be transferred to Italy.[61]

The Partisans found it simply incomprehensible that the British would renege on what they considered an agreement to transfer 670 ill and elderly Jews to southern Italy while, at the same time, they provided planes to transport non-Jewish refugees as well as wounded and ill Partisans. Moreover, ZAVNOH did not want the Partisans to be unfairly blamed for the delays. Thus, although they did not control the transports, the Partisans apologized to the Jews, explaining that they had done all that was humanly possible for the Jewish refugees and that the "world" had no right to insinuate that they had discriminated against the Jews.[62] ZAVNOH authorities even provided evidence that, as Jewish refugees waited in the airport at Topusko, it was the British officers who refused to let them embark, even though the planes were leaving for southern Italy empty.[63] The problem was not Gottlieb's failure to act, but rather that the Allies, in particular the British, for political reasons, refused to evacuate those refugees who most desperately needed medical treatment unavailable in the combat zones of Croatia.

Tito had two objectives in calling attention to the shabby treatment of Jews by the British as compared to the Partisans' self-sacrificing behavior: first, to achieve Allied recognition for his leadership capabilities and humanitarian conduct toward the refugees; and, second, to legitimize his eventual regime.[64] His intention was to let the world know of his deep commitment to brotherhood and unity and his special effort to shield the Jews. Jewish Communities in Palestine and around the world offered both criticism of the British and assistance to the refugees. The Italian Army's chief military rabbi rebuked the British government for holding to its White Paper quota of Jews at a time of desperate need.[65]

The Jewish Committee for Assistance (DELASEM) and the Federation of Zionists of South Italy made donations of 300,000 lire ($2,305). Jews in Haifa and Tel-Aviv contributed funds for two hospitals, each fully equipped with one hundred beds. These two hospitals were to be erected in southern Italy, since the transport of the wounded to Palestine was not feasible.[66] Nevertheless, these contributions, including hundreds of packages, as well as the efforts of large numbers of humanitarian organizations seemed insufficient to reverse the plight of the Jewish refugees. The economic embargo imposed on territories still fighting the Germans and the Ustaše was an additional hurdle.

CIVILIAN POPULATION IN THE UNITED STATES MOUNTS PRESSURE ON CONGRESS

In April 1943, the Allies held a secret conference in Bermuda to discuss resettlement possibilities for Jewish refugees who had reached neutral countries. The U.S. supported the idea that Jewish refugees who reached Italy be offered temporary sanctuary in Libya, but nothing came of it— or indeed of the entire conference. The U.S. was unwilling to relax its immigration laws, and Britain feared raising the Palestine issue. The following year, the War Refugee Board (WRB) pressed the British to take action to expedite the relocation of Jewish refugees in Mediterranean countries, an area for which they were responsible. But the British argued that strong Arab opposition, not their own failure to act, prevented Jews from relocating to Libya, or to any other Muslim country, even for a brief period.

Meanwhile, mounting pressure in the United States on behalf of the Jewish refugees in Yugoslavia met with what seemed an insurmountable obstacle. Namely, in 1940, the U.S. had closed its immigration quotas for all groups, and it would take an act of Congress to reverse the policy.[67] To avoid bringing the immigration issue before Congress, because the idea of "haven" was likely to be unpopular with them and the public, in early 1944, President Roosevelt established the WRB, a government entity with sufficiently broad authority to rescue approximately 1,000 of the Jewish survivors who were stranded in Italy.[68] Executive Order 9417 authorized the newly created entity:

> with carrying out the policy of this Government [which is] to take all measures within its power to rescue the victims of enemy oppression who are in imminent danger of death and otherwise to afford such victims all possible relief and assistance consistent with the successful

prosecution of the war.... It shall be the duty of the State, Treasury and War Departments, within their respective spheres, to execute at the request of the Board.[69]

In addition to initiating and executing rescue operations through its representatives in Europe, the WRB was to appeal to Allied leaders to issue war crime warnings to countries known to be collaborating with Nazi Germany, primarily those—such as Hungary, Romania and Bulgaria—that joined the Axis powers.[70] The WRB soon realized the many obstacles it faced in carrying out its mandate. Above all, Jewish refugees were unwelcome in most countries, making relocation extremely difficult. Nevertheless, the WRB's financing of rescue operations played a crucial role in saving approximately 200,000 Jews, including some in Yugoslavia.[71] Furthermore, the WRB's presence in Europe strengthened the activities of the Joint Distribution Committee (JDC; Joint) and the International Red Cross (IRC). For example, it cooperated with these agencies in places like Lisbon, a transfer point for French Jews fleeing through Spain and on to North Africa. They also collaborated in Istanbul, an escape route for Jews from the Balkan countries, including Yugoslavia.[72]

In March 1944, Anthony Eden, then leader of the House of Commons, informed the British Cabinet that WRB publicity implied that British actions were impeding America's humanitarian efforts. Eden also observed that assisting the refugees might impede the economic embargo, resulting in real benefit to the enemy.[73] In a memo of November 7, 1944, however, ZAVNOH informed Partisan authorities in the regions of Baranja and Kordun—the areas where Jews were concentrated—that the Allies had landed four planes with commodities to be distributed to needy Jews.[74] This air convoy perhaps signaled that it was now time to provide much needed aid to the entire country and that the intensity of political considerations was dwindling.

In April 1944, journalist Samuel Grafton, editorial page editor of the *New York Post* and a syndicated columnist who appeared in more than a hundred papers, brought widespread attention to the plight of refugees with his promotion of "free ports":

A "free port" is a small bit of land, a kind of reservation, into which foreign goods may be brought without paying customs duties. . . . Why couldn't we have a system of free ports for refugees fleeing the Hitler terror? The refugees, Jewish and other, ask only for a few fenced-in acres of the poorest land in America. They don't want to keep it. They just want to sit on it until they can go home again.[75]

Other New York papers—the *Herald Tribune* and the *Times*—soon joined the call for free ports, as did the *Christian Science Monitor,* the entire Hearst chain, syndicated columnist Dorothy Thompson, several radio commentators, as well as the *New Republic,* the *Nation, Commonweal* and the *Christian Century.* The Jewish press and all major Jewish organizations also supported the plan, as did a number of non-profit organizations, including the Federal Council of Churches, the Church Peace Union, the National Board of the YWCA, the Catholic Committee for Refugees, the Friends and Unitarian service committees, the President's Advisory Committee on Political Refugees, the AFL, the CIO, and the National Farmers Union. While support for the idea grew, and public opinion was in agreement with the media and humanitarian organizations, the WRB failed to react to Grafton's idea.[76]

With the pressure for free ports as background, on May 26, 1944, representatives of the U.S. Army told President Roosevelt that the concentration of refugees in Italy had created a bottleneck that hindered the success of other rescue missions. Italy was the only territory where East European Jewish refugees had a chance of survival. But if Italy was filled to capacity, there was no room for other survivors. Thus, Roosevelt almost immediately ordered the army to reopen the refugee flow across the Adriatic. As a first step, the U.S. would open its borders for a group of nearly one thousand refugees congregated mostly in Bari and DP camps in southern Italy. After further discussions with other governments and humanitarian agencies such as the JOINT, as well as with the army, and after considering several possible locations for temporary resettlement, Roosevelt recommended the empty Fort Ontario camp in Oswego, New York. He then sent a letter prepared by the WRB to Congress explaining the dire situation in Italy. In addition, the president explained to Congress and the nation that this was a temporary arrangement; once the war had ended, the refugees would have to return to their homes overseas.

Journalist Ruth Gruber, who accompanied the refugees on their journey from Naples to the U.S., recalled how on August 3, 1944, 982 refugees looked to the horizon to catch the first glimpses of New York Harbor. At that moment she recited to them the poem written by Emma Lazarus:

> Give me your tired, your poor,
> Your huddled masses yearning to breathe free,
> The wretched refuse of your teeming shore,
> Send these, the homeless, tempest-tossed, to me:
> I lift my lamp beside the golden door.[77]

When the ship, the *Henry Gibbins*, docked, it was met with a fanfare of photographers, journalists, and reporters who had come to see the refugees. Luna Kabiljo-Kahana, originally from Sarajevo, was barely five years old when she arrived in the U.S. with her parents, an aunt, and a cousin. Sixty years later, Luna vividly remembered the days when the news of their arrival occupied the columns of newspapers and magazines.[78] Excitement—and the anticipation of families being reunited—permeated every corner of the ship, encompassing everyone aboard: the refugees, wounded soldiers returning home, and the ship's officers and crew. The refugees were soon on their way by train to Fort Ontario, which was located on the shore of Lake Ontario, not far from Syracuse and adjacent to the town of Oswego.[79] The Oswego contingent encompassed a cross-section of the refugee population that had reached southern Italy. Most had fled originally from Austria, Czechoslovakia, Germany, Poland, and Yugoslavia.[80] In age, they ranged from infants to octogenarians, although young men of military age were notably absent. Nearly 90 percent were Jewish; the rest were Catholics.

The refugees had been told about their anticipated postwar repatriation before they left Italy. This led to considerable resentment, especially among the Jews, less from the Christians among them, since most had no desire to return to countries that had disowned them, and where they had experienced great suffering—above all, the loss of family members. The refugees also feared renewed persecution due to prewar antisemitism that had been exacerbated by the Nazi regime. Furthermore, more than half of the refugees had relatives living in the U.S., who in many cases were their only surviving family members. More than one hundred of the refugees had immediate family members in the U.S.; a husband or wife in seven cases; brothers or sisters in 73 cases; and children in 35 cases. Fourteen of the refugees had sons in the American Armed Forces.[81]

The decision to rescind the repatriation scheme was finally made after the war in Europe had ended in May 1945, under the presidency of Harry Truman. Following the election of a new British Labor government under Prime Minister Clement Attlee on July 26, 1945, President Truman called on Britain to permit 100,000 Jews to immigrate to Palestine in order to help relieve the pressure in Europe. It seemed inappropriate for Truman to ask Britain to make such large concessions while keeping the doors to America closed to fewer than a thousand refugees. On December 5, 1945, Truman ruled that the Oswego refugees would be eligible for entry into the U.S. under unused immigration quotas.

The American Christian Committee for Refugees and the Catholic Committee for Refugees made arrangements for the Catholics.[82] Sixty-six out of the 362 refugees that came from Yugoslavia chose to return home, although some of them subsequently left for Israel or other countries. Luna Kabiljo-Kahana, her parents, her aunt Flora Atias and daughter Laura, were among those who chose to return and search for surviving family members. Flora Atias reunited with her husband upon their return to Sarajevo.

With the war still raging, Roosevelt, Churchill, and Stalin met at Yalta from February 4 11, 1945, to discuss the future of postwar Europe, including the borders that might emerge from the battlefields. They had no clear solution for the territories of Yugoslavia. The expectation was that Tito would join forces with the Yugoslav government-in-exile in London. Instead, he began consolidating his power by purging his government of non-communists. The subsequent meeting of the now victorious Big Three powers in Potsdam, from July 17 to August 2, 1945, determined Yugoslavia's future. At issue was whether Tito was living up to the standards of the Declaration on Liberated Europe, by which the Allies meeting at Yalta had pledged to hold free elections in countries under Allied influence. Churchill argued that Yugoslavia had fallen short by this measure: there was no election law; a closed group of ardent communists had chosen the Assembly of the Council; legal procedures had not been re-established, and Tito's Communist Party and its police created a dictatorship that controlled the administration and the press. Churchill wanted to invite Tito and representatives of the new Yugoslav government to Potsdam to explain their intentions. Truman, who in the interim since Yalta had become president, understood that Tito was the dominant force in a country that was already effectively under the Russian sphere of influence. And since Stalin's support was still needed in the war against Japan, Yugoslavia became part of the East European nations affiliated with U.S.S.R. block.[83]

The war and their exile ended, many of the survivors were eager to return to the places and loved ones they had left behind. They were poorly prepared for the devastation that had befallen the Jews of Yugoslavia.[84] Isak Samokovlija, a physician and writer, survived the war and returned to his beloved Sarajevo. Traumatized by the enormity of the Jewish calamity, he wrote:

> Once upon a time I knew everyone here, every man, every child, every chicken, as people say....Look, many houses still exist, all the streets from my childhood, my youth, but none of the same people are here any more. Everyone is new, strange to me. Where are they? Killed, murdered, destroyed, dispersed. These who are moving around— they neither know me nor I them... [85]

7

Summary and Conclusions

Yugoslavia's promise to unite the South Slav nations after World War I failed for several reasons, but primarily because of its complex demographic composition, most notably the mistrust—sometimes spilling over into violence—between the two largest groups, the Serbs and the Croats. Conflicting interests between various ethnic and religious groups and urban and rural residents, and sharp differences in education and standards of living further exacerbated tensions. Yugoslavia's heterogeneity complicates comparisons with other European countries under Axis occupation. The very complexity of Yugoslavia—deserving of the label "Balkanization"—made the task of the occupiers much easier, but may also have made the imposition of the Final Solution more difficult, thus helping to explain the relatively large number of Jews who survived in the face of so many entities that were intent on annihilating them.

This study has examined the ways in which the Ustaše, with their roots in Yugoslavia's nationality conflicts and politics, differed from the Nazis in political aims, as well as in ideology. Nonetheless, Croatia's Jews, like those throughout Nazi-occupied Europe, were annihilated in great numbers. Nazi ideology identified the Jews as an infectious agent threatening the superior race of Aryans. There could be no compromise in regard to the Jewish Question and the Final Solution: no Jews deserved rescue. Thus, the Nazi propaganda machine advocated that Jews must be exterminated for the good of the German people. Given Hitler's self-imposed mission to annihilate European Jewry, he allowed no opposition to this program. Those who dared to defy German commands suffered severe penalties.

Well before the outbreak of war in Yugoslavia, Nazi Germany strategically began the economic penetration of Yugoslavia, accompanied by a propaganda initiative that sought to mobilize the Volksdeutsche as a fifth column. German plans for eventual war and occupation followed. Hitler's agents understood the ethnic and religious divisions within Yugoslavia and exploited and manipulated them to advance the Third Reich's hold in the Balkan Peninsula.

My research has confirmed the view of other historians and those who lived through the occupation that the Nazis intentionally incited greed among ordinary citizens of the NDH. By rewarding self-interest and avarice, they encouraged individuals to acquiesce to, or even commit, the cruelest acts of torture and murder. Nazi sympathizers at all levels, from Pavelić to the lowliest citizens, became preoccupied with looting and plundering Jewish assets. Numerous testimonies describe a craze to possess Jewish belongings and assets. Greed in combination with opportunities drove some ordinary citizens to abandon traditional ideas of morality as well as any ideals they may have held for building a free Croatia. Judge Srećko Bujas, the appointed trustee of the Sephardic Jewish Community in Sarajevo, spoke to this change in his testimony before the postwar National Commission:

> In our country, the anti-Jewish decrees and ordinances were undertaken by people without any professional qualifications, people without judgment of right and wrong. These young people, once righteous and idealistic, instead of channeling their capabilities and talents for the benefit of their people and homeland, chose for themselves a selfish objective: self-enrichment and self-gratification in the shortest time possible and without careful consideration of the consequences for the future. They understood that the so-called Racial Laws placed the Jews totally outside the realm of the law, regarding their very existence worthless and their earthly possessions as belonging to the individual Ustaše.[1]

The resulting atrocities—including the murder of thousands in concentration camps—were horrendous, but despite the opportunities to loot and plunder, indeed the threats of heavy punishments for those caught assisting Jews, ordinary citizens from a variety of ethnic, religious, and socio-economic backgrounds demonstrated a willingness to offer a chance of rescue for NDH's Jews. The rescuers also included officials in the NDH government, Archbishop Alojzije Stepinac and others in the Catholic Church in Croatia, national and international humanitarian organizations, the Italian 2nd Army, and the Croatian Partisans. These individuals and entities acted for a number of reasons and utilized different means. They offered shelter, provided food, obtained forged exit visas, transported Jews across enemy lines, shielded them in camps, and helped them reach territories liberated by the Partisans. Yet all those who reached out and helped Jews took risks and put themselves in harm's way.

Nonetheless, the complex political, religious, and social environment in the NDH interacted with the Nazis' genocidal intent to annihilate 30,000 Jews. Although contemporary Holocaust historiography understandably focuses on genocide, at least 9,500 Jews in NDH territory survived under the most difficult circumstances. Both the survivors and the rescuers who made their survival possible should be considered indelible parts of Holocaust history in Croatia and Bosnia-Herzegovina. For this reason, it is important that these rescuers be identified and acknowledged. As this book has shown, the rescue of a Jew was rarely due to the efforts of one person. More often, it required the cumulative efforts of many, over a period of years. Each assisted in a specific moment, forming a link in a long chain of rescuers.

The degree of control exercised by Nazi forces in their occupied territories varied from one area to another, depending to some extent on the level of local collaboration. As headquarters for the German Army, Sarajevo was under close control by the SS and the Gestapo. Moreover, the Nazis relied on the local Muslim elite, as illustrated by a speech by Ismet Muftić, the mufti of Zagreb, published in a Sarajevo newspaper on April 24, 1941, just after the arrival of German troops into the city: "The

Muslim faces were covered with tears of joy because Bosnia-Herzegovina was included in the newly created NDH. The Muslim people are asked to greet the German Army as if they were their own brothers."[2]

As this book has demonstrated, the Nazi regime in Sarajevo and other cities in Bosnia had no interest in the future of the NDH or the good of the local population; its sole interest was to loot, liquidate, and sell Jewish assets, depositing the proceeds in German banks. Their allies among the Muslim political and religious leadership pocketed their share of the loot, dividing it among family members and friends, and leaving the rest of the population in dire poverty and need.[3] While the plunder and looting went on, twenty-eight successive transports over a period of eight months sent approximately 70 percent of the Jewish men, women and children of Sarajevo to their deaths. Nevertheless, non-Jews undertook heroic acts of rescue, undeterred by the penalties levied against those who were caught assisting Jews.

One such story is from Dr. Vedran Deletis, whose father, Ratimir Deletis, a Catholic and a local judge in Tuzla, Bosnia, rescued over one hundred Jews.[4] Tuzla was a city with a diverse ethnic and religious population, but whose citizens co-existed in neighborly relationships. It was natural that Tuzla's Jews would approach Judge Deletis for assistance. On January 14, 1942, Deletis heard that all Jews in Tuzla and nearby Travnik would be rounded up and sent to Jasenovac, with the exception of those who had obtained official exemptions. Deletis promptly headed for Zagreb, intending to obtain at least two hundred exemptions directly from Dido Kvaternik, the head of the Ustaše Security Services. Before departing, he asked an influential colleague who was a friend of Pavelić, to join him. After a long discussion with Kvaternik, they obtained permission to free sixteen Jewish families provided they converted to Catholicism or Islam. Deletis identified the families with that largest number of children and those he rescued. Fortunately, both the Catholic Church and Muslim imams issued conversion certificates.

Despite the reprieve, most of the families that received exemptions nonetheless sought to relocate to the Dalmatian coast. Again with Deletis's help they were able to obtain travel permits. Among the families he saved were the Domanis, Wieslers, Hirschbeins, Altarzs, and Danons. For help rendered to Jewish persons during the period of the Holocaust, the Commission of the Designation of the Righteous awarded Ratimir Deletis with the title of "Righteous Among the Nations."[5]

In other areas, German influence and control over the apparatus of government was relatively moderate, at least in the beginning. For example, in Osijek between 1941 and mid-1942, the city's Jews acting in concert with other residents were able to protect themselves as well as several hundred Jewish children from Sarajevo. The Osijek Jewish Community exemplifies what was possible under a relatively low level of Nazi control. Jews, together with the local police, worked closely to ensure that living conditions in the nearby Djakovo concentration camp were less harsh and more humane than those in other camps. For example, women from the Osijek Jewish Community visited the camp, bringing provisions and assisting the sick; as they were leaving the camp, they often took with them—one by one—children from Sarajevo who had been interned there and housed them with local Jewish families. Dr. Zdenko Sternberg from Osijek, whose parents perished with the August 1942 transport, willed himself to survive and tell the world his parents' selfless story. They had made all the necessary preparations to leave Osijek—purchased the train tickets and obtained the documents needed to cross the border to the Italian zone. But at the last minute his father decided to delay their departure in an attempt to save the few children remaining in the Djakovo camp. He managed to rescue the children from the hell of Djakovo, but was unable to rescue himself, his wife, and the children from the Volksdeutsche collaborationists of Osijek.

Clearly the Jews of Osijek had many more opportunities for escape than those in other areas, yet many were reluctant to seize their opportunities. Rabbi Charles Steckel, formerly the rabbi of Osijek, recalled:

The Nazis were masters at spreading and fostering illusions among their victims.... The Jews of Osijek were trapped when the Ustaše offered them the village of Tenje, near Osijek. They were told that they could build their own settlement there which would serve as their own community until the end of the war. The Ustaše liquidated the settlement after a few months and deported the Jews to Auschwitz, Jasenovac and Loborgrad.[6]

Thus, in August 1942, the Ustaše rounded up more than 1,200 unsuspecting Jews from Osijek, of whom approximately 700 were children, 350 of them from Sarajevo. Under cover of darkness, they were taken to the railroad station and sent to an unknown destination; nothing more was heard from them after that fatal night.

With hindsight, one might wonder how it was possible that Croatia's literate and well-informed Jews—informed about world affairs, aware of Nazi antisemitism and knowing firsthand that the region was a hotbed of Volksdeutsche sympathies—could be so naïve as to believe that they were safe. Why then did Osijek's Jews believe the Ustaše claim that Tenje would be theirs in perpetuity? If only they had spent the money and the energy they poured into building the settlement on purchasing exit visas, the destiny of many would have been very different. But ifs are irrelevant because in such situations the Jews are optimists. Nahum Goldmann, American Jewish activist said: "This optimism is one of the reasons for the Jews' ability to survive in the Diaspora for hundreds of years."[7]

Zagreb's situation was different from that in Sarajevo or Osijek. Not only was Zagreb the seat of the NDH government, but a third of the city's 12,000 Jews converted to Catholicism, and at least a thousand were involved in mixed marriages. By and large, the Nazis allowed the Ustaše to run the city. But when in time the Ustaše lost their appetite for the murder of Jews, their conduct greatly displeased the Nazi representatives in Zagreb. On May 5, 1943, Heinrich Himmler arrived in Zagreb to request that Pavelić hand over to the SS all the remaining Jews, including the protected ones, in exchange for financial and economic assistance. Pavelić accepted Himmler's offer, excluding only those in mixed marriages.

Despite the risk of punishment for rescuing Jews, Zagreb resident Vera Valentičić Oberiter saved a Jewish-Austrian girl, Suzana Kroll, living under the Croatian name Sofia Ribarić. The girl's mother and step-father were acquaintances of Vera's husband, Ludvik Valentičić. In December 1944, he, along with other Croats, were captured for allegedly helping the Partisans. Vera's parents, who also lived in Zagreb, urged her to give up the child because being the wife of a "traitor" made her a suspect. But she refused, telling her parents: "If only I could remove just one tear in this sea of suffering, I'll do that." On January 12, 1945, Vera was herself arrested and imprisoned for a month. Her elderly parents, who had earlier urged her to give up Sofia, cared for the child, who remained with the family till the end of the war.[8]

The Holocaust and the multiple atrocities perpetrated by the Axis partners Hitler and Mussolini, as well as by their collaborator Pavelić, are notorious for illustrating the evil of which humans are capable. However, as I have aimed to show, the Holocaust also provided opportunities—if less frequent—for behavior that was compassionate and even noble. In relating the details of their experiences during the Holocaust—the greatest tragedy that the Jewish people have ever suffered—most survivors attributed their survival, first, to their will to live, persisting even when they were traumatized beyond description, and to their need to tell the world the story of the Holocaust.

Despite the ethnic and religious differences enumerated above, three overarching variables played key roles in the nature and extent of rescue in the NDH:

- First, Nazi-instigated propaganda struggled to gain traction, even among the Ustaše, a factor attributable to the weakness of pre-war antisemitism, the high rate of assimilation among Croatian Jews, especially the large number of mixed marriages—even Pavelić's wife was half-Jewish—and to the Ustaše's need for the Jews' professional skills.

- Second, even though the Nazis systematically exploited greed to encourage collaboration, many Croatians did not succumb to it. Their reluctance to assist the occupiers and the Ustaše, and their willingness and courage to disobey, helped some Jews to hold on until they could be rescued.

- Third, the initiative on the part of Jews who fled to the Italian zones or to the Partisans—even at the cost of abandoning their property or members of their families—increased their odds of survival. Opportunities for escape were scarce, but they existed, and those who seized the moment improved their chances for survival.

The stories of heroic rescues in this book are specific to Croatia and Bosnia-Herzegovina during World War II. They do not ignore the roles that monetary compensation and sheer luck played in Holocaust survival. Nonetheless, I hope that readers will take from this study an appreciation that people of conscience courageously resisted racist and fascist regimes and toppled dictators. Historians of the Holocaust have a duty not only to research and commemorate the lives of those who are lost, but also to make known the stories and identities of those who acted as rescuers, even when they only signed their name on a petition on behalf of their Jewish fellow citizens. The Croatian peasants, along with many others, formed a link in a long chain of rescuers that Maestro encountered over four arduous years. Similarly, Indig-Ithai's account of his five-year experience with the children known as the *Children of Villa Emma* makes clear that the rescue of these children would have been impossible without ongoing help from Croatian, Slovenian, and Italian non-Jews.

The oral histories of the Croatians I interviewed provided the impetus for my treading into the uncharted territory of the rescue of Jews in NDH as a contribution to Holocaust history. In the hostile circumstances prevailing in the collaborationist NDH, it was the Italians and their army, the Croatian Partisans, and the national and international humanitarian organizations who assisted in the rescue of Jews. However, the actual rescuers were the individuals of all ages and walks of life: government officials, Catholic prelates, and ordinary citizens of all faiths who put their own lives and those of their families in harm's way. Thanks to their courage and perseverance, nine thousand five hundred Jews were rescued and survived. The collective effort confirms that dictators like Hitler, Mussolini, and Pavelić can be defeated when countries unite and challenge the misguided ideologies that intend to divide the world into races, ethnicity, and religion.

Appendix A

A letter of discontent over the Racial Laws signed by 20 Croats against the discrimination. The letter requests the release from concentration camp on the Island of Pag, of Stjepan Levi, an expert forester, whom they considered a good friend and honest Croat. (HDA, RUR 252, 28951, ZO.2227)

28951

Preporoditelju Hrvatske.

p. 2/3

4/I 988

Dr. A N T E P A V E L I Ć.
Poglavnik
Nezavisne države Hrvatske.

U Z a g r e b u .

Podpisani gradjani, posjednici, namještenici, i radnici, iskristilizirani Hrvatski sinovi, Istočne periferije Hrvatske metropole obraćamo se Vama sa ovom opširno obrazloženom

M o l b o m .

Vašim radom za oslobodjenje nas Hrvata, i uspostavljenjem Nezavisne Države Hrvatske, kao i za dobrobit sviju nas, stvoriliste i stvarate sve zakone, sprovadjate obečane odluke u djelo, koje krča sve zapreke koje stoje na putu za napredak i procvat naše ljepe Domovine.

Medju prvima storili ste zakon o židovima, kojim zakonom opravdano pogadjate oduzete vele-kapitala stečenog u Hrvatskoj, i na grbaći Hrvat_ -skih sinova, te ih istim zakonom silite na spoznanje fizičkog rada i re- -da na kome se osniva budučnost i blagostanje naše Domovine.

Ovaj zakon zahvatio je i našeg sugradjana, našeg sumišljenika, i prijatelja, STJEPANA LEVIA, nastanjenog u Sveticama Br.34.

Imenovani sproveo je sa nama i medju nama čitavo svoje djetin- -stvo i mladost, poznajemoga kao Hrvatskog patriotu, kao uzornog i soli- -dnog čovjeka, te primjernog skrbnika svoje Majke i 26. godišnjeg brata koji je 100./% invalid, čiju sliku prilažemo.

Imenovani Stjepan Levi, neposjeduje nikakovog pokretnog ni nepokretnog imetka, već jedino imade svoju skromnu naradu, koja mu je jedini izvor zarade za pokriće njegovih teških obaveza.

Izvršenjem zakona, STJEPAN LEVI je 21./ VI. O.g. po ustaškom redarstvu sproveden na prisilni rad, na otoku Pagu, gdje se još i danas nalazi.

Podpisani duboko smo uvjereni poznavajući Vašu strogost, odlu- -čnost, i stalnost, no poznajemo i Vašu veliku sklonost za pravednost

p.3|3   28951

pogotovo za bjedne i nemočne, to smo više nego uvjereni da će te
ovu našu molbu kao hitnu u pretres uzeti, i naložiti Vašim podod-
-redjenim da se Stjepan Levi,Vašom odlukom amestira sa prisilnog
rada, i da se povrati k nama i medju nas,da se vrati svojoj majci,
i svome nemočnom bratu, kojima je on jedini hranioc.

    Vašu odluku poštivat će mo u cjelosti pa ma kako glasila,
te u tom očekivanju ostajemo i jesmo

                                 ZA DOM SPREMNI.

Zagreb.10./ VII.1941.

Appendix B

Gjuro Jelinek, dentist, requested NDH authorities to grant him Aryan Rights. His friends seconded his request; forty-one signed the petition. Their request was approved. (HAD, RUR 252, 27087, ZO5317)

V 3|3 27087

ske i materijalne izdatke .

        Podupirao sam uvijek i svakom prilikom sva kulturna na-
stojanja hrvatskog naroda i njegove socijalne ustanove, o čemu sve-
doči moje članstvo u sljedećim društvima: Hrvatski liječnički zbor -
Društvo Strossmayerovog Sveučilišta - hrvatska akademska menza - Društvo čovječnosti - Društvo sv.Vida - Materinstvo - Društvo za spašava-
nje - Prehrana - Društvo za podizanje spomenika Kralju Tomislavu -
Društvo za podizanje spomenika A.G.Matošu, a podupiratelj sam Matice
Hrvatske i Hrvatskog ženskog lista, te mislim da mogu mirne duše i sa
punim pravom reći, da sam zaista srastao sa hrvatskim narodom i sa
ovom zemljom, isto tako kao i svaki čistokrvni Hrvat.

        Uvijek sam tiho i skromno radio i ničim se nepovoljnim
nijesam isticao, ali sam sada primoran da to sve navedem, kako bih
opravdao svoju molbu, da mi slavni naslov podijeli dozvolu da mogu
trajno ostati u svojoj ordinaciji i stanu, jer bi jedno eventualno po-
novno seljenje u neko od grada udaljeno područje onemogućilo meni
daljnji opstanak, a isto tako i mojim pacijentima,koji već kroz dece-
nije dolaze k meni, ne bi više bilo moguće da se i dalje obraćaju na
liječnika svog povjerenja.

        Zato još jednom molim slavni naslov - a ovoj molbi pri-
ključuju se niže potpisani pacijenti - za dobrohotno hitno riješenje
moje molbe, te zahvaljujući najtoplije na tome i obećajući, da ću i
nadalje upotrijebiti svoje znanje i svoje skromne sile na dobrobit
hrvatskog naroda, bilježim se sa dubokom odanošću

                        U Zagrebu, dne 27 svibnja 1941.   Dr.Gjuro Jelinek

ISPOSTAVA
USTAŠKOG REDARSTVENOG POVJERENIŠTVA
ŽIDOVSKI ODSJEK
    Br. 142
...................................194..

Ne odobrava se.
    Zagreb,29.V.1941.

                                                liječnik zubar
                                                Martićeva ulica 4/III

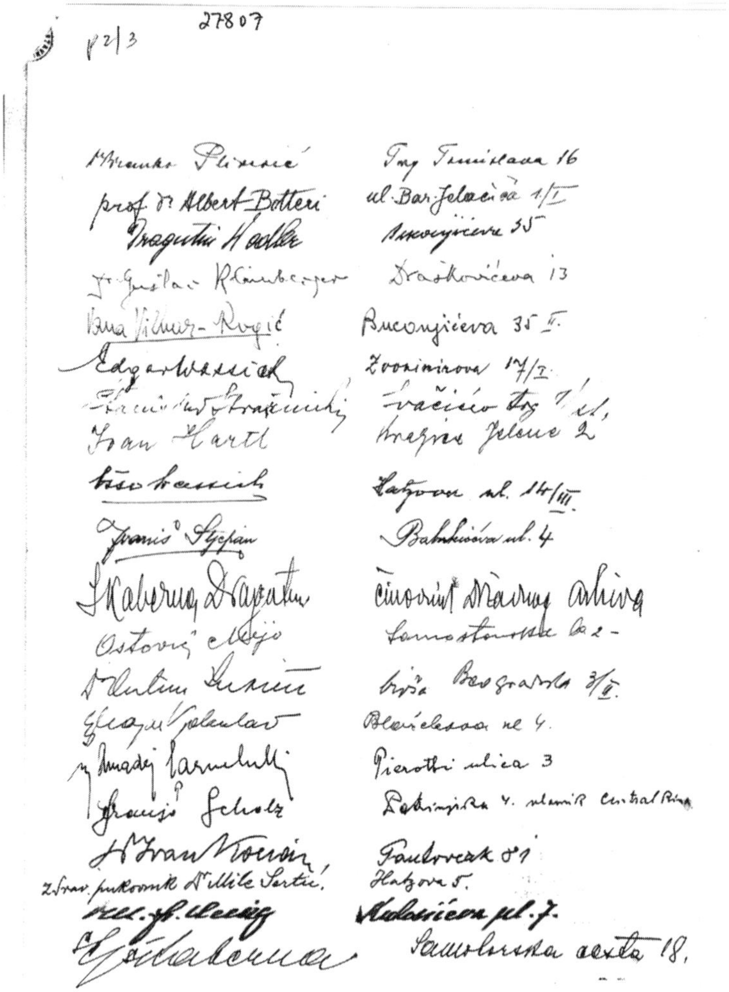

27807

p2/3

Branko Plišević	Trg Tomislava 16
prof. Dr. Albert Botteri	ul. Bar. Jelačića 1/I
Dragutin Hadler	Buconjićeva 35
Dr. Gustav Kleinberger	Draškovićeva 13
Ana Vilmar-Rogić	Buconjićeva 35 II.
Edgar Wassich	Zvonimirova 17/I.
[illegible]	Ivačićev trg [illegible]
Ivan Hartl	Kneginje Jelene 2
[illegible]	Hatzova ul. 14/III.
Franić Stjepan	Babukićeva ul. 4
Skaberna Dragutin	činovnik državnog arhiva
Ostović Mijo	Samostanska [illegible] 2 -
Dr. Antun [illegible]	[illegible] Beogradska 3/II.
[illegible] Vjekoslav	Bleiweisova ul 4.
Ing. Amadej [illegible]	Pierottijeva ulica 3
Franjo Scholz	Petrinjska 4. ulaz u Central Kino
Dr. Ivan [illegible]	[illegible] 81
z. Vrav. pukovnik Dr Mile Sertić	Hatzova 5.
[illegible]	[illegible] ul. 7.
[illegible]	Samoborska cesta 18.

Appendix C

Employees of the Higiea Company requested the release from concentration camp of their technical expert, Vilim Berger, claiming he was indispensible to the future of their company. (RUR 252, 27479, ZO).

y.2/3 27479

Zagreb,dne 25.lipnja   1941.

Predmet:Molba radnika tvornice
HIGIEA D.D.Zagreb,radi oslobo-
djenja tehničkog činovnika VI-
LIMA BERGERA.

USTAŠKO REDARSTVENO POVJERENIŠTVO
Židovski otsjek
na ruke savjetnika g.I.Barakovića

Z A G R E B.

 U vezi molbe tt.Higiea tvornica čepova d.d.,Zagreb od 23.o.mj.potvrdjenoj po,Industrijskoj komori u Zagrebu,radi oslobodjenja uhapšenog tehničkog činovnika gornje tvrtke Vilima BERGERA,potpisani radnici tvornice mole naslov,da se VILIM BERGER kao neophodno potreban tehnički stručnjak oslobodi,jer o tome ovisi daljnji rad poduzeća a time u vezi i naš opstanak osamdeset radnika tvornice.

 Molimo naslov,da hitno odredi potrebno za oslobodjenje Vilima BERGERA,kako bi se rad u tvornici mogao nesmetano odvijati i time osigurati naš opstanak.

 Unapred zahvaljujući ostajemo

za DOM - spremni !

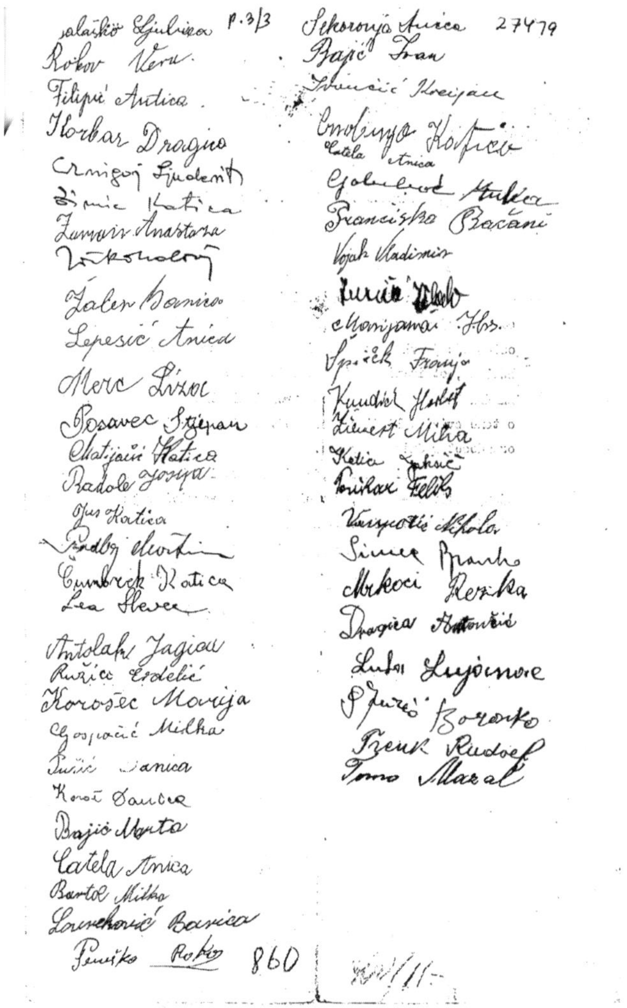

[illegible]alaško Ljubica p.3/3
Rokov Vera
Filipić Antica
Horbar Dragica
Crnigoj Ljudevit
Žimić Katica
Zamair Anastaza
[illegible]
Zalen Danica
Lepesić Anica
Merc Liza
Posavec Stjepan
Matijašić Katica
Radole [illegible]
Jus Katica
[illegible] Martin
Cumbrek Katica
Lea Slevec
Antolak Jagica
Ružica Erdelić
Korošec Marija
Gospočić Milka
[illegible] Danica
Koroš Danica
Bajić Marta
Catela Anica
Bartol Milka
Lovreković Barica
Peničko Rokov 860

Sekoronja Anica 27479
Bajić Ivan
Ivančić [illegible]
[illegible] Kotica
Catela Anica
Golubović Anka
Franciska Bračani
Vojak Vladimir
Jurčić [illegible]
Marijana Hrs.
Spiček Franjo
[illegible]
Zimert Milka
Katica Juhač
[illegible] Felix
[illegible] Nikola
[illegible] Branko
Mikoci Rezika
Dragica Antonić
Luka [illegible]
[illegible] Boranko
Prenk Rudolf
Tomo Mazal

Appendix D

Stepinac's correspondence.

Stepinac's circular from January 11, 1939, is a request for charitable contributions to provide basic support for the refugees (mostly Jews) fleeing the Nazi regime in Europe. (Copy. The actual letter bore Archbishop's signature.)

3

Zagreb, 11. siječnja 1939.
Okružno pismo nadbiskupa Stepinca o prikupljanju pomoći izbjeglim i prognanim Židovima početkom II. svjetskog rata. Ovo pismo svjedoči kako nadbiskup Stepinac nije bio "germanofil", ljubitelj Nijemaca, nego je dapače sve učinio da zaštiti Židove i sve one koje su Nijemci iz bilo kojeg razloga proganjali.

Izvor: AP, sv. C, str. 711 (preslik); spis je pronađen među dokumentima izbjegle Vlade NDH u Leibnitzu 1945. godine.

Poštovani Gospodine,
Uslijed žestokih i nečovječnih progona morao je veliki broj ljudi ostaviti svoju domovinu. Ti su jadnici ostali ne samo bez domovine nego i bez sredstava za život. Lutaju po svijetu da nađu zemlju koja će im dati mogućnosti da stvore sebi i svojima novu egzistenciju. Velik broj takovih boravi privremeno u Jugoslaviji. Mnogi su od njih sa ženom i djecom. Njihova je tragika teška, a bijeda neopisiva.
Svaki se dan obraća na nas veliki broj takovih emigranata tražeći savjeta, intervencije, preporuku, pripomoć u novcu ili u naravi. Ima među njima i intelektualaca, i takovih koji su negda dobro stajali.
Naša je kršćanska dužnost da im pomognemo. Stoga držim za potrebno obratiti se na ljude dobra srca i plemenitih osjećaja s molbom za pripomoć spomenutim bijednicima. Slobodan sam obratiti se i na Vas, Poštovani Gospodine, kao člana naše Crkve, koji ćete najbolje shvatiti tragiku ovih ljudi bez doma, bez sredstava, bez pravoga cilja, da dadete svoju potporu fondu koji će biti upotrebljen u korist emigranata.
Molim da na priloženom listu označite svoj dobrovoljni mjesečni doprinos kojim ćete podupirati ovu tako potrebnu akciju.
Uz odlično poštovanje

Dr. Alojzije Stepinac
(vlastoručni potpis)
Nadbiskup[1]

Archbishop Alojzije Stepinac admonishes the NDH Minister of the Interior, Andrija Artuković, for the conduct of the government towards the Jews, stating: "it is said that even Germany's conduct towards the Jews is more humane and civil than in Croatia." (HDA, Ivo Politeo, Stepinac file, sent to Yad Vashem.)

NADBISKUPSKI DUHOVNI STOL U ZAGREBU

117

Zagreb,22 svibnja 1941

55

Gospodine Ministre,

      Dne 23 travnja o.g. pod br.103/BK imao sam čast obratiti se na Vas predstavkom kojom sam molio da se kod donošenja protužidovskih zakona uzme obzira na one pripadnike židovske rase koji su prešli na kršćanstvo.Međutim su proglašeni zakoni od 30 travnja koji se ništa ne obaziru na vjersku pripadnost. Tada nam je bilo rečeno da su radi razloga neovisnih o nama ti zakoni morali biti proglašeni u ovoj formi,ali da primjena njihova u praksi neće biti tako okrutna.No uza sve to mi vidimo da gotovo svaki dan dolaze sve strože i strože odredbe koje pogađaju jednako i krive i nedužne.Današnje su novine donijele odredbu da svi židovi,bez obzira na starost i spol,te nā vjeru kojoj pripadaju,moraju nositi židovski znak.Tih mjera ima već toliko,da poznavaoci prilika vele da ni u samoj Njemačkoj nisu rasni zakoni provedeni bili takovom strogošću i takovom brzinom.
      Razumije se samo po sebi da će svatko odobriti nastojanje da u jednoj narodnoj Državi vladaju sinovi toga naroda i da se uklone svi štetni utjecaji koji rastaču narodni organizam.Svatko će sigurno odobriti nastojanje da privreda bude u narodnim rukama,da se ne dopusti gomilanje kapitala kod nenarodnog i protunarodnog elementa,te da strani elementi ne odlučuju o Državi i narodu.Ali da se pripadnicima drugih narodnosti ili drugih rasa oduzme svaka mogućnost egzistencije i da se na njih udara žig sramote,to je već pitanje čovječnosti i pitanje morala.A moralni zakoni vrijede ne samo za život pojedinca nego i za državnu upravu.Današnje društveno uređenje i opći moralni pojmovi koji vladaju ne udaraju žig sramote ni na robijaše koji su pušteni iz tamnice na koju su bili suđeni radi ubojstva,jer se želi da i takovi opet budu korisni članovi ljudske zajednice.Nisu obilježeni vidljivim znakom ni konkubinarci,ni poznati preljubnici,pa ni same javne bludnice. Pa kad se to ne čini s onima koji su svojom ličnom krivnjom zavrijedili da ljudsko društvo od njih zazire,zašto da se to čini s onima koji su bez svoje krivnje članovi druge rase? Tu bi trebalo ipak voditi računa da će se,osobito kod omladine koja je još u godinama razvoja i koja je tim mjerama pogođena,u velikoj mjeri razvijati i instinkt osvete i t zv. "Minderwertigkeitskomplex",a te će stvari porazno djelovati na njihovu duševnu formaciju.Imamo li mi pravo na takav atentat na čovjekovu ličnost?
      U vezi s izloženim molim Vas,Gospodine Ministre,da

./.

Gospodin
Dr Andrija A r t u k o v i ć,
Ministar unutarnjih poslova
Z a g r e b

When several survivors suggested that Archbishop Stepinac be granted the award, "The Righteous Among the Nations," many wrote letters to Yad Vashem on his behalf, describing how they were saved while he risked his life to free them from certain death. Among the letters was one written by Dan Baram from Jerusalem and another by Ljudevit Stein who resides in Zagreb. (The letters for this appendix were randomly selected.)

Svjedočanstvo Dana Barama,[2] židovskog građanina i političkog djelatnika od 3. lipnja 1995. o zaštiti koju je nadbiskup Stepinac pružio ugroženim Židovima.
Izvor: Pismo Dana Barama, Jeruzalem, 3. lipnja 1995. u: CP, Fascikl: Novoprikupljeni dokumenti - Nadbiskup Stepinac i Židovi, nenumerirano.

Mr. Dan Baram
Schlein 6
96223 JERUSALEM

Jerusalem, 3. lipnja 1995

Dr. BATELJA JURAJ
Viale GIOTTO 27
00153 ROMA

Poštovani i dragi Velečasni!

Oprostite što je malo zakašnjenje, ali imao sam namjeru početkati sve podatke za pok. gosp. SLAVKA RADEJA od njegove supruge Dr. PODKAMINER Elizabet. Pok. SLAVKO RADEJ bio je za·vrijeme II. svjetskog rata i za vrijeme NDH, za vrijeme ustaško-fašističke okupacije u Hrvatskoj sakriven i spasen u Kuriji NA KAPTOLU, kao židovski mladić. Spasio ga je, sakrivao i brinuo se za njega, a i još par židovskih omladinaca - NADBISKUP ALOJZIJE STEPINAC. Znam da je čak bio u kaptolskom "KORU" i tamo pjevao i ministrirao u Katedrali. Posebne podatke, kako sam pisao na početku, nadam se dobiti od Dr. Podkaminar.

Sada moje svjedočanstvo, jer nažalost, svi oni što su bili umiješani u taj plemeniti čin Nadbiskupa Stepinca su već preminuli: moji roditelji, Erna i Miroslav Radičević (bivši Fuks), umrli u Jeruzalemu, moja tetka Gross Elza i njezin muž Fridrich Gross, rođeni katolik u Austriji i za vrijeme rata direktor Simensa u Hrvatskoj.
Pomoć i intervencija u Kaptolskim dvorima od gospode: F. Gross, Rihard Fuks, odvjetnik u Zagrebu gospođe Lele Sopianec kod Nadbiskupa Stepinca dala je pozitivne rezultate. Prema njegovoj odluci cijela familija naša, porijeklom ŽIDOVI, dobili smo nove dokumente (u toku 1941. godine) na prezime RADIčEVIć kao Arijevci i kršćani. (Sjećam se da smo moji roditelji i ja prekršteni u crkvi sv. Petra u Vlaškoj ulici. Datum je bio falsificiran, tako da je izgledalo da smo rođeni kršćani. Oca su unatoč toga ustaše uhapsili. Bio je po zatvorima par godina.) Majku i mene je Nadbiskup Stepinac poslao kod župnika Dragutina Jesiha u župu Šćitarjevo gdje smo bili sakriveni kao kršćani iako je dr. Jesih znao da smo Židovi. Župnik dr. Jesih Dragutin zaklan je na zvjerski način od ustaša koncem 1944. i bačen u Savu. Iznakažen i zaklan pokopan je na groblju u Šćitarjevu pokraj župnog dvora i crkve. Majka i ja nastavili smo se skrivati u rafineriji "OLEX" u sv. Klari koja je bila vlasništvo gosp. F. SOPIANCA i gospođe LELE.
Početkom 1945., kada je otac moj izašao iz zatvora, pomoću dokumenata i pomoću Nadbiskupa Stepinca bili smo do konca rata skrivani i otac je bio zaposlen u rafineriji "OLEX", tamo smo i stanovali, a i u RATKAJEVOM PROLAZU u prostorijama "Olexa", u tzv. vatikanskim kućama.

Svjedočanstvo Židova Ljudevita Steina, kojega je u svibnju 1943. iz zatvora na Savskoj cesti u Zagrebu spasio nadbiskup Stepinac.
Izvor: Blaženi Alojzije Stepinac, Glasnik Postulature, 6 (1999), 1-2, str. 2./

Zovem se Ljudevit Stein, i rođen sam 23. 05. 1935. godine u Zagrebu, od oca Bela i majke Margite rođene Glass.

Živjeli smo u Zagrebu, u Vlaškoj ulici 63, gdje je moj otac imao svoju limarsko-vodoinstalatersku radionicu. Otac je bio poznati zagrebački obrtnik, imao je svoje izume koje je patentirao.

Mirno smo živjeli do proljeća 1941. godine, kada je stvorena tako zvana NDH. Tada su počeli nemiri i progoni Židova. Mnogi su, da bi spasili život pobjegli i nagovarali moga tatu da i on ode, a on im je odgovarao: Ja sam obrtnik, imam svoju radionicu, pa neće valjda i mene - zanatlija uvijek treba.

U rano ljeto iste 1941. godine moji roditelji, ja, i mnogi Židovi koji su ostali u Zagrebu odlazili smo u Katedralu na Kaptol na vjeronauk, kako bismo bili pod zaštitom Katoličke crkve i izbjegli progon kao Židovi. To je sve organizirao tada nadbiskup zagrebački Alojzije Stepinac. Međutim, to nije uspjelo. Jedini rezultat je bio da mi djeca nismo više trebali nositi oko rukava žutu traku sa slovom Ž.

Početkom jeseni 1941. godine počela su velika hapšenja i progon Židova. Prvo su odveli moju baku Reginu Stein, staricu od 70 godina, u Staru Gradišku, i od tada se za nju više ništa ne zna. Par dana kasnije došli su po moga tatu Bela Steina i njegova brata Filipa Steina i odveli ih u logor Jasenovac, a moju mamu i mene istjerali su iz stana; majka je smjela uzeti samo ono što je mogla u rukama ponijeti. U onoj uzbuđenosti uzela je dokumente koji su već biti priređeni, i dva mala svijećnjaka koja imam još i danas.

Moj tata i njegov brat bili su u Jasenovcu od 1941. do 1945. godine i radili su u zatočeničkoj grupi I. Lančarija. Bili su živi sve do pokušaja oslobođenja logora i dolaska partizanske vojske u Jasenovac. Mamu i mene prihvatila je sestra moga tate Margita Stilinović, koja se udala za katolika, a živjela je u Zagrebu, na Trešnjevki, u Pazinskoj ulici 52.

U proljeće 1942. godine mama je htjela otići kod svojih roditelja i sestara u Suboticu, koja je bila pod mađarskom okupacijom, jer tamo još nije bilo progona Židova. No prilikom prelaska hrvatsko-mađarske granice, bili smo uhićeni od strane mađarskih graničara i predani ondašnjim hrvatskim graničarima i smješteni u zatvor u Petrovaradinu. Mama je pisala mojoj teti Margiti Stilinović da dođe po mene u Petrovaradin, jer mene puštaju iz zatvora, što je teta i učinila, te me odvela u Zagreb. Ondje sam zadnji puta vidio moju mamu, i više nikada nisam čuo za nju. Želim napomenuti da od mnogobrojne mamine obitelji, 1943. godine su svi uhapšeni, odvedeni i nestali, samo se pukim slučajem iz logora Auschwitz uspjela spasiti najmlađa sestra Barbara Kereshi, koja je 1949. godine otišla u Izrael i umrla ove godine.

U noći između 14-og i 15-og svibnja 1943. godine uhapšen sam i odveden u zatvor na Savskoj cesti. Te noći bila su velika i masovna hapšenja preostalih Židova, za koje su tadašnje vlasti znale. Iz zatvora sam pušten 18-og svibnja 1943. godine, za što posjedujem izvornu otpusnicu. Za vrijeme suđenja nadbiskupu Alojziju Stepincu, koje je bilo prenošeno preko radija, teta Margita Stilinović mi je rekla: "Kod njega sam išla moliti da nešto učini za tebe, da te puste iz zatvora." Uvijek sam u sebi nosio poštovanje prema Kardinalu, sada blaženom Alojziju Stepincu, da spasi moje roditelje i mene, što je i uspio.

Moja supruga Zlatica i ja bili smo u 8. mjesecu 1990. godine u Krašiću, u kući i sobi u kojoj je blaženi Alojzije Stepinac boravio i živio. Soba je bila tako uređena i pospremljena,

Archbishop Stepinac writes to Ante Pavelić protesting the order that all Jews have to wear the yellow identification tag. He reminded Pavelić that even in the Third Reich the citizens of the Reich were exempt from such a debasement.

Donosimo prijevod teksta:

Antisemitske mjere

Nakon izvršenja popisa Židova u Hrvatskoj, donesena je odluka da svi Židovi s prebivalištem u Zagrebu, bez obzira na vjeru koju ispovijedaju moraju od 28. ovog mjeseca nositi na lijevoj strani prsa i leđa distinktivna obilježja od dva kvadratića platna žute boje veličine oko 2 centimetra kvadratna sa zvijezdom Siona i slovom Ž (Židov). Čak su i Nijemci poštedjeli Židove Reicha ovog ponižavajućeg zahtjeva koji je izazvao negodovanje dobrog dijela hrvatske javnosti, pa i samih pristalica vlade koji su ga proglasili sadističkim. Time je još dodatno pojačana napetost koja je već vladala između "Kaptola" (sjedište nadbiskupa i Prvostolnog kaptola) i članova vlade kao revnih katolika. Ta napetost se očitovala povodom nedavnog posjeta Rimu dr. Ante Pavelića. Zagrebački nadbiskup Mons. Stepinac, koji je bio pozvan da se priključi delegaciji zaduženoj da preda hrvatsku krunu jednom princu iz obitelji Savoie, odbio je poziv i poslao na svoje mjesto jednog od pomoćnih biskupa. Zlobnici su izmislili da je taj otpor Kaptola željama Poglavnika rezultat utjecaja dvaju kanonika članova slobodne masonerije ili bojazni Kaptola da im vlada ne oduzme neke posjede. S druge strane, sasvim su dovoljni i drugi razlozi materijalne prirode da bi opravdali ovakvo ponašanje. Zaista je Crkvi teško dopustiti takve mjere kao što je odredba prema kojem valjanost svakog vjerskog prijelaza (novog preobraćenja) podliježe prethodnoj upravnoj dozvoli.

Uvjeravaju me, da je Crkva osudila nedavne mjere po kojima su Židovi bili prisiljeni nositi ponižavajuća obilježja i Kaptol da se zauzima za ublaživanje tih odluka vlasti. Međutim, treba reći da usprkos tome što nova vlada teži reputaciji inkorupcije, događa se da se bogati Židovi uspijevaju osloboditi obveze nošenja obilježja na što su prisiljena njihova subraća. Takvi vrlo lako i legitimno ishode potvrdu o arijskom podrijetlu, odričući se svoga.   Rim, 9. srpnja 1941.

The Jewish Community in Zagreb asked Stepinac to write to his contacts and to the Holy See to intervene with the Italian authorities on behalf of 200 orphan Jewish children who could be saved in Italy.

| 1187

U Zagrebu ima oko 200 djece u dobi od 7 – 17 godina. Najveći dio te djece ovdje je bez očeva, stanoviti broj bez očeva i bez majki.

Naša je namjera odobrenjem nadležnih vlasti sukcesivno preseliti ovu djecu u Kr. Italiju.

Prva bi grupa od neko 50 djece pod vodstvom određenih pedagoških i stručnih sila trebala da ode po mogućnosti u što skorijem vremenu. Ostala djeca putovala bi naknadno, opet u grupama od 30-40 sa potrebnim odgojnim osobljem, kad bi prve grupe bile smještene. Djeca će biti podpuno opremljena, obskrbljena odjećom na duže vrijeme te učilima i svima što je potrebno.

Kao mjesto smještavanja dolazi u obzir Firenza, gdje tamošnja Židovska općina posjeduje nekoliko zgrada u kojima je bio prije smješten rabinski seminar ili Padova, gdje općina takodjer posjeduje xxxxxxxxxxx neke zgrade. Za kasnije smještavanje bilo bi najpovoljnije koje imanje, kako bi imladina mogla dobiti poljodjelsku izobrazbu.

Novčano osiguranje ovih omladinskih grupa preuzet će na sebe židovske pripomočne organizacije.

(izvještaj Žid.Bogoš.općine u Zagrebu
- predan u svrhu intervencije.)

Br. 5997/46
Prepis se slaže sa izvornikom.
Zagreb, dne 1 listopada 1946.

Appendix E

**Physicians Recruited to Serve in the NDH Syphilis Mission
in Bosnia-Herzegovina**
Information Obtained from the Croatian National Archives (HDA RUR,252)

X=alive
D=dead,
?=destiny unknown

First Group sent to Bosnia to curb endemic syphilis(group I).

Status	Name	Specialization	Date 05.07.41	Place	File No.	ZO No.
			05.07.41			
D	Adler Antun	Neurologist	05.07.41	Zagreb	29171	3358
X	Barmaper Herman	Neurologist	05.07.41	Zagreb	29171	3358
X	Betlheim Stjepan	Neurologist	05.07.41	Zagreb	29171	3358
D	Bluhweiss Bruno	Internal med.	05.07.41	Zagreb	29171	3358
D	Deutsch Dajc Miroslav	Gynecology	05.07.41	Zagreb	29171	3358
D	Deutsch Edo	Internal med.	05.07.41	Zagreb	29171	3358
D	Frolich Albert	Orthopedic	05.07.41	Zagreb	29171	3358
X	Gruner Teodor	Pediatrician	05.07.41	Zagreb	29171	3358
X	Hafner Ziga	GP, Clinic	05.07.41	Zagreb	29171	3358
X	Hahn Arpad	Radiologist	05.07.41	Zagreb	29171,27986	3358
X	Kohn Bela	Surgeon	05.07.41	Zagreb	29171	3358
D	Low Ivan (Ivo)	Internal med.	05.07.41	Zagreb	29171	3358
D	Neumann Ljuba	Lab. Tech.	05.07.41	Zagreb	29171	3358
D	Nisk Alfred	GP	05.07.41	Zagreb	29171	3358
X	Podvinec Srecko	Internal med.	05.07.41	Zagreb	29171	3358
D	Rausnitz Jelena	Internal med.	05.07.41	Zagreb	29171	3358

X	Reich Emil	GP		05.07.41	Zagreb	29171	3358
D	Schlesinger Brandler Marija	GP		05.07.41	Zagreb	29171	3358
D	Schlesinger Miroslav	GP		05.07.41	Zagreb	29171	3358
X	Schwartz Aleksander	Oculist		05.07.41	Zagreb	29171	3358
X	Svecenski Branko	GP		05.07.41	Zagreb	29171	3358
X	Tempel S. Ignac	Neurologist		05.07.41	Zagreb	29171	3358
X	Weiss Aleksander	Neurolog release from CC			Zagreb	29171	3358
D	Winter Miroslav	Neurologist			Zagreb	29171	3358

Total 24, 12 alive, 12 dead

Second Group sent to Bosnia to curb endmic syphilis(group II)

Status	Name	Specialization	Date 28.08.41 09.07.41	Place	File No.	ZO No.
X	Baum H. Vilko	Surgeon	09.07.41	Vukovar	28017	4143
D	Bauer Marko	Oculist	28.08.41	Zagreb	29171	3358
X	Brajer Karlo	Gynecologist	09.07.41	Zagreb	29171,28017	3358,4143
X	Cegledi Heimer Margita	Pediatrician	28.08.41	Zagreb	28017	4143
?	Citrin Henrich	Internal med.	09.07.41	Zagreb	29171,28017	3358,4143
X	Deszo Juraj	Psychiatrist	28.08.41	Zagreb	28017	4143
X	Desider Julius	Neurologist	09.07.41	Zagreb	29171,28017	3358,4143
D	Deutsch Miroslav	Internal med.	09.07.41	Zagreb	28017	4143
X	Deutsch Samuel	Internal med.	09.07.41	Zagreb	29171,28017	3358,4143
X	Dezso Juraj	Neurologist	28.08.41	Zagreb	29171	3358
X	Eisenstadter Vlatko	GP	28.08.41	Zagreb	29171,28017	3358,4143
X	Fiscer Feliks	Pediatrician	28.08.41	Banja Luka	28017	4143
D	Fischer Zlatko	GP	09.07.41	Sisak	28017	4143
X	Fles M. Josip	Urologist	28.08.41	Zagreb	28017, 28409	4143, 7390
X	Frank Oto	Internal med.	09.07.41	Zagreb	29171	3358

D	Froilich Iso	Internal med.	28.08.41	Zagreb	28017	4143
X	Goldner Milan	Physiotherapist	28.08.41	Zagreb	29171	3358
X	Goldschmidt Zora	GP	09.07.41	Novigrad	28017	4143
?	Gostel Branko	Neurologist	09.07.41	Vrapce	28017	4143
D	Gostl Hinko (J. Romano)	GP	09.07.41	Zagreb	29171,28017	3358,4143
X	Gostl Josip	Neurology		Zagreb	29171	3358
X	Grunfld Julije	GP	09.07.41	Zagreb	29171	3358
D	Gutman Dorde	GP	09.07.41	Zagreb		
D?	Herskovic Isak	GP	28.08.41	Zagreb	29171	3358
X	Herzog Pavao	Internal med.	09.07.41	Zagreb	29171,28017	3358,4143
?	Jurkovic Nada	GP	28.08.41	Osiek	28017	4143
X	Kaufer Leopold	GP	09.07.41	Zagreb	29171	3358
X	Kallay Laszlo	Internal med.	09.07.41	Zagreb	28017	4143
X	Karanfilovic Hirschl Elza	GP	09.07.41	Zagreb	29171	3358
D	Kolman Slavko	Otolaryngologist	28.08.41	Zagreb	29171	3358
D	Konforti Jakob	GP	28.08.41	Mostar	28928	2143
D	Kraus Gustav	GP	09.07.41	Zagreb	28017	4143
D	Kraus Lederer Julija	Plastic surgeon	27.07.41	Zagreb	28017	4143
D?	Leimdorfer Gustav	GP	09.07.41	Zagreb	29171	3358
X	Levental B. Zdenko	hirurg	09.07.41	Zagreb	28017	2397
X	Neufeld Alfred	Internal med.	28.08.41	Zagreb	29171	3358
X	Neufeld Spicer Eta	Med. student	28.08.41	Zagreb	29171	3358
D	Pollak Stejpan	Internal med.	09.07.41	Zagreb	28017	4143
X	Prochnik Ignac	venerolog	26.07.41	Zagreb	28017	4143
X	Rechnitzer Mirko	Internal med.	09.07.41	Zagreb	29171	3358
X	Remenji, Schwartz Suzana	Internal med.	28.08.41	Zagreb	28017	4143
D	Rosner Rudolf	Neurology	09.07.41	Zagreb	29171	3358
X	Rosenzweig Erih	Gynecologist	09.07.41	Zagreb	28017	4143
X?	Rotman Pavao	Otolaryngologist	09.07.41	Zagreb	29171	3358
X	Stein Andrija	GP	09.07.41	Zagreb	29171	3358
D	Stein Mavro	GP	28.08.41	Zagreb	29171	3358

X	Steiner M. Stjepan	GP	09.07.41	Zagreb	29171,28017	3358,4143
X	Szekler Robert	Internal med.	09.07.41	Zagreb	28017	4143
D	Vinski Marija	GP	28.08.41	Zagreb	29171	3358
D	Viola Nikola	Otolaryngologist	28.08.41	Zagreb	29171	3358
D	Weinberger Draga	Venerologist	09.07.41	Zagreb	28017	4143
X	Weiss Arabela	GP		Sisak	28017	4143
X	Weiss Milan	Otolaryngologist		Zagreb	29171	3358

Group II total 53, 31 saved, 14 died, 8 destiny unkown, 5 died in Partisans, 2 in concentration camps)

Total number of physicians sent from Zagreb in grups I and II is 81.

Physicians sent from all parts of NDH to Bosnia to curb endemic syphilis

Status	Name	Specialization	Date	Place	File No.	ZO No./Locat.
X	Altarac Jakob	Internal med.	09.07.41	Vakuf	J. Romano	Tuzla
X	Atias Sisher Lola	GP	09.07.41	Sarajevo	J. Romano	Banja Luka
D	Atias Izdor Albert*	GP	09.07.41	Zagreb	J. Romano	Jajice
X	Atias Moric-Branko	GP from Bugojno	09.07.41	Zagreb	J. Romano	Bugojno
X	Bader Artur	Podiatrist		Zagreb	J. Romano	Tuzla
X	Baum Vilko	Surgeon		Zagreb	J. Romano	Tuzla
X	Bergstein Naftali	GP	23.05.42	Zagreb	J. Romano	Pazaric, Most
X	Bernhaut J. Izidor	Internal med.	10.11.41	Karlovac	J. Romano	Banja Luka
X	Deutsch Edo	GP	26.01.42	Zagreb	29485	4110
X	Deutsch Andrije	GP	09.07.41	Zagreb	29485	4110
?	Frank Oto	GP	1941	Zagreb	28658	0008
X	Fischbach Lav Jonas	Internal med. was in CC	09.07.41	Zagreb	J. Romano	Maglai
X	Fischer Duro	GP	09.07.41	Zagreb	J. Romano	Bosna
X	Fischer -Lederer S. Klara	GP	09.07.41	Zagreb	J. Romano	Odzake
X	Fischer Otton	Internal med.	09.07.41	Zagreb	J. Romano	Odzake

D	Frajnd David	GP		Sremska-Mitro	J.Romano	Modrica
X	Ginsberger Ervin	Surgeon	27.10.41	Zagreb	J. Romano	Gradacac
X	Grin Ernest	Dermatologist	09.07.41	Sarajevo	J. Romano	Banja Luka
D	Gross Mavro	GP	17.01.43	Zagreb	28154,4786	Bosna
D	Gruner (Griner) Simon*	Bacteriologist	09.07.41	Zagreb	J. Romano	Tuzla
X	Grunfeld Julijo		09.07.41	Zagreb	302/10221	Jajice
X	Grun(Grin) Ernest*	Dermatologist	09.07.41	Zagreb	J. Romano	Banja Luka
D	Herlinger Dragutin (Drago)	hirurg	09.07.41	Zagreb	J. Romano	Bihac
X	Herlinger Ivo	Internal med.	1941	Zagreb	J. Romano	Bihac
D	Hirschl Milan	Internal med.		Zagreb	J. Romano	Gracanica
X	Hirschler Slavko	Stomat	09.07.41	Ko-privnica	J. Romano	Tesanj
X	Jungwirth Gustav	Internal med.	12.08.42	Zagreb	29195	3396
X	Kaufer S. Leopold*	Surgeon	09.07.41	Zagreb	J. Romano	Pazaric
D	Kisicki Zigo	Dentist	27.07.41	Zagreb	29790	
D	Kraus S. Gustav	Dentist		Zagreb	J. Romano	Varos
X	Kraus G. Zdenko	GP	28.08.41	Zagreb	28017/4143	Bosnia
X	Lederer Ladislav	GP	09.07.41	Belisce	J. Romano	Modrica
D	Low Ivan (Ivo)	GP	28.08.41	Zagreb	28017,4143	4143
D	Lev L. Ivo	Internal med.	09.07.41	Zagreb	J. Romano	Doboj
X	Levent9l Zdenko	GP		Zagreb	28017,4143	Bosnia
X	Levi T. Haim (Bukus)			Zagreb	J. Romano	Banja Luka
X	Levi Izdor	GP		Cazin	J. Romano	Cazin
X	Maric Hinko	Gynecology	09.07.41	Varazdin	J. Romano	Gracanica
D	Neuman Ljuba	Internal med.	09.07.41	Zagreb	J. Romano	G. Vakuf
D	Neumann Vladimir	GP	09.07.41	Zagreb	Dotrscina	Tuzla
X	Nik I. Alfred	GP		Zagreb	J. Romano	Visoko
X	Orenshtein M. Karlo	Roentgenology	09.07.41	Zagreb	J. Romano	Banja Luka
D	Papo Mordehai	GP	02.08.41	Sarajevo	J. Romano	Sarajevo
X	Pinto B. David	Internal med.	09.01.42	Zagreb	J. Romano	Tuzla
X	Rausnic Jolana	Internal med.	09.07.41	Zagreb	27969,2882	Sarajevo
X	Reich Emil	honorarnom	09.07.41	Zagreb	28745,0550	Bosanska K

X	Romano J. Mario		09.07.41	Zagreb	J. Romano	Visoko
X	Rozencvajg M. Erih	Gynecologist		Zagreb	J. Romano	Banja Luka
X	Salom D. Mento	GP	28.08.41	Zagreb	J. Romano	Tuzla
X	Samakovlija Isak	GP	09.07.41	Sarajevo	J.Romano	Alipasin Most
X	Schlezinger Albert	GP		Zagreb	28017	4143
X	Schmukler M. Vilim	GP		Zagreb	J. Romano	Gracanic
D	Spicer Milan	Gynecology		Osijek	J. Romano	Dervnta Gradac
X	Templ Salamon Ignac	Dermatologist		Zagreb	J. Romano	Kakanj, Travnik
X	Vajsler-Najfeld Stela	GP		N. Gradiska	J. Romano	B.Gradi, Mostar
X	Zupic Klara	GP		Zagreb	J. Romano	Busovaca

Total 57; 42 survived the war, 14 killed, 1 destiny unkown.

Physicians Released from concentration camps(CC) and sent to Bosnia in 1942 to curb endemic syphilis

Status	Name	Specialization	Date 20.02.42 15.10.42	Place	File No.	ZO No.
X	Fuchs Milan	Pharmacist, Banja Luka	29.07.42	Mostar	29386	3877
X	Hass Zarko, Domo-branstvo	GP	24.02.42	Varazdin	29969	5654
X	Hochstadter Bela	GP	24.02.42	Zagreb	302/10154	5050
D	Konforti Jakob	GP	28.01.42	Zagreb	28928	2143
X	Maric Hinko	GP, Banja Luka	27.10.41	Varazdin	28929	2145
?	Milhofer Bela	GP	15.05.42	Bjelovar	28330,29117	7066,3135
?	Polak Stanko	GP	15.10.42	Karlovac	29117	3135
?	Salom Jesua	Pharmacist, Banja Luka	07.11.41	Zagreb	29323	3754
?	Rosenbaum Elizabeta	GP	16.03.42	Varazdin	29969	5654
X	Schwarz Milan	GP	02.03.42	Logorgrad	28309	6902
?	Tergeslav Ada	GP		Sarajevo	29057	2639
X	Weiss Aleksander	GP in Banja Luka		Zagreb	28969	2270

Total 12; 6 alive, 1 killed, 5 destiny unkown

Physicians in the Service of the NDH, Domobranstvo (home gurad units)

Status	Name	Specialization	Date	Place	File No.	ZO No.
X	Bader Artur	Psychiatrist	15.07.42	Zagreb	29850	5252
X	Binenfeld Rudolf	Dentist	15.07.42	Vukovar	J. Romano	Sanski Most
D	Bischitz Franjo	Neuropsychiatrist in Vrapce	26.01.42	Vrapce	29821	5126
X	Deutsch Samuel	GP	12.06.42	Zagreb	29874	3740
?	Frank Oto	GP	26.01.42	Zagreb	28810	1071
?	Freiberger Nikola	GP	13.11.42	Zagreb	29531	4250
X	Heim Oskar	GP	21.11.41	Zagreb	28810	1071
?	Horvat Artur	GP	41	Zagreb	302/Inv.30014	5867
?	Izrael Izak, (died while on duty)	GP	04.08.42	Travnik	302/30020	5925
X	Kajon Ezra	GP	13.05.42	Travnik	J. Romano	
?	Kett Dragutin	GP	26.01.42	Zagreb	29755	4960
D	Klein Bruno	pricuvani Ljekar	26.01.42	Zagreb	29344	3790
X	Kohn Artur	GP	26.01.42	Zagreb	28810	1071
?	Kohn Benko	GP	16.07.42	Zagreb	28810	1071
?	Kurschner Milan	GP	14.01.42	Zagreb	28810	1071
?	Nahmias, ?	GP	26.01.42	Travnik	29683	4743
?	Neufeld Filip	GP	29.08.42	Zagreb	28738	0515
X	Njemirovski Herman	GP	31.01.42	Zagreb	28810	1071
X	Pollak Slavko	Ljekar, Popovac 1943, Dakovo	18.02.42	Zagreb	29857	5247
D	Reichl Raic Artur	GP	06.01.42	Zagreb	29810	5105
X	Rechnitzer Mirko	GP	11.04.42	Zagreb	29036	2560
X?	Sebastian General Mantel	GP retired from duty	26.06.42	Zagreb	29259	3533
X	Singer Sinjski Gustav	GP	26.01.42	Zagreb	29165	3344
?	Spitzer Ivan	GP	07.02.42	Zagreb	29570	4410
?	Stajner Samuel	GP	Date ?	Zagreb	28810	1071
?	Sternberg	GP	Date ?	Sarajevo	29655	4654
?	Zohr Milan	GP	Date ?	Zagreb	29708	4829

Total 27, 11 survived, 3 killed, 13 destiny unkown

Notes

NOTES FOR INTRODUCTION

1.   Croatia is situated between central, southern and Eastern Europe. Because of its distinct horseshoe-like shape, it has many neighbors: Slovenia, Hungary, part of Serbia and Montenegro, Bosnia-Herzegovina, and Italy across the Adriatic.

2.   Bosnia-Herzegovina is located in southeastern Europe on the Balkan Peninsula, between Croatia, Serbia, and Montenegro, and the Adriatic coast.

3.   See Chapter 1 for a more detailed discussion of Pavelić and the Ustaše.

4.   Documents and historiographies of fascism frequently use the term "Quisling"—after Norway's collaborationist leader Vidkun Quisling—to refer to the Ustaše regime.

5.   Narcisa Krizman-Lengel, "A Contribution to the Study of Terror in the So-Called Independent State of Croatia: Concentration Camps for Women in 1941–1942," (Jerusalem: Yad Vashem Vol. XX, 1990), 2-4. See also, Vlado Strugar, *Jugoslavia: 1941–1945* (Belgrade: Vojnoizdavacki zavod, 1969), 349.

6.   Jozo Tomasevich, *War and Revolution in Yugoslavia, 1941–1945: Ocupation and Collaboration* (Palo Alto, CA: Stanford University Press, 2001), 593-594. See also Hannah Arendt, A *Report on the Banality of Evil: Eichmann in Jerusalem,* (New York: Penguin Group, 1977), 183-184.

7.   Nathan Rotenstreich, "Summary Lecture," *Holocaust and Rebirth, A Symposium* (Jerusalem: Yad Vashem, Hacohen Press Ltd., 1974), 197.

8.   See my Ph.D. dissertation, Esther Gitman, *Rescue and Survival of Jews in the Independent State of Croatia, (NDH), 1941–1945,* (The City University of New York, 2005), 10.

9.   In 1942, Dr. Ivo Petrić had to flee Croatia because he assisted in the rescue of Jewish physicians. Rescues by government officials are discussed in Chapter 3.

10.   Frano Kritić, *Dita* (Osijek: Komputerska odrada i tisak, Gradska tiskara Naklada, 1997 primjeraka [preliminary free copy]), 21.

11.   HDA, ZKRZ-GUZ 2235-45, box 10, Jasenovac.

12.   Josef Indig-Ithai, "Children of Villa Emma," in Ivo Herzer, *The Italian Refuge, Rescue of Jews During the Holocaust* (Washington, D.C.: The Catholic University of America Press, 1989), 180.

13.   HDA, ZKRZ, GUZ 2235/10-45, Zemaljska Komisija NR Hrvatske za utvrdjivanje zločina okupatora i nhihovih pomagača (hereafter National Commission), Zagreb: Jasenovac, zapisnici svejedoka, Alberta Maestra.

14. Ljerka Auferber, interview, Zagreb, Croatia, February 20, 2003.

15. Dubrovnik is an ancient city on the Adriatic coast; during World War II the city was under Ustaše administrative rule and Italian military control in an area designated as Zone II. Out of the 81 pre-World War II Jewish citizens in this region, 23 survived. Many Jewish refugees fled there from inland territories.

16. Milislav Ercegović, interview, May 27, 2003, Zagreb, Croatia.

17. Jaška Kalogera, interview, January 23, 2003, Zagreb, Croatia.

18. Slavko Goldstein, interview, August 19, 2003, Zagreb, Croatia.

19. Theodora Klayman (Teodora Basch-Vrančić), interview, February 24, 2010, Washington, D.C.

NOTES FOR CHAPTER 1

1. The idea of Yugoslavism (unification of the South Slavs) was conceived first by Josip Juraj Strossmayer, who became bishop of Bosnia Srijem, with his seat in Djakovo, in 1849. Despite his Bosnian bishopric, he was ethnically a Croat, and his motto was: Everything for the faith and the homeland. In 1860 he was chosen as the leader of the Croatian People's Party, which favored the unity of the Croatian and Serbian people, provided Serbs merged with Croats.

2. Jozo Tomasevich, *War and Revolution in Yugoslavia, 1941–1945: Occupation and Collaboration* (Stanford: Stanford University Press, 2001), 8-9.

3. Rudolf Horvat, *Hrvatska na mučilištu* (Zagreb: Kulturno Historijsko Društvo "Hrvatski Rodoljub"), 124–129.

4. Fredo Šišić, *Dokumenti of postanku Kraljevine Srba: Hrvata i Slovenaca, 1914-1918* (Zagreb: Matica Hrvatska, 1920), 196-198.

5. Richard Pattee, *The Case of Cardinal Aloysius Stepinac* (Milwaukee: The Bruce Publishing Company, 1953), 6–7. In December 1519, Pope Julius II promised the Croatian leader [Ban], that "the Head of the Catholic Church will not allow Croatia to fall, for they are the *Antemurale Christianitatis* (shield and bulwark of Christianity)." The bond between the Croats and the Vatican remained strong.

6. Ivo Banac, *The National Question in Yugoslavia: Origin, History, Politics,* (Ithaca: Cornell University Press, 1984), 22, 85-89.

7. Phyllis Auty, *Yugoslavia* (London: Walker, 1949). See also Ivo Banac, *The National Question in Yugoslavia: Origins, History, Politics* (Ithaca, Cornell University, 1984) [short cite]; Harriet Pass Feidenreich, *The Jews of Yugoslavia: A Quest for Community* (Philadelphia: Jewish Publication Society, 1979); Robert Lee Wolff, *The Balkans in Our Time: History of Yugoslavia* (New York: Cambridge University Press, 1966); Jozo Tomasevich, *Peasants, Politics, and economic Change in Yugoslavia* (Stanford: Stanford University Press, 1955).

8.   Glen Curtis, ed., *Yugoslavia: A Country Study*, (Washington, DC: Federal Research Division, Library of Congress, 1992), 29.

9.   As an inducement to join the Western Allies, the secret Treaty of London in 1915 promised Italy territories on the eastern Adriatic coast that had significant Italian minorities. The postwar treaties awarded Italy Zadar, Istria, Trieste, and several Adriatic islands, and it took Rijeka after protracted struggles. Yet Italy resented that it had not received all the territories it had been promised and continued to support Croatian, Macedonian and Albanian extremists in the hope of stirring unrest that would undermine the Yugoslavian Kingdom.

10.   Fredo Šišić, *Dokumenti of postanku Kraljevine Srba, Hrvata i Slovenaca, 1914-1918* (Zagreb: Matica Hrvatska, 1920), 99, 196.

11.   Viktor Novak, *Antologia jugoslavenske misli in narodnog jedinstva, 1390-1930* (Belgrade: 1930).

12.   Fredo Šišić, *Dokumenti of postanku Kraljevine Srba: Hrvata i Slovenaca, 1914-1919*, (Zagreb: Matica Hrvatska, 1920), 201, 216-217, 275, 309. See also Aleksa Djilas, *The Contested Country*, 108-109. A vast historiographic literature is available on the formation of Yugoslavia and on nationalism before and after unification. Since many issues are still contested, it is imperative to review the Serb, the Croat and some in between versions in order to try to understand the aspirations and the conduct of each entity.

13.   Banac, *The National Question*, 168-171.

14.   Ante Nazor and Zoran Ladić, *History of the Croatians: Illustrated Chronology* (Zagreb: Multigraf, 2003), 325-376. [Published in Croatian and in English]

15.   Curtis, ed., *Yugoslavia*, 32-33.

16.   Aleksa Djilas, *The Contested Country*, 59-65.

17.   Jozo Tomasevich, *Peasants, Politics, and Economic Change in Yugoslavia*, 205. See also Banac, *The National Question*, 23. In July 1919 the Croatian Communist paper *Istina* (Truth), in Zagreb, published an editorial arguing that both the Croatian and Serbian national consciousnesses were "feudal" and "medieval" in origin; both were rooted in the past and had little or no relevance to the present, yet they persisted.

18.   Marcus Tanner, *Croatia: A Nation Forged in War* (2ⁿᵈ ed.; New Haven and London: Yale University Press, 2001), 123-124.

19.   Ibid., 125.

20.   Blaž Lorković, *Ustaški pokret u borbi za oslobodjenje Hrvatske* (The Ustaše Movement in the Struggle for the Liberation of Croatia) (Zagreb: 1942), 10-12.

21.   Aleksa Djilas, *The Contested Country*, 150-151.

22.   Gavro Schwarz, *Povijest zagrebačke židovske općine od osnutka do 50-tih godina 19. vijeka* (Jews and Minorities Rights) (Zagreb: Štamparija Gaj, 1939), 372-373. Ibid., 69.

23. Yakir Eventov, *A History of Yugoslav Jews: From Ancient Times to the End of the 19th Century* (Tel-Aviv: "Davar," 1971), 179.

24. Norman Stillman, *Jews in Arab Lands: History and Source Book* (Philadelphia: Jewish Publication Society of America, 1979), 25-26. The Pact of Umar, which protected the Jews was considered a writ of protection extended by Allah's community to their protégés (*ahl al-dhimma* or *dhimmi*).

25. Ibid., 90, 97. Jews in most of the Ottoman Empire's Arab provinces also lived independent communal lives, as did other ethnic groups.

26. Moric Levi,"Fragmenti iz života sefarada," in *Spomenica La Benevolencija* (Sarajevo: Jewish Community, 1924), 16-24.

27. Gavro Schwarz, *Povijest zagrebačke zidovske opčine of osnutka do 50-tih godina 19 vijeka* (Zagreb: Štamparija "Gaj," 1939), 8-9.

28. Melita Švob, *Židovi u Hrvatskoj* (Zagreb: Židovskih Opčina, 1997), 168-170.

29. Jaša Romano, *Jevreji Jugoslavije 1941–1945: Žrtve genocida i učesnici narodnooslobodilačkog rata* (Belgrade: The Federation of Jewish Communities in Yugoslavia, 1980), 14. There are minor disagreements among historians about the exact number of Jewish Communities, but greater differences between historians and statisticians regarding the number of Jews in Yugoslavia. David Levi Dale estimated a population of approximately 75,000 Jews in Yugoslavia in 1918, while historian Albert Vise estimated that there were only 71,000 in 1941, two decades later. The figures above baffled Gerald Reitlinger, American Historian who emphasized that: "In no country of Axis-occupied Europe is the fate of Jewry more difficult to trace than in Yugoslavia." The final figures of losses and survivals are accordingly more difficult to assess.

30. "Statistika Jevrejstva Kraljevine Srba, Hrvata i Slovenaca" (KSHS) (Statistics regarding the Jews in the Kingdom of Serbs, Croats and Slovene), *Jevrejski Almanah*, (O.S.), (Jewish Almanac), 1929-30, 225.

31. "Kraljevine Srba, Hrvata i Slovenaca" (KSHS), *Jevrejski Almanah*, (O.S.), 1929-30; General Population Distribution 1941, 574.

32. Ivo Goldstein and Slavko Goldstein, *Holokaust u Zagrebu* [Holocaust in Zagreb] (Zagreb: Novi Liber & Židovska Opčina, 2001, p. 26).

33. *Židov* (a Jewish weekly), "Statistika 40."

34. David Perera, "Jevrejski almanah" (Belgrade: Savez Jevrejskih opčina, 1968-70). The more detailed distribution was: Public Employees, 571 (0.8 percent); Commerce and Business, 6,835 (9.5 percent); Skilled Workers, 2,288 (3.1 percent); Physicians, 528 (0.7 percent); Lawyers 381 (0.5 percent); Pharmacists, 101 (0.08 percent); Veterinarians, 50 (0.05); Engineers, 145 (0.02 percent); Laborers, 3,548 (4.9 percent); Pupils, 6,713 (9.4 percent); University Students, 709 (0.9 percent).

35. Jaša Romano, *Jevreji Jugoslavije 1941-194: Žrtve genocida i učesnici narodnooslobodilačkog rata* (Belgrade: The Federation of Jewish Communities in Yugoslavia, 1980), 573.

36. *Hrvatski dnevninik* (Croatian Daily), October 6, 1940.

37. *Spomenica 50, 1919-1969* (Belgrade: Savez jvrejskih opština Yugoslavije, 1969), 39-42.

38. Because a sizable number of Jewish individuals prospered under the Austro-Hungarian Empire, they shared some of this wealth with their less fortunate coreligionists by supporting talented but disadvantaged children.

39. *Politika* (daily newspaper, published in Belgrade), XXVI, no. 7599 (July 1, 1929): interview by Jakob Landau, director of the Jewish Telegraphic Agency, with Vojislav Marinković, Minister of External Affairs.

40. R. Mitrović, "The Fate of Jews in Areas Where German Minority Groups (Volksdeutsche) Assumed Power in April 1941," *Zbornik 2, Studije i gradja o učešću Jevreja u natodnooslobodilačkom ratu* (Belgrade: JIM, 1973), 265.

41. *Nezavisnot* (Indpendence) 30:1938.

42. *Spomenica 400* [400-years Commemoration] *godina of dolaska jevreja u Bosnu i Hercegovinu,* (400 Years of the Jews in Bosnia), *Beograd, 1566-1966* (1966), 211.

43. HDA, Ispostava Ustaškog redarstvenog povjereništva Židovski odsjek, RUR 252, Inv. Br. 27309 ŽO 383, 4.6.1941 (June 6). The list of converted Jews to Catholicism was compiled by the Jewish Community in Zagreb (ŽOZ); they list 3,400 names.

44. Jaša Romano, *Jews of Yugoslavia, 1941–1945: Victims of Genocide and Freedom Fighters* (Belgrade: The Federation of Jewish Communities in Yugoslavia, 1980), 574. More than twenty Jews participated in the Hungarian revolution in 1919, and a larger number took part in the October Revolution in Russia. A considerable number of Yugoslav Jews joined the Yugoslav Socialist Students' Club, formed in 1919.

45. Zvi Loker, *Pinkas Hakehillot* (Jerusalem: The Holocaust Heroes' Remembrance Authority, 1988), 215.

46. Zdenko Lowenthal (Levental), *Jewish Resistance During the Holocaust: Proceedings of the Conference on Manifestations of Jewish Resistance* (Jerusalem: Yad Vashem, 1971), 301-310.

47. HDA, fond ZKRZ GUZ, # 306 box 15, 3722. See also the list of converted Jews in ŽOŽ (Jewish Community Archive, Zagreb).

48. Albert Vajs, Jevreji Jugoslavije, [*The Jews in New Yugoslavia*] (Belgrade: Savez Jevrejskih opština Jugoslavije, 1954), 28-29.

49. *Židov*'s editors between 1927 and 1941 were Dr. J. Rosenberg, A. Gross, A. Singer, S. Spitzer, and Zeev Gluck from 1927 to 1941.

50. *Židov*, March 26, 1936.

51. *Jevrejski glas* was published from 1928 to 1941. Its editor, Dr. Braco Poljokan, attempted to blend Zionist education and training in preparation for emigration

to Eretz Israel with activities aimed at improving living conditions for Jews in the Diaspora. *Židovska svest*, Belgrade's weekly, took on bigots and antisemites.

52.   H.J. Zimmels, *Ashkenazim and Sephardim* (London: Oxford University Press, 1958) contains a full discussion of differences between these two branches of Judaism.

53.   Maček "O antisemitizmu" (editorial), *Židov* (August 12,1936).

54.   Šime Djodan, *Ekonomska Politika Jugoslavije* (Zagreb: Školska knjiga, 1970), 50-51.

55.   "Murder in the Parliament," HDA, *Memorandum*, 1935.

56.   "Vjesnik hrvatskih revolucionaraca" February 1931.

57.   Djilas, *The Contested Country*, 110-127. "Vjesnik hrvatskih revolucionaraca," February 1931.

58.   Ivo Goldstein and Slavko Goldstein, *Holocaust in Zagreb* (Zagreb: Novi Liber i Židovska općina, 2001), 68-69.

59.   Tanner, *Croatia*, 125.

60.   NARA, D-2005526, Counter Intelligence Corps. Rome Detachment, Zone 5, A.P.O. 512 U.S. Army. August 29, 1947, Case 5650. Confidential, RG. 319 Stack IRR Persona –File, Box 173, Rile XE 001109.

61.   Tanner, *Croatia*, 125-126.

62.   Josip Kolanović, *Holocaust in Croatia: Documentation and Research Perspectives*, (Zagreb: Hrvatski Državni Arhiv, 1996), 161.

63.   Dr. Samuel Pinto, *"Zločini Okupatora I Njihovih pomagaća izvršeni nad Jevrejima u Bosni i Herzegovini,"* (Crimes by the Forces of Occupation and their Collaborators Committed Against the Jews of BiH), Sarajevo, 1952. HDA, ZKRZ-GUZ 2235/2-45, box 10.

64.   R. Mitrović, "Sudbina Jevreja u krajevima gde su Folksdojceri preuzeli vlast April 1941" (The Fate of the Jews in Areas where German Minority Groups (Volksdeutsche) Assumed Power in April 1941), Beograd: *Zbornik* 2 (1973), 265. See also, M. Janković, *Rat špijuna u Kraljevini Jugoslavije* (The Spy War in the Kingdom of Yugoslavia) (Belgrade: JIM 1982,) 246.

65.   *Zbornik* 2 (1973), 266. See also Chapter 2 in the testimony of Leon Kabiljo and his former Volksdeutsche employee Josip Eberhardt.

66.   Glen Curtis, ed., *Yugoslavia: A Country Study*, Federal Research Division, Library of Congress, 1992, 37-39.

67.   Dr. Samuel Pinto, HDA, ZKRZ-GUZ 3335/2-45, box 10, p.2-5. Pinto's work was published in 1952. *Testimonies* he obtained confirm that Tito's government, after the war placed the entire blame for collaboration on the Croats in Croatia thus absolving the Ustaše Muslims in Bosnia-Herzegovina of their contributions to German and Ustaše success.

68.   *Balkan*, June 8, 1938.

69.   *Katolički Tjednik* (Catholic Weekly), April 6, 1941, 4.

70.   Samuel Pinto, "Zločini okupatiora i njihovih pomagaca izvršeni nad jevre-jima u BiH," 9. HDA, ZKRZ-GUZ 3335/2-45, box 10.

71.   Zvi Loker, ed., *Pinkas Hakehillot–Yugoslavia* (Jerusalem: Yad Vashem, 1988), 216. See Hrvoje Matković, *Povijest Jugoslavije, Hrvatski Pogled*, 132.

72.   Joseph Rothschild, *East Central Europe between Two World Wars* (Seattle: University of Washington Press, 1974), 250-267.

73.   Joseph Schechtman, *The Mufti and the Fuehrer: The Rise and Fall of Hajj Amin el Husseini* (New York, 1965). See also Jennie Lebel, *Hajj Amin and Berlin* (Tel-Aviv: Technosdar, Ltd., 1996), 25, 128-145. On July 26, 1931, Hajj Amin el Husseini organized an international convention of Muslim leaders in Jerusalem. Twenty-two delegates from Yugoslavia attended. Hajj Amin formed strong relationships with some of the Bosnian delegates, a relationship that lasted throughout the war, with implications for the fate of the Jews of Sarajevo. In Lebel (p. 25), see the letter "Unser Fuehrer" (Our Leader) from the Muslim's to Hitler.

74.   HDA, Military file, Volksdeutsche Activities.

75.   Dr. Samuel Pinto, HDA, ZKRZ-GUZ 2335/2-45, box 1012-13.

76.   Menahem Shelah, *History of the Holocaust: Yugoslavia* (Jerusalem: Yad Vashem, 1990), 327.

77.   Galeazzo Ciano, *Diary 1937-1943*, 350, 417, 418.

78.   Ciano, *Diary*, 417-418.

79.   *Službene novine kraljevine Jugoslavije* (Business Newspaper of the Kingdom of Yugoslav), October 15,1940.

80.   *Hrvatski dnevnik* (Croatian Daily), 6.10.1940.

81.   Menahem Shelah, *The Murder of the Croatian Jews by the Germans and Their Helpers During the Second World War* (Ph.D. Dissertation, Tel-Aviv University, 1980), 21-25. This unpublished dissertation was written in Hebrew.

82.   Ante Nazor and Zoran Ladić, *History of Croatians* (Zagreb: Multigraf, 2003), 350.

83.   Srdja Trifković, *Ustaša: Croatian Separatism and European Politics, 1929-1945* (London: and Aiken, SC: The Lord Byron Foundation for Balkan Studies, 1998), 99.

84.   Winston S. Churchill, *The Grand Alliance*, Vol. 3:162. Both the Serbs and many Croats had strong affinities with Western Europe and to the U.S., strengthened by immigrants to America, and the Jews were convinced that the West would come to their rescue.

85.   Abteilung Landesverteidigung was the department under the Wehrmacht High Command (OKW) that formulated Hitler's war directives.

86. Jozo Tomasevich, *War and Revolution in Yugoslavia, 1941–1945: Occupation and Collaboration* (Stanford: Stanford University Press, 2001, 48-49.

87. Nazor and Ladić, *History of Croatians*, 350.

88. Galeazzo Ciano, *The Ciano Diaries 1939-1943*, 247. See also, Hrvoje Matković, *Povjest Jugoslavije, 1918-1991* (Zagreb: Naklada Pavčić, 1998), 244.

89. See the letter from Edmund Glaise von Horstenau, Germany's plenipotentiary general in Croatia, November 26, 1941, to Colonel Friedrich von Mellenthin, Wehrmacht High Command (OKW). U.S., Department of State, *Documents on German Foreign Policy, 1918-1945* [hereafter DGFP] (Washington, D.C., 1960-64), Series D, Vol. 12:515-517.

90. U.S. Department of Commerce, Economics & Statistics Division, January 1994, National Trade Data Bank (NTDB) CD-ROM, Su Doc C1.88: 994/1/V.2, processed 02/16/1994 by RCM (UM-St. Louis Libraries) AAHB0147.

91. Gerald Reitlinger, *The Final Solution: The Attempt to Exterminate the Jews of Europe, 1939-1945*, (New-York: Beechhurst Press, 1953), 358.

92. Jaša Romano, *Jevreji Jugoslavije, 1941–1945* (Belgrade: Jevrejski Istorički Musej, JIM, 1980), 201. (Belgrade: The Federation of Jewish Communities in Yugoslavia, 1980), 5-14. Because historians cannot agree on the size of Yugoslavia's pre-war Jewish population, estimates of casualties and survivors varies by as much as 20 percent. This book follows the numbers suggested by Jaša Romano, who gives the following estimates for the Jewish population on the eve of World War II: 39,500 (25,000 in Croatia and 14,500 in Bosnia-Herzegovina; 9,500 of this total Jewish population survived.

NOTES FOR CHAPTER 2

1. Menahem Shelah, ed., *History of the Holocaust: Yugoslavia* (Jerusalem: Yad Vashem, 1990), 138. See also Fikrita Jelić-Butić, *Ustaše I Nezavisna Država Hrvatska* (The Ustaše and the Independent State of Croatia) (Zagreb: Sveučilišna Naklad Liber, 1977), 173. See also the daily news, "Hrvatski Narod," 24.6.1941.

2. HDA, ZKRZ-GUZ, 2235/2-45 box 10, 123.

3. *Zbornik i Zakoni, zakonske odredbe, naredbe itd.* (A compilation of laws and decrees) (Zagreb: NDH, 1941), 42, 134,142. The most exhaustive and comprehensive bibliography on the subject of NDH anti-Jewish legislation is L. Kopsa, "O organizaciji ustaskog aparata vlasti na provotenju terora u tzv."

4. Narcisa Krizman–Lengel, "A Contribution to the Study of Terror in the So-Called Independent State of Croatia: Concentration Camps for Women in 1941-1942" (Jerusalem: Yad Vashem Vol. XX, 1990), 2-4.

5. *Novi list*, April 18, 1941. Dr. Samuel Pinto described these actions in a memorandum for the postwar National Commission for the Ascertainment of Crimes by

the Occupiers and their Collaborators against the Jews. See his *"Zločini okupatora i nji-hovih pomagača izvršeni nad Jevrejima u Bosni i Hercegovini,"* HDA, ZKRZ-GUZ 2235-2/45, box 10.

6. NARA, RG59, 860H.4016/64, PS/RJH, "Persecution of Jews in Croatia, Zagreb, June 13, 1941." See also HDA, ZKRZ-GUZ 2235-2/45, box 10, Dr. Samuel Pinto, National Commission memorandum, 18.

7. HDA, ZKRZ, 2235, 12 April, 1945, 483-510.

8. The proclamation was published in Zagreb's daily newspaper *Novi list,* 18, 05.16.41 representing the voice of the regime.

9. National Archives and Records Administration (NARA), 860H.4016/63, 1686, telegram sent from Berlin, May 2, 1941 to the Secretary of State, Washington, D.C.

10. *Zbornik Zakona i Naredaba Nezavisne Države Hrvatske* (Listings of NDH rules, decrees and regulations (Zagreb: NDH).

11. Ulrich Von Hasel, *The Von Hassel Diaries 1938-1942: The Story of the Forces Against Hitler Inside Germany,* English trans. of *Von Anderem Deutschland,* intro. by Allen W. Dulles (Westport, CT: Greenwood, 1971). Von Hassell served in the diplomatic corps in Belgrade and Rome; he was executed as a member of the German Resistance.

12. Srdja Trifkovic, "The Real Genocide in Yugoslavia," in DGFP, D, 12; *Minutes of Hitler's talks with Pavelić, June 6, 1941.*

13. Tomasevich, *War and Revolution in Yugoslavia,* 54-56.

14. Many Bosnian Muslims were Ustaše. They included NDH Vice President Osman beg Kulenović (April 16, 1941 to October 7, 1941), who was followed in this position by his brother Dzafer beg Kulenović until May, 1945; Mehmed Alajbegović, Minister of Foreign Affairs (May 5, 1944 to May 1945) and previously NDH general consul in Munich (January 1942 to October 1943); And Hilmija Beslagić, Minister of Transportation (July 1, 1941 to October 11, 1943). A number of Muslims held high positions in the Ustaše governance of Bosnia and Herzegovina. Bosnian Muslims participated in genocidal actions agains Serbs, Jews, and Gypsies. In addition, 50,000 Bosnian Muslims fought in the Axis forces that invaded the Soviet Union.

15. G. Victor Rosenzweig, *Naš život* (Our Life) (Zagreb: Cultural Society Miroslav Šalom Freiberger & Jewish Community, 2001), 14.

16. Nahum Goldmann, "The Influence of the Holocaust on the Change in the Attitude of World Jewry to Zionism and the State of Israel" *Holocaust and Rebirth, A Symposium,* (Jerusalem: Yad Vashem, Hacohen Press Ltd., 1974, 82.

17. Ivo Goldstein and Slavko Goldstein, *Holokaust u Zagrebu* (Zagreb: Novi Liber, 2001), 78-88.

18. Zdenka Novak, *When Heaven's Vault Cracked* (Cambridge: England, Merlin Books Ltd., St. Ives, 1995)31.

19. Zdenka Steiner-Novak, interview, Haifa, Israel, October 14, 2003. (Unless otherwise indicated, all interviews in this book were conducted by the author.) Until the last day of her life, Zdenka was preoccupied with one thought: What could she have done to save her family? (A few days after this interview, Zdenka passed on.)

20. David Levi Dale, "The Jews of New Yugoslavia," in *Spomenica 1919-1969* (Belgrade: Savez Jevrejskih opština Jugoslavije, 1972), 225. (English summary of Chapter 3.) JOINT American Jewish Joint Distribution Committee (JDC or Joint), HICEM was formed with the merger of three Jewish migration associations, based in New York: HIAS (Hebrew Immigrant Aid Society), ICA (Jewish Colonization Association) based in France and Emigdirect, a migration organization based in Berlin. The name HICEM is an acronym of the three mentioned above.

21. Žuži Jelenik, interview, Zagreb, January 23, 2003.

22. Branko Polić, interview, Zagreb, February 22, 2003. Branko converted to Catholicism in 1936, followed by his parents in 1938.

23. Jevrejski glas, December 13, 1940.

24. Rabbi Šalom Freiberger, *Židov*, October 2, 1940.

25. Mišo Montiljo, interview, Zagreb, Croatia, Hazoreah, Israel, September 11, 2002.

26. ZKRZ, Srečko Bujas, 2235/2/1-45, box 10.

27. Ivo Andrić, "Introduction," in Isak Samakolija, *Tales of Sarajevo* (Portland, OR: Vallentine Mitchell &Co. LTD, 1997) 3.

28. Michael (Mišo) Montiljo, interview, Zagreb, February 18, 2003.

29. Richard Breitman, *The Architect of Genocide: Himmler and the Final Solution* (Hanover, NH: Brandies University Press, 1991), 224.

30. David LittleJohn, *Foreign Legions of the Third Reich, Albania, Czechoslovakia, Greece, Hungary and Yugoslavia,* (San Jose, CA: R. James Bender Publishing, (1994), vol. 3, 210-215.

31. HDA, PONOVA, Jewish Section, 386/1076 5.4.1941.

32. HDA, RUR 252 No. 28026 ŽO 4178, 29. VIII. 1941.

33. HDA, RUR 252 No. 27673 ŽO 1342, 14. VII. 1941.

34. HDA, RUR 252 No. 28704 ŽO 278, 23. VII. 1941.

35. HDA, RUR 252 No. 28237, ZO5985, 23. IX. 1941.

36. HDA, RUR 252, 28524, ZO.7990 [date illegible].

37. Stjepan Steiner, interview with Esther Gitman, Zagreb, December 16, 2002.

38. Josip Kolanović letter in HDA, Roma, ASAE, AG Croazia 35: Condizione degli ebrei in Croazia VI.1941–V.1943.

39. USHMM, 1998.A.0027, Reel 1 file 4.

40. HDA, ZKRZ-GUZ, 2235/2-45, box 10, 3.

41. Mira Kolar-Dimitrijević, "The Material Losses of the Jewish Population of Croatia during World War II," *Voice*, No. 4 (Zagreb, Winter 2002/2003), 43-46.

42. HDA, ZKRZ-GUZ, box 15, 3732-3733. The other two deputies were Ivan Britvić and Ivo Baraković.

43. National Commission for the Ascertainment of Crimes Committed by the Occupiers and their Collaborators against the Jews of NDH.

44. Croatian National Archive (HDA), ZKRZ-GUZ 2235/45, Box 10: Auschwitz.

45. In his testimony of September 1945, Mann revealed that the Jewish Community in Zagreb identified one of the board members as an informer who provided the Ustaše information on Jewish assets and which ones should have larger assessments. The original amount of gold requested was 500 kg. The informer gave the Ustaše the idea of raising the basic demand from 500 to 1,000 kg. The informer's name was known to the board, but Mann did not reveal his name in order not to embarrass any possible surviving family members.

46. In an interview on March 2, 2003, Branko Polić described the day his family was expelled from their villa. Before leaving, they had time to distribute their valuables among neighbors, who after the war faithfully returned every single item. There are many accounts of such incidents. Because they distributed their assets in this way, they never paid the "contribution."

47. HDA, ZKRZ-GUZ, 2235/2-45, box 10.

48. HDA, ZKRZ-GUZ, 2235/2-45, box 10, Mann testimony.

49. Branko Polić, interview, Zagreb, February 22, 2003.

50. Goldstein and Goldstein, *Holokaust u Zagrebu*, 158. The authors argue that Mann exaggerated the number of exit visas issued by Kuhnel, but they provide no evidence to substantiate their claim.

51. HDA, ZKRZ-GUZ, 2235/2-45, box 10, Hinko Mann, 9. Mann expressed surprise when he heard from others that Kuhnel had asked to be paid. See also HDA, 1549 ZiG NDH, Box 62.

Vilko Kuhnel. Mann's testimony was corroborated by Yehuda Bauer, *American Jewry and the Holocaust: American Jewish Joint Distribution Committee, 1939–1945* (Detroit: Wayne State University Press, 1982), 280-281.

52. HDA, ZKRZ-GUZ, 2235/2-45, box 10, Mann testimony, 5.

53. Marion Kaplan, *Between Dignity and Despair: Jewish Life in Nazi Germany* (New York: Oxford University Press, 1998), 40-43.

54. Narcisa Krizman–Lengel, "A Contribution to the Study of Terror in the So-Called Independent State of Croatia: Concentration Camps for Women in 1941-1942," *Yad Vashem Studies*, vol. 20 (1990), 2-4.

55. Regina Perera, written testimony (Montreal, Canada, September 20, 2008) sent to the author. Regina and her brother did not discuss the rescue with their mother,

and many pertinent details are missing from her testimony, such as the names of the Muslim friend and village where they hid. Nor is it clear how sincere the conversion to Islam was. Regina and her family identify themselves as Jews and in fact after the war for a while they lived in Israel and then relocated to Canada where her mother had two brothers. Chapter 6 discusses the Italian chapter of the Pereras' story, when the children were older. The friends they made in Italy kept in touch with them through the years.

56.   Šarika Kaveson-Stern, interview, Kibbutz Shaar-Hamakim, Israel, October 6, 2003.

57.   Regina Kamhi, interview, Zagreb, October 25, 2002. In subsequent meetings, Regina filled in this formal interview with stories and anecdotes about the Sephardic Jews of Sarajevo.

58.   Nada Grgeć, interview, Zagreb, December 29, 2002. Nada's father, Samuel Sterk, was an illegimite son of a Jewish father and Christian mother; he married a Jewish woman, Netika Klein, who was Nada's mother. Before the family converted to Christianity in 1943, two people living in their apartment house joined the Ustaše in order to obtain preference in ration cards. They then shared the food they received with other neighbors. Even before her mother converted to Christianity and her Jewish documents miraculously disappeared, their Ustaše neighbors warned them to leave the neighborhood. They were fortunate to live in a neigborhood in which nobody provided information to the Ustaše.

59.   Lotika Papo-Latinović, interview, Sarajevo, August 10, 2003.

60.   Slavko Goldstein, interview, Zagreb, September 19, 2003.

61.   Ella Finci-Koen, interview, Sarajevo, August 12, 2003.

62.   Ibid. Ella said that when her family searched for Sokol after the war, they were told that the Partisans had killed him for his service with the Ustaše.

63.   HDA, RUR 252, #28453 ŽO, 7537. The District of Sarajevo informed the Office for Law and Order on November 9, 1941, that the city's remaining Jewish male population over age 16 was: 100 employees of the Jewish Community of Sarajevo; 267 elderly men (60 and above); 51 ill and hospitalized men; 16 awaiting official recognition as Aryans; 28 married to Aryans; 78 in forced labor; 44 working for the NDH; and smaller numbers of skilled employees, including railroad experts, physicians, and pharmacists, for a total of 622 adult Jewish men.

64.   Jakica Danon, interview, Sarajevo, August 14, 2003.

65.   The hospital of the Sisters of Mercy, such hospitals were spread over Croatia.

66.   Zlata Romano, interview, Lod, Israel, September 28, 2003.

67.   Romano, *Jews of Yugoslavia: Victims of Genocide and Freedom Fighters* (Belgrade: Federation of Jewish Communities in Yugoslavia, 1980), 281,289.

68.   Eva Grlić, interview, Zagreb, February 2, 2003.

69.   Vesna Domani (Eva Grlic's daughter), interview, Zagreb, February 8, 2003.

70. HDA, ZKRZ-GUZ 2235/45 Box 10, Auschwitz.

71. HDA, RUR 252, #28453 ŽO, 7537.

72. HDA, Hans Helm Folder, *Izvještaj* br. 20, Zabreb, April 15,1943, 355-357.

73. HDA, Hans Helm Folder, *Einsatzkommando Zagreb*, September 1,1944. 354.

74. JIM, for further information on the subjects see documents: K62.6-1, 1-76, K62.6-1, 1-179, K62.6-1, 1-155, K62.6-1, 1-126, K62.6-1, 1-127, K62.6-1, 1-120, K62.6-1, 1-87, K62.6-1, 1-65, K62.6-1, 1-191, K62.6-1, 1-244, K62.6-1, 1-251, K62.6-1, 1-213, K62.6-1, 1-107, K62.6-1, 1-183.

75. JIM, K62.6-1, 1-112, K62.6-1, 1-142.

76. JIM, K62.6-1, 1-204.

77. JIM, K62.6-1, 1-249.

78. JIM, K.62.6-1/1-227, hospital's number 881/43.

79. JIM, K.62-6-1/1-291, hospital's number 1135/43.

80. Ante Fulgosi, interview Zagreb, March 3, 2003.

81. The file cards completed by survivors immediately upon returning to their homes, in this case Sarajevo, played a vital role in assisting the refugees, but they are also valuable historical documents.

82. Danilo Nikolić (president of the Jewish Community in Sarajevo), interview, Sarajevo, Bosnia-Herzegovina, August 12 and 14, 2003. Nikolić reported that approximately 200 Jews who survived the war and returned to Sarajevo refused to register with the Jewish Community.

83. See note above.

84. Excluding the 200 mentioned above, the number of survivors from Sarajevo is not clear. Some left for Palestine in 1944, the U.S. in 1944, and various other countries. Many served in Tito's new administration and resided in Belgrade. Still others changed their surnames when they converted or when they gave up any affiliation with the Jewish Community and its organizations.

85. Various National Commissions were created after the war. One that was exclusively dedicated to the investigation of the atrocities committed against Jews. In this chapter the focus is on Jews only.

86. Reitlinger, *The Final Solution*, 358.

87. David Levi-Dale, "The Jews of New Yugoslavia," in *Spomenica 1919-1969* (Belgrade: Savez Jevrejskih opština Jugoslavije, 1972), 7-21.

88. Albert Vajs, "The Jews in Yugoslavia," in *Spomenica 1919-1969*, 125-136.

89. Jaša Romano, *Jevreji Jugoslavije 1941–1945: Zrtve genocida i učesnici narodno-oslobodilačkog rata* (Belgrade: Jewish Historical Museum and the Federation of Jewish Communities in Yugoslavia, 1980), 201.

90.   Dotrščina files were opened by the Croatian National Archives (HDA); they list the names of Jews annihilated during the war.

91.   Djuro Schwarz, "Death Rate, Natural and Normal," Jewish Community of Zagreb (ŽOZ) *Bulletin,* no. 39 (May-June 1995).

92.   The files of the National Commission in Yugoslavia and the testimonies recorded by such Holocaust archives as the Shoah Foundation Institute at the University of Southern California or the United States Holocaust Memorial Museum in Washington, DC, hold many such stories.

NOTES FOR CHAPTER 3

1.   Jozo Tomasevich, *War and Revolution in Yugoslavia, 1941–1945* (Stanford, CA: Stanford University Press, 2001), 593-594. See also, Raul Hilberg, *Perpetrators, Victims, Bystanders: The Jewish Catastrophe 1933-1945* (New York City: Harper Collins Publishers, 1992), 86.

2.   Hannah Arendt, *Eichmann in Jerusalem* (New York: Penguin Books, 1964), 183-184. Arendt attributes the destruction of Croatia's Jewish Community in Zagreb to the Ustaše's conferring the "Honorary Aryans" title, which then encouraged assimilated Jews to stay until it was too late to get out.

3.   HDA, Hans Helm File, Subject Mixed Marriages sent to Berlin, 25.3.1943.

4.   HDA, MUP NDH, Pr. 21378/41, box 25. See also, RUR 30068-30072 a list of 2,519 individuals who requested various exemptions.

5.   In mid-1943, Heinrich Himmler, on a visit to Zagreb, made a deal with Pavelić to exchange economic support for giving up the protected Jews. See later in this chapter for a more detailed discussion.

6.   HDA, ZKRZ-GUZ, 2235/2-45, box 10, 1-20, Hinko Mann's testimony to the National Commission in Chapter 2.

7.   *Narodne novine,* June 19, 1941.

8.   Hrvoje Matković, *Povjest Jugoslavije, Hrvatski pogled* (Zagreb: PIP Naklada Pavčić, 1998), 216-217.

9.   Ibid., 137-139. This picture had changed little since 1921, when 80.4 percent of Croatians earned their livelihood from agriculture. Yugoslavia in the 1930s remained one of the most backward countries, and the situation was most dire in Dalmatia.

10.   ZKRZ-GUZ, 2235/2-45, box 10, Samuel Pinto, *Zločini okupatora,* 52.

11.   Menahem Shelah, ed., *The History of the Holocaust—Yugoslavia* (Jerusalem: Yad Vashem, 1990), 212. See also Matković, *Povijest Jugoslavije,* 137.

12.   *Spomenica 400, 400 godina of dolaska jevreja u Bosnu i Hercegovinu, Beograd, 1566-1966, odbor za proslavu,* (Sarajevo, 1966), 225. Also see Fikreta Jelić-Butić, *Ustaše*

Nezavisna Država Hrvatska, 1941–1945 (Zagreb: Sveučelišna Naklada Liber, 1977), 183-185. See HDA, ZKRZ-GUZ 2235/2-45, box 10, Srećko Bujas, 12.

13.   *Narodne novine*, (newspaper), June 19, 1941.

14.   *Spomenica 400*, 226. Most of these letters came from Zagreb, a few from other cities and towns in Croatia. I initially wondered why similar petitions were not sent from Sarajevo or other parts of Bosnia-Herzegovina. After extensive research, I found an answer, which is explained later in this chapter.

15.   HDA, RUR 252, 28145, ŽO 4767; also RUR 252, 27667 ŽO 1334, 16.VI.1941; 27963 ŽO 2834, 12.XII.1941; 28145 ŽO 4767, 11.VII.1941.

16.   HDA, RUR 252, 28145, ŽO 4767.

17.   HDA, RUR 252, 27479,ZO.

18.   HDA, RUR 252, 27685, ZO 1362.

19.   HDA, RUR 252, 27479, 14, VII. 1941.

20.   HDA, RUR 252, 28829 ZO not marked.

21.   HDA, RUR 252, 27938, ŽO 2647, July 31, 1941.

22.   HDA, RUR 252, 28769, ŽO 794, January 17, 1942.

23.   HDA, RUR 252, 27610, ŽO 1177, July 8, 1941.

24.   HDA, RUR 252, 29823, ŽO 345, March 24, 1942.

25.   HDA, RUR 252, 29461, ŽO 4067, May 3, 1942.

26.   HDA, MUP 302/30022, ŽO 5935, November 24, 1942.

27.   HDA, RUR 252, 29448, ŽO 4329, June 17, 1942.

28.   HDA, RUR 252, 29501, ŽO 4159, June 19, 1942.

29.   Gotz Aly and Susanne Heim, *Architects of Annihilation: Auschwitz and the Logic of Destruction* (Princeton: Princeton University Press, 2002), 11.

30.   HDA, ZKRZ-GUZ 2235/2-45, Box. 10, Srećko Bujas, 1944.

31.   Menahem Shelah, ed., *History of the Holocaust, Yugoslavia* 153.

32.   HDA, ZKRZ-GUZ 2235/2-45, box 10, Srečko Bujas testimony, 18.

33.   HDA, PONOVA (Jewish File), doc's # 56231/42, 56232/42, 56233/42, 56234/42, Zagreb, July 1942.

34.   HDA, PONOVA, (Jewish File), doc. # 5946/42, District of Bijeljina, 25 (July 1942).

35.   JIM, 2188-K-22-2-1/8-63-101. See also Shelah, ed., *History of the Holocaust*, 152-153.

36.   HDA, ZKRZ-GUZ, 2235/45, box 10. Judge Srećko Bujas submitted his report to the National Commission in Bosnia-Herzegovina.

37.   Fikreta Jellić-Butić, *Ustaše i NDH* (Ustaše in the NDH), 197.

38.   Esther Gitman, "The Rescue of Jewish Physicians in the Independent State of Croatia (NDH), 1941–1945," in *Holocaust and Genocide Studies* 23, no. 1 (Spring 2009), 76-91.

39.   Jaša Romano, "Jevreji Zdravstveni radnici Jugoslavije 1941–1945", *Zbornik* 2 (1973), 73-257.

40.   See HDA, RUR, 302/Inv. 10154/1941, ŽO 5050, which documents the deportation to a camp of Dr. Bela Hochstader on July 15,1941; RUR 252, 29117, ŽO 3135 (Dr. Stanko Pollak); and 28266, ŽO 6408 (Dr. Hinko Marić). There were probably many such examples, since I found documentation of 13 physicians who were rescued from concentration camps and sent to serve in Bosnia. (Jaša Romano states that on the eve of World War II the number of Jewish physicians, veterinarians, nurses, pharmacists, and medical students in Yugoslavia was approximately 1,150. He does not provide any approximation of their number in the NDH.

41.   Stjepan Steiner, interview, Zagreb, October 1, 2003.

42.   Dr. Miroslav Schlesinger had been involved in social activities while a medical student in Vienna. After returning to Zagreb, he promoted the causes of working people, continuing his activism into the war years. Both he and his wife Dr. Maria Schlesinger, as well as their daughter, were killed while serving with the Partisans.

43.   HDA, RUR 252, # 27710, ŽO 1467, July14,1941. A letter from Dr. Petrić, sent to Baraković, who was at that time, a high official in UNS with the knowledge and approval of Minister of Internal Affairs Andrija Artuković, recommended that Dr. Steinhardt and his family receive "Aryan rights."

44.   In 1942 Dr. Petrić escaped the NDH and immigrated to South America.

45.   *Narodne novine*, no.16, April 30,1941.

46.   HDA, RUR 252, 27710 ŽO 1467, July14,1941. According to the written tesimony I received in 2006 from Dr. Ibre Dizdarevic, from Bosnia-Herzegovina based on his conversation with Dr. Ante Vuletić in 1962, when Vulatić came to see Dr. Petrić, the latter exclaimed: "You are an expert on endemic syphilis; you must organize an action which would ameliorate this disease among the Bosnian Muslims. I request that you liquidate the disease within a period of two years."

47.   Saša Jevtović, "Djelovnje Židovskih ljećnika u Bosni i Hercegovini 1941-1942" (The participation of Jewish Physicians in Bosnia-Herzegovina, 1941-1942), *Novi Omanut*, no.46, (June/July 2001), 9-10.

48.   A copy of the list and the invitations are in HDA, RUR 252 29195 ŽO 3396, and HDA, RUR 252 28017 ŽO 4143, respectively. As soon as the invitations to join the syphilis mission had been sent to Jewish doctors, a letter from the Ministry of Health was sent to the Office of Law and Order and Security asking them to stop sending the physicians to labor or death camps. HAD, 252 28017.

49.   Dr. Teodor Gruner, interview, Zagreb, January 14, 2003.

50.   USHMM, 1998-A-0019, contains a copy of the instructions to all Law and Order officials to refrain from deporting to concentration camps the Jewish physicians in the service of the NDH Ministry of Health.

51.   HDA, ZKRZ-GUZ, 2235/45 box 10, sample contract between the NDH Government and the physicians. Dr. Teodor Gruner's contract, June 26, 1941. Each employment contract (*Ugovor službe*) bore three signatures, those of the physician as employee, the government administrator, and the minister of health as the employer.

52.   HDA, RUR 252, 28601, ŽO, 38245, "Dr. Najfeld's " contract of employment. HDA, RUR 252, 28601, ŽO 8245, instructions for departure, November, 4, 1941.

53.   HDA, RUR 252, 28929658, ŽO 8, November 10, 1941.

54.   HDA, ZKRZ GUZ, 2235-45/2 box 10, Dr. Gruner's contract DDXXXVII-2115-Z; legal decrees of December 1941.

55.   HDA, RUR 252, 29184, ŽO 3379. Physicians, who were recruited to serve in the home-defense army (*Domobranstvo*), had similar privileges as did the engineers. See document: HDA, RUR 252 29904, ŽO, 5421, Zagreb, September 15, 1942.

56.   USHMM, 1998.A.0024, Reel 4, documents, 586-587. In testimony before the National Commission on March 19, 1946, Dr. Bela Hochstader described his capture in June 1941 in Zagreb and subsequent detention in the concentration camp on the Island of Pag. Among the few to survive, he was transferred to Jasenovac. Due to the Institute's efforts, he was released in June 1942, and immediately joined his colleagues in Bosnia.

57.   HDA, RUR 252, #28810, ŽO 1071, 26.01.1942. This subject merits further research in the military files, as does the number of Jewish engineers in the home-defense force.

58.   HDA, RUR 252, 29184 ZO.3379; HDA, RUR 252, 29790 ZO.5071; HDA, RUR 252, 28017 ZO.4143. Most of the letters in these files were from physicians requesting the release of family members from concentration camps. Other documents inform wives of their husbands' release.

59.   I want to thank Dr. Gruner for letting me see his own copy of *Vjesnik*. The Zagreb physicians were unaware that the program had been extended to include physicians from other parts of Croatia. Very few were from Bosnia-Herzegovina.

60.   *Vjesnik*, no. 4, published by the Institute to Combat Endemic Syphilis, Banja Luka, 1942, p. 37.

61.   Dr. Teodor Gruner, interview, Zagreb, Croatia, January 14, 2003.

62.   HDA, Dotrščina. Dr. Draga Weinberg was captured in Zenica, sent to Auschwitz in 1944, and killed in 1945.

63.   HDA, RUR 252, 23 XII 1941, 28929, ŽO 2145, 5721/dr.T.1942; HDA, RUR 252, #29078, Z0 2712, 20 III 1942, # 4281-V-1/1942; HDA, RUR 252, #29184, Z0 3379, 17, IV, 1942, # 48044-Iib-1-1942.

64.   HDA, RUR 252, 29165, ŽO.334.

65.   HDA, RUR 252, 29790, ŽO.5071. These documents contain the names of 12 family members who were released at about the same time; both the individual's family members and the Institute were notified.

66.   HDA, RUR 252, 29790, ŽO 5071, July 12, 1942. In his interview, Dr. Gruner also mentioned the help of Archbishop Stepinac and the assistance of Dr. Karlo Lutelski, the son-in-law of Dido Kvaternik, head of the Ustaše Police. In fact, in appreciation of the Institute's services, Dr. Gruner received the thanks of Minister of Health Dr. Ivan Petrić, in communications to Deputy Minister Dr. Mladen Petras and to the Institute's director, Dr. Stanko Sielski.

67.   HDA, RUR 252, #29864, ŽO 5288, September 31, 1942.

68.   HDA, RUR 252 #28946, ŽO 2240, February 28, 1942.

69.   HDA, MUP 302/Inv.10154/1942 ZO. 5050.

70.   Darko Fišer, interview, Osijek, Croatia, January 21, 2003.

71.   HDA RUR 252, 29864 ŽO 5288, September 31, 1942. Dr. Heimer-Cegledi's request to release her 11-year-old niece, whose parents had died in concentration camps, was granted even though the girl was not a member of Dr. Heimer-Cegledi's immediate family.

72.   HDA, RUR 252, # 29221, ŽO 3436, April 23,1942; HDA, RUR 29592 ŽO 4463, HDA RUR 29057., ŽO2639. The request and releases were not unique events; the Institute personnel pursued every request sent to them by the physicians who worked for the Institute.

73.   HDA, RUR 252, 29790 ŽO. 5071. List of family members released from concentration camps.

74.   Dr. Teodor Gruner, private collection. Doc. # 3806-1943, signed Dr. Stanko Sielski, Director, urging him to leave his current post immediately.

75.   HDA, RUR 252, 28762 ZO749: Cantor Gruner's letter to the Ministry of Health asking about of his son. On the back of the original letter is a reply dated January 20, 1942.

76.   The HDA and the U.S. Holocaust Memorial Museum (USHMM) have many documents on this subject, but since they are organized chronologically rather than thematically it is hard to find them.

77.   Stjepan Steiner, interview, Zagreb, October 1, 2003.

78.   Ante Sorić, *Židovi na tlu Jugoslavije* (Zagreb: Muzejski prostor, 1988), 211. From May 7-13, 1943, some 4,500 Jews were deported from NDH territories to Auschwitz.

79.   Ivo Goldstein and Slavko Goldstein, *Holokaust u Zagrebu* (Zagreb: Novi Liber 2001), 215.

80.   Zdenko Lowenthal, (Levental), "Lekari na suzbijanju endemskog sifilisa u BiH, i njihovo učešće u NOB", (Physicians on a mision to aleviate syphilis in Bosnia-Herzegovina), *Zbornik* referata 11, (Beograd: statistika, naučnog društva za istoriju zdrastvene kulture Jugoslavije), 1963, 84.

81.   Samuel Daić, (Deutsch) "Jevrjski lječnici i akcija za subijene endemskog sifilisa u Bosni," Jevrejski Pregled, Beograd: 1970, 1-2.

82.   Jaša Romano, "Studies and Facts and Figures on Participation of Jews in the People's Liberation War" (*studije I grada o ucescu Jevreja u Narodnooslobodilackom Ratu*), in *Zbornik* (Belgrade: Federation of the Jewish Communities in Yugoslavia, 1973, 112-115. See also Eta Najfeld, "Sečanja iz vremena Drugog Svetskog Rata," *Jevrejski Pregled*, nos. 1-2 (1975), 6-10.

83.   Zdenko Lowenthal (Levental), "Debate," in *Jewish Resistance During the Holocaust: Proceedings of the Conference on Manifestations of Jewish Resistance, April 7-11, 1968*, eds., Yisrael Gutman and Efraim Zuroff (Jerusalem: Yad Vashem, 1971), 339.

84.   Based on my findings in the HDA and USHMM archives, 142 Jewish physicians served in the Bosnian expedition. Accepting the accuracy of these documents, Lowenthal's figures show a discrepancy of 62 physicians (or 44.8 percent).

85.   Ivo Goldstein, and Slavko Goldstein, *Holokaust u Zagreb* (Zagreb: Novi Lieber 2001), 218-219. See p. 219 for a record of all the items confiscated from Jewish medical practices.

NOTES FOR CHAPTER 4

1.   Celestin Tomić, *Prophetic Spirit of Aloysius Stepinac,* October 3, 1938, (during Lent in 1938 Stepinac spoke to a group of students from the University of Zagreb.

2.   For general background on Stepinac during the war and the postwar controversy, Ivo and Slavko Goldstein, *Holokaust u Zagrebu* (Zagreb: Novi Liber i Židovska općina, 2001), 559-578; Michael Phayer, *The Catholic Church and the Holocaust, 1930–1965* (Bloomington and Indianapolis: Indiana University Press, 2000), 31–40; Stella Alexander, *The Triple Myth: A Life of Archbishop Stepinac* (Boulder, CO: East European Monographs, 1987); Menachem Shelah, "'Christian Confrontations with the Holocaust: The Catholic Church in Croatia, the Vatican and the Murder of the Croatian Jews," *Holocaust and Genocide Studies* 4, no. 3 (1989), 323–39; Aleksa Benigar, *Alojzije Stepinac: Hrvatski kardinal* (Rome: Zajednica izdanja Ranjeni labud, 1974); Jonathan Steinberg, *All or Nothing: The Axis and the Holocaust, 1941–1943* (New York: Rutledge Taylor and Francis, 1990); Martin Mark Biondich, "Religion and Nation in Wartime Croatia: Reflections on the Ustaša Policy of Forced Religious Conversions, 1941–1942," *The Slavonic and East European Review* 83, no. 1 (2005), 71–116; Stan Granic, "Representations of the Other: The Ustaše and the Demonization of the

Croats," *Journal of Croatian Studies*, no. 34 (1998), 3–56; Ronald J. Rychlak, *Hitler, the War, and the Pope* (Columbus, MO: Genesis Press, 2000); Richard Pattee, *The Case of Cardinal Aloysius Stepinac* (Milwaukee: The Bruce Publishing Company, 1953); Vladimir Dedijer, *The Yugoslav Auschwitz and the Vatican* (Buffalo, NY: Prometheus Books, 1992).

3.   Alexander Djilas, *The Contested Country: Yugoslav Unity and Communist Revolution, 1919–1953* (Cambridge, MA: Harvard University Press, 1991), 92.

4.   Patricia A. Kluck, "Yugoslavia: A Country Study," (Washington, DC: Government Printing Office, Department of the Army, 1982), Chapter 2E, Religion.

5.   Alojzije Stepinac, *By Their Fruits You Shall Know Them* (in Croatian). (Reprint, Chicago: 1980).

6.   Jakob Blažević, *Mač a ne mir: Za pravnu sigurnost gradjana* (Sword, and not peace: for the legal security of citizens) (Zagreb: Mladost, 1980), 161. Blažević was Stepinac's chief prosecutor.

7.   Jasper Ridley, *Tito: A Biography* (Zagreb: Prometej, 2000), 302.

8.   Fikrita Jelić-Butić, "Uloga Katoličke crkve," in idem., *Ustaše i NDH, 1941–1945* (Zagreb: [publisher],1977).

9.   Neil Barnett, *Tito* (London: Haus Publishing, 2006), 79.

10.   Anthony H. O'Brien, *Archbishop Stepinac: The Man and His Case* (Westminster, MD: The Newman Bookshop, 1947), 5.

11.   Miroslav Akmadža, "The Position of the Catholic Church in Croatia, 1945–1970," *Review of Croatian History* 2, no. 1 (2006), 96.

12.   NARA, RG 59, Microfilm, 860H.00/11-2746, 10.

13.   "The Silent Voice," *Time*, February 22, 1960.

14.   NARA, (National Archive II), RG 59 [U.S. State Dept.], Lot file No. 62 D33, Legal Adviser Relating to War Crimes, Box 33, (location 250/49/25/7), 12-13.

15.   HDA, Hans Helm File, box 33-str 5-7, book XIII. The same source contains other letters indicating Stepinac's close contacts with Partisans.

16.   HDA, Hans Helm File, box 33-str 5-7, book XIII, 17–34.

17.   Jonathan Steinberg, *All or Nothing: The Axis and the Holocaust, 1941–1943* (New York: Rutledge Taylor and Francis, 1990), 80. In 1936 thousands of refugees fleeing Nazi Germany and Austria began flocking to the territories of Yugoslavia. Upon seeing their plight, Stepinac wrote a fundraising letter to his parishioners, requesting their support for the Jews and other refugees.

18.   Josip Kolanović, (Source): HDA, Roma, ASAE, AG Croazia 35:

19.   NARA, RG. 59, Microfilm 860H.404/79, telegram no. 7382, November 23, 1943. See also, RG 59 [State Dept.], Lot file no. 61 D33, Legal Adviser Relating to War Crimes, box 33, location: 250/49/25/7, 14. See also Phayer, *The Catholic Church*, 38.

20.   Hans Helm, on October 11, 1943, sent the following information to Berlin, letting his superiors know of the new and open rift between the Ustaše regime and Archbishop Stepinac. HDA, Hans Helm File, box 33-str5, book (knjiga) XIII.

21.   NARA, Microfilm 860H.40416/59, enclosure No. 181, from the American Embassy, Cairo, August 5, 1944, concerning the policy of the Catholic Church in Yugoslavia, cover page.

22.   NARA, Microfilm 860H.40416/79, enclosure No. 181. The testimony was obtained by J. Jukich, a former undersecretary for foreign affairs in the Yugoslav government.

23.   The Catholic weekly was taken over by the government when Pavelić came to power. For the English translation, see Pattee, *The Case of Cardinal Aloysius Stepinac*, 258–60.

24.   Phayer, *The Catholic Church*, 35. Because he did not mention Rapotetz, he must have obtained this information from another source.

25.   Steven K. Pavlowitch, *Unconventional Perceptions of Yugoslavia, 1940–1945* (New York: Columbia University Press, 1985). Alexander, *The Triple Myth*, 92–93, Pavlowitch conducted personal interviews with Rapotec after the war.

26.   Goda, "The Ustaše," 206. Stepinac's disappointment was understandable. Diplomatic dispatches indicate that in September 1942, at the urging of Archbishop Stepinac, Augustine Juretić, a Croatian priest, left the NDH and settled in Switzerland. Via the Vatican mail, Stepinac informed Juretić of his work on behalf of the victims.

27.   Alexander, *The Triple Myth*, 102.

28.   NARA, RG 59 [U.S. State Dept], Lot file no. 61 D33, Legal Adviser Relating to War Crimes, box 33, location: 250/49/25/7, 3.

29.   NARA, Microfilm Roll 25, 860H.404/79, enclosure 181, 2. See also Phayer, *The Catholic Church*, 38. Stepinac strongly urged his priests to refrain from taking sides in the conflict.

30.   NARA, RG 59 [State Dept.], Lot file no. 61 D33, Legal Adviser Relating to War Crimes, box 33, location: 250/49/25/7, 15.

31.   Goda, "The Ustaše," 207.

32.   NARA, (National Archives II) RG 59 [U.S. State Dept.], Lot file No. 62 D33, Legal Adviser Relating to War Crimes, box 33, (location 250/49/25/7), 12-13.

33.   NARA, Microfilm 860H.404/79, telegram no. 7382, twenty-third, Enclosure to Dispatch no. 181 from the American Embassy, Cairo, dated August 5, 1944, concerning the policy of the Catholic Church in [Croatia] Yugoslavia.

34.   Alexander, *The Triple Myth*, 82. On the criticism of papal pronouncements, see "The Catholic Episcopate," 8–10. See also, Goda, "The Ustaše," 207.

35.   NARA, RG 226, entry 210, box 94, 974345.

36.   NARA, Microfilm 860H.40416/59, enclosure No. 181, from the American Embassy, Cairo, August 5, 1944, concerning the policy of the Catholic Church in Yugoslavia, cover page.

37.   Raul Hilberg, *Perpetrators, Victims, Bystanders: the Jewish Catastrophe, 1933-1945,* (New York: Harper Perennial edition, 1993), 260.

38.   Pattee, *The Case of Cardinal Aloysius Stepinac,* 311. See also Kasche's report, Micr., T-120, Roll 5787.Frs. H302, 156–57.

39.   HDA, Ivo Politeo, file A. Stepinac, document 1026, October 26, 1941. See also, Circular Letter no. 1722a, dated February 4, 1942.

40.   HDA, Ivo Politeo, (Archbishop Stepinac file) Predmet Stepinac.

41.   Gitman, "Archbishop Alojzije Stepinac," 11. See also Benigar, *Hrvatski kardinal,* 197.

42.   O'Brien, *Archbishop Stepinac,* 15. See also, Alexander, *The Triple Myth,* 90.

43.   HDA, Kaptol, AP. sv. C, str. 711 (preslik). The letter was found among other documents left by the fleeing NDH regime in Leibnitz, a town in Austria, in 1945.

44.   *Hrvatica* 3, March 1940, Archbishop Stepinac.

45.   HDA, Ivo Politeo, file of A. Stepinac.

46.   Shomrony's testimony is in HDA, Ivo Politeo, file of A. Stepinac. Shomrony left Yugoslavia before Stepinac's trial in 1946, but he volunteered to come to Zagreb as a witness for the defense. He was urged not to come out of fear that the communist government would arrest him; in any event, his testimony would not be heard. Other émigrés who volunteered received similar advice.

47.   Štambuk-Škalić et al., *Proces Alojziju Stepincu,* 264–66.

48.   HDA, Ivo Politeo, file A. Stepinac, documents prepared for Yad Vashem. See also, O'Brien, *Archbishop Stepinac,* 19. O'Brien suggests that Stepinac strongly condemned antisemitism. See Hans Helm File. See also, Phayer, *The Catholic Church,* 85.

49.   Pattee, *The Case of Cardinal Aloysius Stepinac,* 206.

50.   HDA, MUP 3RH, I-49 and MUP RH, I-22.

51.   During the years 1941 to 1945, Stepinac stood unequivocally for the rule of law and for the God-given right of every people and every race to exist. For further information, see Ljubo Krašić, ed., *Croatian Almanac 1999, Stepinac: The Man for this Time* (Chicago: Croatian Franciscan Publications, 1999). See also, HDA, Ivo Politeo, Rezolucija Hrvatske biskupe konferencije o Židovima, Vrhovni Sud NRH stup 6/1946, 863.

52.   Hilberg, *Perpetrators, Victims, Bystanders,* 45, 261.

53.   Gitman, "A Question of Judgement." See also Krišto, *Katolička crkva,* 330, dokuments 294, 344.

54.   O'Brien, *Archbishop Stepinac,* 20.

55. Phayer, *The Catholic Church*, 32.

56. Ciano, *Diary 1937–1943*, 426.

57. *Glas koncila*, September 16, 1967, interview with Bishop Salis-Seewis.

58. William L. Shirer, *The Rise and Fall of the Third Reich, A History of Nazi Germany* (New York: Simon and Schuster, 1990), 234-235.

59. Dedijer, *The Yugoslav Auschwitz*, 313–36.

60. Pattee, *The Case of Cardinal Aloysius Stepinac*, 384–87.

61. Benigar, 428. See also Ivan Meštrović, "Stepinac, The Spiritual Hero," *Hrvatska Revia* (Buenos Aires) 6, no. 3 (1956), 201–6. Meštrović claimed that Stepinac had prepared this directive for distribution to all parishes.

62. Tomasevich, 577. On October 25, 1975, Tomasevich received an official letter to this effect from Reverend Dušan Kašić.

63. Dedijer, *The Yugoslav Auschwitz*, 313–36.

64. Gitman, "A Question of Judgment," 28–47.

65. HDA, Ivo Politeo, Stepinac file 301681, jacket 12, box 1, 21, 22: personal letter of May 22, 1941, from the archbishop of Zagreb to Minister of Internal Affairs Artuković, box 118.

66. HDA, Ivo Politeo, file Stepinac, 1172 of March 7, 1942. See also, Skalić-Štambuk, et al., *Proces Alojziju Stepincu* (Zagreb: Kršćanska sadašnjost, 1997), 162, document 6.23.1.

67. Pattee, *The Case of Cardinal Aloysius Stepinac*, 194.

68. O'Brien, *Archbishop Stepinac*, 17.

69. Tomasevich, *War and Revolution in Yugoslavia*, 555.

70. *Službene novine* (Kingdom of Yugoslavia) (London), no. 10, Nov. 24, 1942.

71. HDA, Ivo Politeo, file A. Stepinac, 332.

72. Skalić-Štambuk et al., *Proces Alojziju Stepincu*, 164, document 6.23.2. See also, Alexander, *The Triple Myth*, 88–89. Alexander argues that while Stepinac was angered and dismayed by the regime's conduct, outwardly he acted as though Pavelić had no hand in the brutalities.

73. Krišto, *Katolička crkva*, 73, document 59.

74. Židovska Opčina Zagreb (ŽOZ), *Community Books of Registered Conversions*. Ninety percent of the Jews who converted to Catholicism did so in 1938. They did not inform the Jewish Community until 1941. It is assumed that many Jews were preparing themselves for occupation of Yugoslavia.

75. Gitman interview with Nada Grgeć, December 29, 2002, Zagreb.

76. Phayer, *The Catholic Church*, 84.

77. HDA, MPB, NDH, box 15, No. 4778/41.

11

78. Ivo Politeo, HDA file A. Stepinac, documents 1183, 1197.

79. Hilberg, *Perpetrators, Victims, Bystanders,* 261.

80. John F. Morley, *Vatican Diplomacy and the Jews during the Holocaust, 1939–1943* (New York: KTAV, 1980), 161. Stepinac warned those men high in the Ustaše hierarchy who had Jewish wives—for example, Pavelić and Home Guard commander Kvaternik—that they could find themselves in the same predicament.

81. *Review of Croatian History* 2, no.1 (2006), 47–72. A similar letter was sent to the Reichsführer SS, the Chief of Police in Germany, 266–267–RSHA-Amt VI, Amt IV, Berlin: Subject: Mixed Marriages in Croatia, 25.3.1943.

82. Tomasevich, *War and Revolution in Yugoslavia,* 598–99. Abromeit dealt with Helm on these matters.

83. Facts and Views, "Eichmann Crimes in Yugoslavia", 125, 1961, 8–9.

84. Hans Helm file, Mixed Marriages, 24.3.1943, 267. HDA.

85. Phayer, *The Catholic Church,* 84.

86. HDA, Ivo Politeo, file A. Stepinac, prepared for Yad Vashem, no. 1187. See also, Krišto, *Katolička crkva,* 209, document 198, title: "Recognition for the deeds that the representatives of the Holy See and the bishops have done on behalf of the Jews of NDH." The request was made on behalf of thousands of widows and orphans.

87. Krišto, *Katolička crkva,* 242, document 231.

88. HDA, Nadbiskupski Duhovni Stol to Artuković, Zagreb, Doc 9274, July 22, 1942, and 1536/53, February 9, 1943, request for permission to provide shelter for Jewish children in Catholic orphanages.

89. HDA, Ivo Politeo documents, file Alojzije Stepinac, 1187.

90. HDA, Ivo Politeo, subject A. Stepinac, box 25, 120, document 1188.

91. HDA, Ivo Politeo, subject A. Stepinac, document 1175. See also, Skalić-Štambuk et al., *Proces Alojziju Stepincu,* 64, document 62. 23.3.

92. HDA, Ivo Politeo, A. Stepinac file, April 14, 1943, 1588/P/43-Dr.F./DA. From December 1943 to 1947, the former residents of Lavoslav Schwartz lived on church property, where the archbishop became a frequent visitor. HDA, ZKRZ-GUZ 2235/45-2, box 10, Zapisnik, Br. 1771. See also USHMM, 1998.A. 0024, Reel 4.1.

93. HDA, ZKRZ-GUZ 2235/2-45, box 10, Zapisnik, June 9, 1945, 14.

94. HDA, Ivo Politeo, file A. Stepinac. After the burial of Sabina Steiner, the Jews made a collection to honor the dead. The sum collected was donated to an orphanage as gratitude and in honor of Archbishop Stepinac.

95. Krišto, *Katolička crkva,* 300, document 291. On February 28, 1944, Chief Rabbi Herzog, on the eve of his departure from Ankara en route to Eretz, Israel, wrote two letters of gratitude that favorably mentioned Stepinac and thanked him for his activities on behalf of the Jews in Croatia, document 292.

96. Krišto, *Katolička crkva*, 298, document 287, Cardinal Maglione to Apostolic Visitor Marcone, requesting intervention on behalf of 400 Jews.

97. HDA, Ivo Politeo file, subject Alojzije Stepinac. See also, Krišto, *Katolička crkva*, 294, documents 283, 295. As discussed below, Freiberger had volunteered to be deported along with his congregation.

98. HDA, Ivo Politeo, file A. Stepinac, 356. See also, Shelah, *The Holocaust in Yugoslavia*, 292–93.

99. NARA, NARA, RG 59 [State Dept.], Lot file no. 61 D33, Legal Adviser Relating to War Crimes, box 33, location: 250/49/25/7.

100. HDA, Ivo Politeo file, subject Alojzije Stepinac. See also, Krišto, *Katolička crkva*; *Fontes: Izvori za Hrvatsku Povijest*, no. 2 (Zagreb: Hrvatski državni arhiv), 1996.

101. Ljubo Boban, *Kontroverze iz povijesti Jugoslavije*, vols. I–III (Zagreb: Globus, 1990), 431. Corroborated by the testimony of Stjepan Steiner, interview, December 16, 2002, Zagreb. Croatia.

102. Gitman, interview with Stjepan Steiner, interview, December 16, 2002, Zagreb. See also, HDA, Hans Helm, German Police Attaché, box 33, 5, book XIII.

103. Gitman, interview with Teodor Gruner, January 14, 2003, Zagreb. There are many similar stories, too many to be told in detail.

104. Gitman, interview with Olga Rajšek-Neumann, December 26, 2002, Zagreb. Danko Shtockhammer gave sworn testimony on behalf of Olga Neumann in 1998. In April 2004, Olga Rajšek-Neumann was awarded by Yad Vashem "Righteous Among the Nations." It seems strange that she was awarded, and yet the person who was responsible for the rescue was not even mentioned.

105. In an interview on April 21, 1996, with Ivan Miklenić for the periodical *Glas koncila*, Amiel Shomrony was asked, "If Archbishop Stepinac helped so many Jews, why, then, have such a small number of Jews spoken on his behalf?" He responded: "The Jews are neither united nor do they hold the same opinion about their own religion let alone about other matters…." Razgovor s dr. Amielom Shomroniyem, promicateljem istine o Kardinalu Stepincu, Kardianal Stepinac je svetac i mučnik," *Bilten* (June 1996), 44–45.

106. Olga Neumann, Yad Vashem, The Holocaust Martyr's and Heroes' Remembrance Authority, file 9848a.

107. Barnett, *Tito*, 79.

108. Vladko Maček, "Kardinal Stepinac i 'nasilno prekrštavanje pravoslavnih'," *Hrvatski glas* (Croatian voice), Winnipeg, Canada, March 16, 1953.

109. Goda, "The Ustaše," 205.

110. Ivo and Slavko Goldstein, *Holokaust u Zagrebu* (Zagreb: Novi Liber i Židovska općina, 2001).

111. Phayer, *The Catholic Church and the Holocaust, 1930–1965*, 31-40.

112. Goldstein, 560-561.

113. Ibid., 564.

114. Ibid., 567.

115. See below.

116. Goda, "The Ustaše," 205. See also Alexander, *The Triple Myth*, 82.

117. Phayer, *The Catholic Church*, 35.

118. Phayer, *The Catholic Church*, 46-47.

119. Ivo Goldstein wasn't born until 1958, so he had no personal experience in the war. Slavko in 1943, after the capitulation of Italy, joined the Partisans and his father was killed by the Ustaše. Catholics excoriated the book, especially regarding Stepinac.

120. Tomasevich, *War and Revolution*, 555. See Pattee, *The Case of Cardinal Aloysius Stepinac*, 258–56, and *Katolički list*, April 21, 1941, 16.

121. Menahem Shelah, "The Murder of the Croatian Jews by the Germans and their Helpers during the Second World War" (unpublished Ph.D. dissertation, Tel-Aviv University, 1980), xxxii. See in ed., *The Holocaust in Yugoslavia* (Jerusalem: Yad Vashem, 1999), 283–284.

122. Alexander, *The Triple Myth*, 3-5. See also Goldstein, 559.

123. Steinberg, *All or Nothing*, 120.

124. Gitman, "Archbishop Alojzije Stepinac," in Željko Tanjić, ed., *Stepinac, A Witness to the Truth* (Zagreb: Glas Koncila, 2008), 39–40. See also, NARA, RG 59 [U.S. State Dept.], Lot file no. 61 D33, Legal Adviser Relating to War Crimes, box 33, Enclosure no. 1 to Dispatch no. 4 from the American Consulate Zagreb, October 31, 1946, "Trial of Archbishop Stepinac and others at Zagreb." Secret: Speech of Dr. Ivo Politeo in Defense of Archbishop Stepinac before Supreme Court of Croatia on October 8, 1946, 4–5.

125. Joseph L. Lichten, "Question of Judgment: Pius XII & the Jews" (Washington, D.C.: National Catholic Welfare Conference, 1963). See also, Peter White, "An Attack on Pope Pius XII," *Jubilee* (June 1963) and Paul Duclos, *Le Vatican et la seconde guerre mondial* (Paris: Podone, 1955), 221–23.

126. Sir Alec Randall, "The Pope, the Jews, and the Nazis" (London: Catholic Truth Society, 1963), 18.

127. Tomasevich, *War and Revolution in Yugoslavia*, 552.

128. White, "An Attack on Pope Pius XII."

129. Pattee, *The Case of Cardinal Aloysius Stepinac*, 6-7.

NOTES FOR CHAPTER 5

1. Verax, "Italiani ed ebrei in Jugoslavia," *Politica Estera*, Vol. I (1944), 21-29.

2. *Relazione sull'opera svolta dal Ministero degli Affari Esteri per la tutela delle Communità Ebraiche (1938-1943)*, n.p., n.d. Archives of the Italian Foregn Ministry (hereafter AIFM).

3. Leon Poliakov and Jacques Sabille, *La condition des Juifs en France sous l'occupation italienne* (Paris: Editions Du Centre, 1955).

4. Galeazzo Ciano, *Diary 1937-1943* (New York: Enigma Books, 2002), 415. Ciano was also Mussolini's son-in-law.

5. Ibid., 417-418.

6. Ibid., 420.

7. Ibid., 426.

8. HDA, HR, 1547, *Zbirka* RSUP, "Služba državne sigurnosti" Prilike u Anektiranoj Talijanskoj Dlmaciji na granicama ove zone, 2-18.

9. Ciano, *Diary 1937-1943*, 434.

10. HDA, HR, 1547, *Zbirka* RSUP.

11. Memorandum to Ciano, November 3, 1942, AIMF.

12. Poliakov and Sabille, *Jews Under Italian Occupation*, 164: Document CXXVa–67a.

13. Testimony by Judge Srećko Bujas submitted to the National Commission, 210. HDA, ZKRZ-GUZ, 2235/2-45 box 10.

14. Daniel Carpi, "Le Toledot ha-Yehudim be-Split u-be-Sarayevo" (Te'udot Hadashot min ha-Shanim, 1941-1942). *Yalkut Moreshet*, No. 10 (1969), 109-121.

15. Daniel Carpi, "Rescue of Jews in the Italian Zone of Occupied Croatia, Rescue Attempts During the Holocaust," *Proceedings of the Second Yad Vashem International Historical Conference* (Jerusalem, 1971), 475.

16. Dr. Ante Fulgosi saved 15 Jews; for his courage he was recognized by Yad Vashem as Righteous Among the Nations.

17. Written testimony from Dr. Emil Freundlich (Nahariya, Israel, August 20, 2003) to Esther Gitman, followed by several telephone conversations.

18. HDA, ZKRZ-GUZ 2235/2-45 box 10, logbook (Zapisnik), June 9, 1945.

19. Charles W. Steckel, *Destruction and Survival* (Los Angeles: Delmar Publishing Company, Inc., 1973), 21.

20. HDA, ZKRZ-GUZ 2235/20-45, box 12, 1920.

21. HDA, ZKRZ-GUZ 2235/20-45, box 12, page 1915.

22. Milislav Ercegović, interview with Esther Gitman, Zagreb, May 27, 2003. See also the personal diary of Elvira Khon, who was one of the survivors in Dubrovnik.

23.   Ivo Herzer, interview with USHMM, Washington, D.C., September 13, 1989.

24.   Duje Bilić, testimony to the National Commission (November 20, 1945), 1211-1212. HDA, ZKR-GUZ 2235/11-45, box 11, Zapisnik. *Jews on the Island of Pag*, 24.

25.   HDA, ZKRZ-GUZ 2235/16-45, box 12.

26.   Jonathan Steinberg, *All or Nothing: The Axis and the Holocaust, 1941-1943* (New York: Rutledge Taylor and Francis Group, 1990), 7.

27.   Branko Polić, interview with Esther Gitman, Zagreb, March 23, 2003.

28.   Poliakov and Sabille, *Jews Under Italian Occupation*, 132.

29.   Zdenko Levental, ed., *Zločini Fasištčkih Okupatora i njihovih pomagača protiv Jevreja u Jugoslaviji* (Belgrade, JIM, 1952), 227. Levental mentions three exceptions. In June 12, 1942, in the Dalmatian port city of Split, a mob, which included Italian soldiers, devastated the synagogue, attacked the Jews inside, and looted sixty Jewish homes. In the coastal town of Sušak, Italian troops handed over to the Ustaše 200 Jewish refugees from Europe. And the Italian military command in Dubrovnik permitted the transport of 27 Jews to Ustaše paramilitary; subsequently they were killed.

30.   Menahem Shelah, "The Italian Rescue of Yugoslav Jews 1941-1943," in Ivo Herzer, *The Italian Refuge: Rescue of Jews During the Holocaust* (Washington, DC: The Catholic University, 1986), 205.

31.   Jonathan Steinberg, *All or Nothing*, 6-9.

32.   Hannah Arendt, *Eichmann in Jerusalem: A Report on the Banality of Evil* (New York: Penguin Books, The Viking Press, 1964), 161.

33.   Menahem Shelah, ed., *History of the Holocaust—Yugoslavia* (Jerusalem: Yad Vashem, 1990), 227.

34.   Daniel Carpi makes this point in "Rescue of Jews in the Italian Zone of Occupied Croatia: Rescue Attempts During the Holocaust." *Proceedings of the Second, Yad Vashem International Historical Conference* (Jerusalem, 1971), 466.

35.   Hans Helm File, re: Intervention on Behalf of the Jews: letter signed by Kasche sent to several entities including the RFSS-Kom. Sipo Ostufaf Heman. Kasche's letter confirms Ducci's report, p. 351, HAD.

36.   Report of the Italian Legation in Zagreb, August 6, 1942. Archives of the Italian Foreign Ministry (AIFM).

37.   Carpi, "Rescue of Jews in the Italian Zone of Occupied Croatia," 512.

38.   Poliakov and Sabille, *Jews under Italian Occupation*, 164, Document CXXVa—67a.

39.   Ibid., 142.

40.   Report by Castellani, November 18, 1942, AIFM.

41. Vera Fischer, "Kupari 1942-43," *Ha-Kol*, No. 53-54 (March-April, 1998), 16.

42. Zlata Goldstein, "Sječanjima na Kraljevicu," *Bilten*, ŽOZ, 1993.

43. No reliable or quantifiable data exists on how many Jews, out of fear of the imminent arrival of the Nazis and Ustaše, committed suicide. However, the fact that General Roatta hurried to the region confirms that the Jewish morale was low and the suicide rate high.

44. Poliakov and Sabille, *Jews under Italian Occupation*, 138-139.

45. Report signed by Kasche to the Police Attaché, HDA, Hans Helm File, 303.

46. Carpi, "Rescue of Jews in the Italian Zone of Occupied Croatia," 521.

47. To the Ministry of the Interior, USHMM, 1998.A. 0027, reel 1 file 1.

48. Jure Krišto, *Katolička Crkva i Neavisna Drežava Hrvatska, 1941–1945, Dokumenti*, (Zagreb: Hrvatski Institut za Povijest, Dom i Svjet, 1998), Documents 221 and 292, p. 229. See also Margherita Marchione, *Yours Is a Precious Witness: Memoirs of Jews and Catholics in Wartime Italy* (Mahwah, NJ: Paulist Press, 1997), 87.

49. Branko Polić, interview with Esther Gitman, Zagreb, February 22, 2003.

50. NARA, Mic., T-821, 405, 749, Roatta to the Foreign Ministry, September 22, 1942.

51. Carpi, "Rescue of Jews in the Italian Zone of Occupied Croatia," 512.

52. USHMM, 1998.A.0027 reel 1 file 1, page 3.

53. Aleksander Mošić, written testimony on Jews in the town of Korčula, submitted personally to Esther Gitman, Belgrade, August 22, 2001.

54. Dado Maestro, a written testimony, "About the Jewish Refugees in Vela Luka," (known also as Vale Grande or Big Port) 1941-1943, Kibbutz Ein Shemer, Israel 1996.

55. On Korčula, see JIM, 4560, K.24-4B-5/2; on Vela Luka, see Maestro, Vela Luka Personal Diary.

56. JIM, 4559, K24-4B-5/1.

57. HDA, ZKRZ-GUZ, 2235/2-45, Talijanska Zona. See also Branko Polić testimony, February, 22, 2003, Zagreb.

58. Contemporaneous archival lists indicate that 2,660 Jews were interned on Rab; however, postwar data indicates that they did not include the immigrants who began arriving in Yugoslavia with Hitler's rise to power. This was a result of the Italians' obfuscatory efforts to exclude post-1933 immigrants from the records. See also Hans Helm file (HDA), including a letter sent from Zagreb and dated June 10, 1943, in which Helm informed Berlin that the Italians claimed that the Jews were their prisoners of war.

59. "Židovi u logoru na otoku Rabu, žrtve fašizma i taljinskog imperialisma," 1229-1258. ZKRZ-GUZ 2235/12-45, box 11.

60. Jaša Roman, "Jevreji U Logoru na Rabu i njihovo ukjučivanje u Narodnooslobodilački rat," *Zbornik*, No. 2 (1973).

61. Renzo De Felice, *The Jews in Fascist Italy* (New (New York: Enigma Books, 2002), 428-430.

62. Carpi, "Rescue Attempts During the Holocaust," in *Proceedings of the Second Yad Vashem International Historical Conference, April 1974*, 524-525; Steinberg, *All or Nothing*, 158.

63. Ibid., 157. Rosso, as quoted in Ducci's "Verax" essay in *Politica estera*, Vol.1, no. 9 (1944), 8.

64. De Felice, *The Jews in Fascist Italy*, 431.

65. Miloš Haimović, " O razlikama u odnosu i tretmanu ustaske Nezavisne Države Hrvatske prema Jevrejima u Bosni i Hercegoving 1941–1945," *Zbornik*, Studije arhivske i memoarska gradja, Beograd, (Belgrade: Jevrejski Istoricki Musej, 1997), 199-209.

66. Emil Freundlich, written testimony (Nahariya, Israel, August 20, 2003) sent to Esther Gitman.

67. Carlo Spartaco Capogreco, "The Internment Camp of Ferramonti-Tarsia," in Ivo Herzer, ed., *The Italian Refuge: Rescue of Jews During the Holocaust* (Washington, DC: The Catholic University, 1989), 171.

68. Miriam Aviezer-Steiner (born in Zagreb), interview with Esther Gitman, Yad Vashem Office, Jerusalem, October 2, 2003.

69. De Felice, *The Jews in Fascist Italy*, 408.

70. Capogreco, "The Internment Camp of Ferramonti-Tarsia," 174.

71. Emil Freundlich (Nahariya, Israel), written testimony of August 20, 2004, sent to Esther Gitman.

72. Neli née Almoslino Bararon and Nehama Alkalaj. Isak and Regina did not remember the third woman's name. All three survived.

73. The JOINT was founded in 1914 to assist Palestinian Jews caught in the throes of World War I. The JDC began when Henry Morgenthau, the U.S. ambassador to Turkey, sought $50,000 to save Palestinian Jews under Ottoman rule from starvation.

74. Margherita Marchione, *Yours Is a Precious Witness: Memoirs of Jews and Catholics in Wartime Italy* (Mahwah, NJ: Paulist Press, 1997), 75.

75. Renzo De Felice, *The Jews in Fascist Italy* (New York: Enigma Books, 2001), 416-417.

76. De Felice, *The Jews in Fascist Italy*, 418-419.

77. Josef Indig-Ithai, "Children of Villa Emma", in Ivo Herzer, ed., *The Italian Refuge: Rescue of Jews During the Holocaust* (Washington D.C.: The Catholic University, 1989), 184-186.

78. De Felice, 417.

79. Robert Leiber, S.J., "*Pio XII e gli ebreidi Roma, 1943-1944*" (reprint), *Civilta Cattolica*,1961, I (2675), 452-455.

80. Danko Samokovlija, *Dolar Dnevno* (Beograd: Džepna Knjiga, Redakcioni Kolegij, 1956), 92.

81. Recha Freier created the idea of the Aliyath Hanoar (Youth Aliyah) in Berlin in 1933.

82. Josef Indig-Ithai, "Djeca bježe" (Children on the run), *Jevrejski Almanah* (Opština, Yugoslavia: Savez Jevrejskih, 1963-64), 129-136.

83. Lelio Vittorio Valobra, letter sent from Genoa on February 9, 1960, to Ilva Vaccari in Modena. In Yad Vashem Archive, Dalmatia M.70/107-109. This eight-page letter, written in Italian, provides a firsthand description of the "story" of the Villa Emma children.

84. Ibid., Valobra letter, 2-3.

85. Klaus Voigt, "The Children of Villa Emma," in Joshua D. Zimmerman, *Jews in Italy under Fascist and Nazi Rule, 1922-1945* (New York, Cambridge University Press, 2005), 183-198.

86. Ilva Vaccari wrote the first version of the children's story, *Villa Emma* (Modena, Istituto Della Resistenza e Provincia, 1960), 19.

87. After the war, General Pieche received the gold medal of recognition from the Union of the Jewish Communities of Italy for his rescue of the children and for his help in other matters regarding Jews in Italy and in the Italian zones of occupation. See Ilva Vaccari, *Villa Emma*, 19-20.

88. Josef Indig-Ithai, "Children of Villa Emma," in Herzer, ed., *The Italian Refuge*, 189.

89. Klaus Voigt, "The Children of Villa Emma at Nonantola," in Zimmerman, ed., *Jews under Fascist and Nazi Rule, 1922-1945*, 183-198.

90. ORT, an international Jewish organization for vocational education. (Founded in 1880 in St. Petersburg, ORT was active during World War II.) It was important that the children acquire new and practical skills.

91. Voigt, "The Children of Villa Emma at Nonantola," 183.

92. Eliezer Kaveson-Hadas, interview with Esther Gitman, Bet Zaid, near Jerusalem, September 27, 2003.

93. Josef Indig-Ithai, "Children of Villa Emma," 193-194.

94. Klaus Voit, "Jews in Italy under Fascist and Nazi Rule, 1922-1945," 193.

95. Eliezer Kaveson-Hadas, interview with Esther Gitman, Bet Zaid, near Jerusalem, September 27, 2003.

96. Josef Indig-Ithai, "Children of Villa Emma," in Ivo Herzer, *The Italian Refuge*, 201.

NOTES FOR CHAPTER 6

1.   Daniel Carpi, "Rescue of Jews in the Italian Zone of Occupied Croatia," in *Proceedings of the Second Yad Vashem International Historical Conference* (1971), 508.

2.   Vlado Strugar, *Jugoslavija 1941–1945* (Beograd: Vojnoizdavački zavod, 1969).

3.   Ante Nazor and Zoran Ladić, *History of the Croatians* (Zagreb: Multigraph, 2003), 370.

4.   NARA, Micr., T-501, Roll 268, 159.

5.   David (Dado) Maestro, Vela Luka (Vale Grande) personal diary 1941-1943 (Kibbutz Ein Shemer, Israel, 1996).

6.   HDA, ZKRZ-GUZ 2235/18/3-45, box 12, Zapisnik Zagreb, Br. 1148/45.

7.   Drago Gizdić, *Dalmacija 1943, Prilozi historije narodnooslobodilačke borbe* (Zagreb: Epoha, 1962), 762-763.

8.   Erna Gaon, interview, Zagreb, June 6, 2003.

9.   Romano, interview, Lud, near Tel-Aviv, Israel, October 4, 2003.

10.   The United Nations Relief and Rehabilitation Administration (UNRRA) was founded on November 9, 1943, with a mandate to provide aid to areas liberated from the Axis powers. The UNRRA's Welfare Division assisted governments in meeting the special needs of especially vulnerable groups of the population.

UNRRA coordinated the work of 23 separate voluntary welfare agencies, including the Joint Distribution Committee, the Organization for Rehabilitation through Training (ORT), and the Hebrew Immigrant Aid Society (HIAS). The UNRAA discontinued its operations in Europe on 30 June 1947.

11.   JM/24, Yad Vashem Archive, Bari, September 6, 1944, includes donations list from Yugoslav Jews in southern Italy to family members and friends in Lika, Kordun, Topusko, and Barnja. Most transfers were made via the offices of ZAVNOH.

12.   The situation of these refugees in Partisan-held territories is discussed later in this chapter.

13.   David S. Wyman, *The Abandonment of the Jews: America and the Holocaust, 1941–1945* (New York: Pantheon Books, 1984), 227.

14.   Mihajlo Tolnauer, interview, Zagreb, November 27, 2002.

15.   Menahem Shelah, "The Murder of the Croatian Jews by the Germans and Their Helpers during World War II," Ph.D. dissertation, Tel Aviv University, 1980, XIL. See also Shelah, "The Italian Rescue of Yugoslav Jews 1941-1943," in Ivo Herzer, ed., *The Italian Refuge: Rescue of Jews During the Holocaust* (Washington, D.C.: The Catholic University of American Press, 1986). 217.

16.   Jaša Romano, "Jevreji u loguru Na Rabu i njihove uključivanje u Narodnooslobodilački rat" (Jews in the Rab Camp and their Participation in the Liberation War), *Zbornik*, No. 2 (1973), 1-68.

17. Narcisa Krizman-Lengel, "Destiny of Jewish Survivors from the Rab Concentration Camp, 1943-1945," *Voice*: Publication of the Jewish Community in Zagreb (ŽOZ) (Fall, 1998), 66.

18. Marcus Tanner, *Croatia, a Nation in War,* (New Haven, Yale University Press, 1998) 163-165.

19. JM/24 October 31, 1943, Yad Vashem Archive. This file contains a collection of documents and articles on the rescue of Jews after Italy's capitulation. Document #1444 summarizes the "decision" reached by the National Antifascist Army for the Liberation of Croatia with the camp's Jewish representatives to evacuate the Jewish refugees from Rab island to the freed territories of Lika and Kordun.

20. Korčula's greater proximity to southern Italy allowed evacuation with or without the help of Partisans or the Allies.

21. Diary of Elvira Kohn, a photographer and journalist who was interned in the Rab camp. Her papers are now located in the Croatian History Museum in Zagreb.

22. Ivo Herzer, document received from his wife Dorothy Herzer in May 2007.

23. HDA, ZKRZ-GUZ 2235/45 Box 10, Auschwitz. In her testimony, Armuth recounted that, meeting no resistance, the Nazis encircled the island and landed at five different locations, quickly rounding up approximately 180, mainly sick and elderly, Jews. Under threat of retribution, the Nazis demanded the immediate surrender of all remaining Jews—most of whom were eventually found. Armuth's tribute to the antifascist women who supported her in Auschwitz is discussed later in this chapter.

24. Branko Polić, interview, Zagreb, February 22, 2003.

25. HDA, ZKRZ-GUZ 2235/45 Box 10, documents on the Atias family and similar stories. See Chapter 4 on the rescue of Jews by the Catholic Church.

26. Ivo Goldstein and Slavko Goldstein, *Holokaust u Zagrebu* (Zagreb: Novi Liber, 2001), 520.

27. The Jewish Partisans were dispersed into other Croatian units. Another Jewish combat unit formed as a platoon within the Montenegro Battalion of the First Prekomurje Brigade. See Aleksander Demajo, "Jevrejski vod u prvoj prekomorskoj brigadi NOVJ"), *Zbornik 7* (Belgrade: Jevrejski Istorijski Muzej- Beograd, 1997), 185-189.

28. Narcisa Krizman-Lengel, "Destiny of Jewish Survivors from the Rab Concentration Camp, 1943-1945," *Voice*, Publication of the Jewish Community in Zagreb (ŽOZ), fall (1998), 66.

29. HDA, Croatian History Museum, Zagreb, Partisans' file: unnamed newsletter published on March 7, 1945.

30. Menahem Shelah, *The Yugoslav Connection: Immigration of Jewish Refugees to Palestine through Yugoslavia, 1938- 1948* (Tel Aviv: Am Oved Publishers Ltd., 1994), 93.

31. Ibid., 92-93.

32. The Central Zionist Archive, Jerusalem, s25/242: S26/1309, 1255.

33. HDA, ZKRZ-GUZ 2235/2-45, Box 10, Zapisnik, Zagreb June 9, 1945, 14.

34. Shelah, *The Yugoslav Connection*, 111.

35. Ella Finci Koen, Erna Kaveson Debenić, Erna Gaon Latinović, interviews, Sarajevo, Bosnia-Herzegovina, Jewish Community, August 11 and 12, 2003.

36. Slavko Goldstein, interview with *Globus/Zagreb*, July 23, 1991.

37. HDA, ZKRZ-GUZ 2235/2-45, box 10, Zapisnik Zagreb.

38. Lengel-Krizman, "Organizacija i rad pokrajinskog i mjesnog odbora narodne pomoći u Zagrebu: 1941-1942, (1941–1945, Sjeverozapadna Hrvatska u NOB, (Zagreb, 1984), 22, 129-130.

39. Menahem Shelah, "Final Solution" Ph.D. dissertation, Tel-Aviv University, 1980, 313-315.

40. JM/24, Yad Vashem Archive, Bari August 2, 1944.

41. Wyman, *The Abandonment of the Jews*, 294.

42. JIM, Inv. # 3225. K-38.

43. Shelah, *The Murder of the Croatian Jews by the Germans and their Helpers*, 359-361. Shelah suggests that local Partisans did not welcome Jewish paratroopers from Kibbutz Gat in Palestine in 1944.

44. Shelah, *The Yugoslav Connection: Immigration of Jewish Refugees to Palestine through Yugoslavia, 1938- 1948* (Tel Aviv: Am Oved Publishers Ltd 1994), 91.

45. JIM, ZAVNOH, Inv. # 3225, K-38, March 4, 1944, Inv. # 3227, K-38, March 5, 1944.

46. Hinko Gottlieb, "His Ways and Writings" Book I (Tel-Aviv: 1980), 132.

47. Narcisa Krizman-Lengel, "Destiny of Jewish Survivors from the Rab Concentration Camp, 1943-1945," *Voice*, publication of the Jewish Community in Zagreb (ŽOZ), (Fall, 1998), 66.

48. ZAVNOH, Inv. # 3399, K-39, 3358, K39, September 3, 1944, 3533, K-41.

49. JIM, ZAVNOH, Inv. # 3412, K-40, October 10, 1944.

50. JIM, ZAVNOH, Inv. # 3271, K-38, July 7, 1944.

51. Vladimir Velebit, interview, February 4, 2003, Zagreb. See also, JIM, ZAVNOH, Inv. # 3412, K-40, October 10, 1944.

52. Historical Archive of the Jewish People, Jerusalem; File: Jews and Partisans, 14/153.

53. JM 24, Yad Vashem Archive, collection of letters and documents from the Zemaljsko Antifasisticko Vijece, Narodnog Oslobodjenja Hrvatske, ZAVNOH 3.VI.1944.

54. HDA, ZAVNOH, Predsjednistvo Br. 596, July 8, 1944.

55. Shelah, *The Yugoslav Connection*, 95.

56. Letter of July 12, 1944, Inv. # 1132, Croatian History Museum (Muzej Narodne Revolucije). From Bari, Edholm sent a second, similar letter (Inv. # 1130) to an unidentified recipient on August 15, 1944; marked "Top Secret," the letter describes the quantities of wheat that would be shipped once the German retreated from their territories.

57. JM/24, Yad Vashem Archive, Spisak.

58. Wyman, *The Abandonment of the Jews*, 339.

59. *Haaretz* (Tel-Aviv daily newspaper), May 17, 1939, 1-2.

60. Shabtai Teveth, *Ben-Gurion and the Palestinian Arabs: From Peace to War* (New York: Oxford University Press, 1985), 193-194.

61. JM/24, Yad Vashem Archive, letter of September 3, 1944, from Gregorić in Pajo to Gottlib.

62. The Central Zionist Archive, Jerusalem, s25/242.

63. PRO, WO 202/294 104438.

64. Shelah, *The Yugoslav Connection*, 95-96.

65. PRO, WO 202/294, Minutes, December 17, 1944.

66. JM/24, Yad Vashem Archive, letter of June 22, 1944, from Hinko Gottlieb to the representatives of ZAVNOH. See also document 3484, K-40, to the local commander, describing four planeloads of clothing and other items from the Allies to be distributed among the neediest Jews.

67. Charles Steckel, *Destruction and Survival* (Los Angles: Delmar Publishing Company, Inc., 1973), 19.

68. David S. Wyman, *Abandonment of the Jews: America and the Holocaust, 1941–1945* (New York: Pantheon Books, 1984), 268-285.

69. Federal Register, 1/26/44, 935, United States Holocaust Memorial Museum, The War Refugee Board, *The Holocaust Encyclopedia*, http>// www. USHMM.org/ Module=1005143. Access on May 16, 2010.

70. HDA, ZKRZ-GUZ, HR, Zagreb 1547 Zbrika, RSUP, Sluzba drzavne sigurnost. Br. 63/42.B.B. *Top Secret* Report from the NDH Ambassador to Romania's Minister of Foreign Affairs, Mladen Lorković, covering the period October11-18, 1942, regarding pressure from the U.S. government and the Vatican to stop immediately the deportation of Jews.

71. David, S. Wyman, *The Abandonment of the Jews, America and the Holocaust, 1941–1945*, (New York: Pantheon Books), 285.

72. Yehuda Bauer, *American Jewry and the Holocaust: The American Jewish Joint Distribution Committee, 1939–1945* (Detroit: Wayne State University Press, 1981), 405-408.

73.   Shelah, *The Yugoslav Connection*, 102.

74.   JM/24, Yad Vashem Archive, ZAVNOH, Inv. # 3484, K-40, November 11, 1944.

75.   On April 23, 1944, Grafton's column appeared in both the *New York Times* and the *New York Post*.

76.   Wyman, *The Abandonment of the Jews*, 263-264.

77.   Ruth Gruber, *Haven: The Unknown Story of 1000 World War II Refugees* (New York: Signet Book, 1984), 106-107.

78.   Luna Kabiljo-Kahana, interview, October 14, 2003, Haifa, Israel.

79.   Gruber, 117-122.

80.   More than a third (nearly 37 percent) of the refugees came from Yugoslavian territory, most of them from Croatia and Bosnia-Herzegovina.

81.   Wyman, *The Abandonment of the Jews*, 272.

82.   Ibid., 403.

83.   Charles Jr. Mee, *Meeting at Potsdam* (New York: M. Evans and Company, 1975), 146-147.

84.   Life for Jews in postwar Yugoslavia was not much better than under Nazism. Thus, when an opportunity arose, 1,600 of the survivors from Sarajevo left for Israel.

85.   Isak Samokovlija, *Tales of Old Sarajevo* (Portland, OR: Vallentine Mitchell & Co. Ltd., 1997). Samokovlija dedicated this book to the community of Sephardic Jews of Bosnia who disappeared in the Holocaust and who now live only in his stories.

NOTES FOR CHAPTER 7

1.   HDA, ZKRZ-GUZ, 2235/2-45, box 10, 210.

2.   HDA, ZKRZ-GUZ 2235/2-45, box 10, 12-13.

3.   HDA, ZKRZ-GUZ 2235/2-45, box 10, 251-252.

4.   Vedran Deletis, interview, New York City, November 11, 2005. On that same day Vedran called his father who still lived in Tuzla and I had the opportunity to thank him for his selfless pursuit of justice and humanity.

5.   Ratimir Deletis, "Righteous Among the Nations," May 12, 1989, file 3859.

6.   Charles Steckel, *Destruction and Survival* (Los Angeles: Delmar Publishing Company, Inc., 1973), 36, 42-43.

7.   Nahum Goldmann, "The Influence of the Holocaust on the Change in the Attitude of World Jewry to Zionism and the State of Israel," in Yad Vashem *Holocaust and Rebirth, Symposium*, (Jerusalem, Yad Vashem, 1974), 84.

8.   Dr. Vera Oberiter, interview, Zagreb, November 21, 2002.

Bibliography

PRIMARY SOURCES

I. **Hrvatki Državni Arhiv (HDA), Croatian National Archive.**

    1. Archive Hans Helm box 34: Helm, Hans, (In Hans Helm Archive, stored in the Croatian National Archive HDA are found 107 pages of Jews. Among the non-Jews Archbishop Stepinac is mentioned as "Jew Lover" see pages 22, 31, 63, 77, and 87). It also lists Jewish activists who were transporting Jews and information outside Croatia; to the Partisans and British forces, see pages: 130, 136, 137, 189, 192, 207, 208, 261, 262, 300, 361x5, 375, 414, 467,476, 481, 488, 521x 3, 525, 541, 544, 546x 3, 550, 562, and 611.

        Book XIV; Hans Helm, after the liberation of Croatia surrendered it to the Partisans. Box 36 code 341-IV/14 from 1943 through 1944. Content; Četniks in NDH, Activities of NOP, Partisans in NDH, Problem of Jews.

        Hans Helm's notebook Mixed Marriages. Approx. 840 names including Pavelić, p. 114, 222-228, 233, 235, 236, 237-242, 245, 249-255, 256-260, 266-267 (Stepinac) 269-173, 277-280, 281-287, 288-293, 294-297, 298, 301, 302, 303, 305-307, 309-313, 318-320, 324, 328-329, 339, 344, 346-348, 350-352, 354-357, 358-362.

    2. Ustaša Surveillance Services (UNS), Jewish Section Administration of the Detention center—Zagreb (1941–1943); 1941–1943: 5 boxes, approx. 5, 000 pages.

    3. Service Directorate of the Ustaša Constabulary, Constabulary—Jewish Section Zagreb, 1941-1942: 10 boxes, 13,500 items.

    4. Branch-Office in Zagreb—Jewish Section (1941–1942); 1941-1942: 8 boxes, 4,220.

    5. Ministry of the Interior of the Independent State of Croatia Directorate For Public Order and Security —Jewish Section (MUP NDH) Zagreb (1942-1945); 2 boxes, 1,950 pages.

    6. Ministry of Health and Social Services. Directorate for Social Service and Welfare (MU)—Zagreb (1941–1945); 24 boxes, about 23,000 pages. (Approximately 5 percent of this material relates to Jewish issues).

7. Ministry of State Treasury. Department of State Property, misappropriations and Debts Office for Nationalized Property (PONOVA) Zagreb (1941–1945); 751 shelves, about 720,000 pages. (Approximately 50 percent of the material relates to Jewish issues).

8. People's Republic of Croatia, Croatian National Committee for Ascertainment of the Crimes Committed by Occupying Forces and Their Collaborators. (ZKRZ) (1944-1947); total 18 boxes. 9 pertain to Jews and 9 list victims according to the site of crime.

9. Dr. Samuel Pinto, Sarajevo, zločini, okupatora i njihovih pomagaća izveršeni nad Jevrejima u Bosni i Herzegovini, 1946. HDA, ZKRZ-GUZ 2235-2/45, Ministry of the Interior of the People's Republic of Croatia (MUP NRH) Zagreb (1945- 1953); 4 boxes, 2,500 pages.

10. Public Prosecutor's Office of the People's Republic of Croatia–Zagreb (1945-1953); 8 boxes, Indictments: Pavelić-Artuković.

11. History of the Workers' Movement in Zagreb (Zb. PRP) (1945-1950); 24 boxes. (Approx. 45 percent of the archival material relates to the Jews).

12. Documents compiled by the Anti-Fascist Partisan Movement, the Anti-Fascist Council of National Liberation of Croatia (ZAVNOH).

13. Dotrščina lists WWII Zagreb Jews victims 6,537. 154. Ivo Politeo; Indictments of Archbishop Stepinac. Stepinac file, April 14, 1943, 1588/P/43-Dr.F./DA.

14. HDA, Nadbiskupski Duhovni Stol, Catholic Church), Zagreb, Doc 9274, July 1942 and 1536/53, February 9, 1943, request permission to provide shelter for Jewish children in Catholic orphanages.

II. **Državni Arhiv u Zagrebu: State Archive, Zagreb Gradsko poglavarstvo Stambeni ured u Zagrebu (GPSUZ).**

III. **Arhiv Instituta za suvremenu povijest, Zagreb.**

Jareb, Jere, *Državno gospodarstvo povjerenstvo, Nezavisna Države Hrvatske od kolovoza 1941 do travnja 1945. Dokument prikaz*, Dom i Svijet, Zagreb, 2001.

Krišto, Jure, *Katolička Crkva i Nezavisna Država Hrvatska 1941–1945, Dokumenti 1941–1945, Dokumenti*, Hrvatski Institut za Povijest, Dom i Svijet, Zagreb, 1998.

IV. **Arhiv ŽOZ, Archives of the Jewish Community in Zagreb.**

WWII Victims of the Holocaust in Croatia, Zagreb 1946.

Converts to other Religions 1941, Two volumes of converts to Roman Catholicism and 17 names to Islam.

Book of Contributions (Book of the so-called voluntary contributions).

Book of Hevra Kadisa (Burrial Society).

V. **Jevrejski istorijski muzej (JIM) Beograd. (Jewish Historical Museum, Belgrade).**

Jewish Community of Zagreb. (Jewish Community Zagreb).

Files of the inernees in Korcula and Vela Luka 4559 K.24-4 B-5, 4560 K.24-4B-52.

VI. **Sarajevo Jewish Community, Sarajevo, Bosnia-Herzegovina.**

File cards recorded by the survivors upon their return to Sarajevo, 1945-1952.

File, Sarajevo Osijek correspondence prepared by Drs. Pinto Avram and Pinto David.

VII. **Yad Vashem Archives, Jerusalem, Israel.**

1. Italian Foreign Ministry in Croatia: JMO.10 file 1222, 218642. Verax, (Roberto Ducci), "Italiani ed ebrei in Jugoslavia", Politica Estera, I 1944), 21-29.

2. Lelio Vittorio Valobra, Head of DELASEM Genova. On February 1960 the archive sent 8 page summary to Ilva Vaccari regarding the rescue of the children known as the "Villa Emma Children". (See Appendix 7.5.)

3. Dalmatia: M.70/107-109.

4. Dubrovnik: JM/1197 Jewish Assets: 0.10/24-25; 83; 130-149;14; 70/11;53;97;109.

5. DELASM: 0.10/87; 69; 71.

VIII. **The Central Zionist Archive, Jerusalem, s25/242.**

IX. **U.S. Holocaust Memorial Museum, (microfilms, all reels and files).**

1995A

1997A

1998A

1999A

X. **NARA: National Archives and Records Administration.**

NARA, National Archives II, (NACP) RG 59 [State Dept.], Lot file No. 61 D33, box 33, (location 250/49/25/7). Declassified, NND8 97219, NARA 1/23/08.

NARA, (National Archives II) RG 59 [U.S. State Dept.], Lot file No. 62 D33, box 33, (location 250/49/25/7), 12-13.

NARA, 860H.4016/63, 1686, May 2, 1941 to Secretary of State, Washington.

NARA, 860H.4016/64, American Consulate, Zagreb, June 13, 1941, No.546.

NARA, 860H.4016/64, PS/RJH Persecution of Jews in Croatia, June 13, 1941.

NARA, DGFP, D, 12, Minutes of Hitler's talks with Pavelić, June 6, 1941, (Chronicles Online, April 21, 2000).

NARA, RG 59 [U.S. State Dept.], Lot file No 61 D33, Legal Adviser Relating to War Crimes, box 33. Enclosure No. 1 to Dispatch No. 4 from American Consulate Zagreb, October 31, 1946, entitled "Trial of Archbishop Stepinac and others at Zagreb". Secret: Speech of Dr. Ivo Politeo in Defense of Archbishop Stepinac before Supreme Court of Croatia on October 8, 1946, 4-5.

XI. Croatian Daily and Weekly Newspapers.

Hrvatska Gruda, Zagreb 1936, 1940-1945.

Hrvatska straža, tjednik za katolički dom, Zagreb 1933-1943.

Hrvatski dnevnik, Zagreb 1936-1941.

Hrvatski list, 1920-1945.

Hrvatski narod, glasilo hrvatskog ustaškog pokreta, Zagreb 1939-1945.

Hrvatski radnik, Zagreb 1936-1945.

Katolicki list, Zagreb 1849-1945.

Narodne novine, Zagreb 1941–1945.

Židov, (Jew) 1917-1941

Jevrejski glas, (Jewish Voice) 1928-1941.

Jevrejski List. Zagreb, 1934.

Narodna Židovska Svijest. (National Jewish Conscience). Weekly. Sarajevo, 1924-1928.

XII. Israeli News Papers (Palestine 1943-1945).

Davar

Haaretz

Jewish Agency Report (s)

XIII. Interview of Rescuers and Survivors 2002-2010.

Name:	Date of interview	Place of interview
1. Papo Lotika	08. 11. 2003	Sarajevo
2. Papo Laura	08. 11. 2003	Sarajevo
3. Koen- Finci Ela	08. 12. 2003	Sarajevo
4. Erna Debenić-Kaveson	08. 13. 2003	Sarajevo
5. Nikolić Danilo	08. 14. 2003	Sarajevo
6. Albahari Moric	08. 13. 2003	Sarajevo
7. Papo Suada Dada	08. 10. 2003	Sarajevo
8. Danon Jakica	08. 14. 2003	Sarajevo

9. Greta Ferušić	08. 11. 2003	Sarajevo
10. David Kamhi	09. 05. 2001	Sarajevo
11. Jakov Finzi	09. 05. 2001	Sarajevo

1. Eva Nahir Panić	10. 06. 2003	Israel
2. Dr. Shomrony Amiel (Emil Schwarz)	10. 11. 2003	Israel
3. Zlata Romano	10. 04. 2003	Israel
4. Eliezer Hadas-Kaveson	10. 06. 2003	Israel
5. Sharika Stern-Kaveson	09. 27. 2003	Israel
6. Zdenka Novak- Steiner	10. 14. 2003	Israel
7. Dr. Emil Freundlich, (witten test.)	11. 20. 2003	Israel
8. Luna Kahana-Kabiljo	10. 14. 2003	Israel
9. Kabiljo Itzhak (Izika)		

1. Erna Gaon		
2. Montiljo (Mišo) Mihael	09. 11. 2002	Zagreb
3. Dr. Oberiter Vera	11. 21. 2002	Zagreb
4. Mihajlo Tolnauer	11. 11. 2002	Zagreb
5. Mari Radinger	11. 27. 2002	Zagreb
6. Jasa Binenfeld	12. 05. 2002	Zagreb
7. Dr. Stjepan Steiner	01. 10. 2003	Zagreb
8. Dr. Teodor Gruner	01. 16. 2003	Zagreb
9. Olga Neumann	01. 16. 2003	Zagreb
10. Nada Grgec	01. 06. 2003	Zagreb
11. Zdenko Sternberg,	01. 01. 2003	Zagreb
12. Dr. Matilda Gruner (taped-testimony)	05. 12. 2003	Zagreb
13. Jaska Kalodjera	01. 23. 2003	Zagreb
14. Žuži Jelinek	01. 18. 2003	Zagreb
15. Dr. Darko Fischer	01. 23. 2003	Osijek
16. Blanka Auslander (taped testimony)	04. 06. 2003	Zagreb
17. Eva Grlić-Izrael	06. 15. 2003	Zagreb
18. Papo Nada (written testimony)	03. 30. 1995	Zagreb
19. Mladen Čaldarović	10. 20. 2003	Zagreb
20. Ljerka Rajić	09. 28. 2003	Zagreb
21. Lucja Benyovsky	07. 10. 2003	Zagreb

22. Slavko Goldstein	09. 19. 2003	Zagreb
23. Vlasta Kovač	02. 06. 2003	Zagreb
24. Dr. Žarko Stern	02. 06. 2003	Zagreb
25. Zora Dirnbach	02. 06. 2003	Zagreb
26. Regina Kamhi	10. 10. 2002	Zagreb
27. Glik Zlatko	02. 11. 2003	Zagreb.
28. Ljerka Auferber	02. 20. 2003	Zagreb
29. Dr. Ivan Antunac	02. 12. 2003	Zagreb
30. Alfonso Kabiljo, (Alfi)	02. 20. 2003	Zagreb
31. Branko Polić	02. 22. 2003	Zagreb
32. Dr. Ante Fulgozi	03. 03. 2003	Zagreb
33. Berger, Tuković, Branka	03. 03. 2003	Zagreb
34. Berger, Tuković, Lea	03. 03. 2003	Zagreb
35. Dr. Vladimir Velebit	04. 02. 2003	Zagreb
36. Mislav Ercegović	05. 28. 2003	Zagreb
37. Vesna Domani-Hardi	08. 03. 2003	Zagreb
38. Lili Kraus	02. 27. 2003	Zagreb

Serbia

1. Aleksander Mošić	08. 22. 2001	Belgrade
2. Eta Najfeld	08. 20. 2001	Belgrade

United States

1. Isak Danon	05. 21. 2007	Washington, D.C.
2. Dora Klayman	06. 19. 2007	Washington, D.C.
3. Flori Jagoda	06. 21. 2007	Washington, D.C.
4. Berry Berkić	07. 04. 2007	Washington, D.C.
5. Ayana Tuval	06. 20. 2007	Washington, D.C.
6. Miriam Gery-Mayer	06. 20. 2007	Washington, D.C.

Secondary Sources

Alexander, Stella. *The Triple Myth—A Life of Archbishop Alojzije Stepinac*, East European Monograph, New York: Boulder, Distributed by Columbia University Press, 1987.

Andrić, Ivo. *Bosnian Chronicle*, London: The Harvill Press, London edi., 1992.

_____.*The Bridge Over the Drina*, London: The Harvill Press, London edi., 1995.

Arendt, Hanna. *Eichmann in Jerusalem*, New York: Penguin Books, The Viking Press, 1963.

Auty, Phyllis. "Some Aspects of British-Yugoslav Relations in 1941" (In Vasa Cubrilovic, ed., *Ustanak u Jugoslaviji 1941 godine i Evropa* (The uprising inYugoslavia in 1941 and Europe), Belgrade, 1973.

Badoglio, Pietro. *Italy in the Second World War*. London, 1948.

Banac, Ivo. *The National Question in Yugoslavia, Origins, History, Politics*. Ithaca: Cornell University Press, 1984.

Banović, Branimir. "The Export of Labor and the Deportation of People from the Territory of the Independent State of Croatia in the Course of the Second World War" (in Serbo-Croatian), Putovi revolucije, Zagreb, 1963.

Barbić, Ivo. *"Teror nad Židovima u Slavoniji za vrijeme II svjetskog rata,"* in *Zbornik Centra za društvena istraživanja Slavonje i Baranje*, Zagreb: 1/1984, 363-364.

Barnett, Neil. *Tito*, London: Haus Publishing, 2006.

Bauer, Yeuda. *American Jewry and the Holocaust. American Jewish Joint Distribution Committee, 1939-1945*, Detroit: Wayne State University Press 1982.

_____. *Flight and Rescue*, Random House, New York, 1970.

_____. *The Holocaust in Historical Perspective*, University of Washington, Seattle, 1978.

_____. *Out of the Ashes*, Pergamon, Oxford, 1989.

_____ . *Rethinking the Holocaust*, New Haven: Yale University Press, 2002.

Bein, Alex. "On the Future of Our Past," lecture at the Third Congress of Jewish Studies, 27.7.1961, Jerusalem: published in Jerusalem, 1963, by the State Archive.

Benigar, O. *Aleksa. Alojzije Stepinac Hrvatski Kardinal*, Čakovec:Hrvatska Tiskara Zrinski, 1993.

Berenbaum, Michael. ed., *A Mosaic of Victims: Non-Jews Persecuted and Murdered by the Nazis*, New York. 1990, 64-73)

_____. "Germans and Serbs: The Emergence of Nazi Antipartisan Policies in 1941."

Bilandžić, D. *Hrvatska moderna povijest*. Zagreb: Golden Marketing , 1999.

Browning, Christopher R. *Ordinary Men, Reserve Police Battalion 101 and the Final Solution in Poland*, New York: Harper Perennial A Division of HarperCollins Publishers Aaron Asher Books, 1992.

Burgwyn, James H. *Empire on the Adriatic, Mussolini's Conquest of Yugoslavia, 1941-1943*, New York: Enigma Books, 2005.

Butić-Jelić, Fikreta. *Ustaše i Nezavisna Država Hrvatska*, Zagreb: Sveučilišna Naklada Liber, 1977.

Capogreco, Carlo S. "The Interment Camp Ferramonti- Tarsia," in Herzer, Ivo ed., *The Italian Refuge*, Washington D.C.: The Catholic University of American Press 1989.

Carpi, Daniel. "The Diplomatic Negotiations Regarding the Transfer of Jewish Children from Croatia to Turkey and Eretz Israel in the Year 1943," (XII) of Yad Vashem Studies, 1977.

_____. *Between Mussolini and Hitler, The Jews and the Italian Authorities In France and Tunisia*, Hanover: Brandeis University Press, 1994.

_____. "The Rescue of Jews in the Italian Zone of Occupied Croatia," Gutman, ed., Rescue Attempts during the Holocaust. Proceedings of the Second Yad Vashem International Historical Conference, Jerusalem, 1977.

Čengić, Esad, "Sarajevski Jevreji, *Zbornik 4*, Beograd: JIM, 1979, 223-240.

Ciano, Galeazzo. *Diary 1937-1943*, New York: Enigma Books, 2002.

Cornwell, John. *Hitler's Pope: The Secret History of Pius XII*, New York: Viking, 1999.

Čulinović, Fredo. *Jugoslavia izmedju dva rata*, Zagreb: JAZU 1961, Vol. I. 149.

Danon, Cadik (Braco) I., *The Smell of Human Flesh, A Witness of the Holocaust, Memoiries of Jasenovac*, Belgrade: Slobodan Mašić Publishing House, 2002.

Dawidowicz, Lucy S. *The War Against the Jews 1933-1945*, New York: Holt, Rinehart and Winston of Canada, 1975.

Dedijer, Vladimir. *The Yugoslav Auschwitz and the Vatican: The Croatian Massacre of the Serbs during World War II*, Buffalo: Prometheus Books, Ahriman-Verlag, 1992.

Dinnerstein, Leonard. *America and the Suroivors of the Holocaust*. New York: Columbia University Press, 1982.

De Felice, Renzo. *The Jews in Fascist Italy*, New York: Enigma Books, 2001.

Despot, Zvonimir. "Župnik koji je spašavo Židove" je Mijo Seleć, Zagreb; *Vjesnik, Večerni list*, 10.6. 1997.

Djilas, Aleksa. *The Contested Country: Yugoslav Unity and Communist Revolution, 1919-1953*, Cambridge: Harvard University Press, 1991.

Djodan, Šime. *Ekonomska Politika Jugoslavije*, Zagreb: Školska knjiga, 1970.

Domaš, Jasminka. ed. *Family*, Vienna: Kroatisches Kultur-und dokumentationszentrum, A-7000 Eisenstadt, J. Permayerstr. 9/3, 2002. (English version).

Eventov, Yakir. *A History of Yugoslav Jews, From Ancient Times to the End of the 19th Century*, Tel-Aviv: Printed in Israel by "Davar", 1971.

Falconi, Carlo. *Il silenzio di Pio XII*. Milan, 1965.

Feingold, Henry, L. *Bearing Witness: How America and Its Jews Responded to the Holocaust,* Syracuse, NY: Syracuse University Press, 1995.

_____. *The Politics of Rescue, The Roosevelt Administration, 1939-1945,* New Brunswick: Rugers University Press, 1970.

Feldman, Gerald, D. *Allianz and the German Insurance Business, 1933-1945,* Cambridge, United Kingdom, Cambridge University Press, 2001.

Frankel, Jonathan, ed. *The Fate of the European Jews.* Studies in Contemporary Jewry. Vol. 15, Oxford University Press, New York. 1997.

Freidenreich-Pass, Harriet. Belgrade, Zagreb, Sarajevo, *A Study of Jeiwsh Communities in Yugoslavia Before WWII,* New York: Columbia University, 1973.

_____. *The Jews of Yugoslavia, A Quest for Community,* Philadelphia 1979.

Friedlander, Saul. *Nazi Germany and the Jews, The Years of Persecutions, 1933-1939,* New York, Harper Collins Publishers, 1997.

Goda, Norman, J. W. "The Ustaše: Murder and Espionage" in *U.S. Intelligence and the Nazis,* ed. Breitman, Richard, Goda, Norman J. W., Timothy Naftali, and Robert Wol, New York: Cambridge University Press, 2005.

Goldberger, Leo. "Denmark's Good Deed" New York: Museum of Jewish Heritage, NYC Conference on Rescue of European Jews, March 11, 2004.

Gilbert, Martin. *The Holocaust: A History of the Jews of Europe during the Second World War,* New York: Holt, Rinehart and Winston 1985.

_____. *The Righteous, The Unsung heroes of the Holocaust,* New York: Henry Holt and Company, 2003.

Gitman, Esther. "Archbishop Alojzije Stepinac, 1941–1945, Under the Lens of Historians and Diplomats." In Željko Tanjić, ed., *Stepinac, A Witness to the Truth,* (A Collection of Papers from the International Conference), Zagreb: Glas Koncila, 2008.

_____. "The Rescue of Jewish Physicians in the Independent State of Croatia (NDH), 1941–1945" in *Holocaust and Genocide Studies*: Oxford University Press in association with the United States Holocaust Memorial Museum, Vol. 20, number 3,2006, 76-91.

_____. "A Question of Judgment: Dr. Alojzije Stepinac and the Jews," in *Review of Croatian History,* Zagreb: *Hrvatski institute za povijest,* Croatian Institute of History II. No.1 2006.

Goldhagen, Daniel Jonah. *Hitler's Willing Executioners, Ordinary Germans and the Holocaust,* New York: Alfred A., Knoph, 1996.

Goldstein, Ivo and Goldstein, Slavko. *Holokaust u Zagrebu,* (Holocaust in Zagreb), Zagreb: Novi Liber, Židovska Općina Zagreb, 2001.

Goldstein, Ivo. "*Memorija i obitelj u povijesti*", *Obitelj (Family),* Zgreb: Novi Liber 2003.

_____. "Stjepan Radić i Židovi," *Radovi* ZHP 29, Zagreb 1996, 208-216.

_____. "The Genocide of the Jews in the Independent State of Croatia," Zagreb: *Vjesnik*, 1996, 30-35.

Goldstein, Slavko. "Beatifikacija kardinala Alojzija Stepinca," *Ha-kol* 55-56/1998, 15-16.

_____."Iskustva holokausta u Hrvatskoj," Bilten, Zagreb: ŽOŽ 28-29/1993, 4-5.

Gottlieb, Hinko. "Kaddish in the Serbian Forest-The Massacre of European Jewry": *An Antology*, Israel: Kibbutz Merchavia, 1963.

Aly Gotz and Heim Susanne. *Architects of Annihilation, Auschwitz and the Logic of Destruction*, Princeton: Princeton University Press, 2002.

Gruber, Ruth. *Haven, The Unkonwn Story of 1000 World War II Refugees*, New York: Signet Books, 1984.

Gutman, Yisreal, Arad, Yitzhak, and Margaliot, Avraham. "Documents on the Holocaust," Jerusalem: Yad Vashem, 1981.

Herzer, Ivo. ed. *The Italian Refuge, Rescue of Jews During the Holocaust*, Washington D.C.: The Catholic University of America Press, 1986.

Hilberg, Raul. *The Destruction of the European Jews*, New York: Holmes & Meier Publishers, Inc.,1985.

_____. *The Politics of Memory: the Journey of a Holocaust Historian*, Chicago: van R. Dee, 1996.

_____. *Perpetrators, Victims, Bystanders: The Jewish Catastrophe*, New York: Aaron Asher Books, HarperCollins, 1993.

Hughes, S. H. *Prisoners of Hope, The Silver Age of the Italian Jews 1924-1974*, Carmbridge: MA, Harvard University Press, 1996.

Isaić, Vladimir. "Časno djelo sestara franjevki na Rabu," Zagreb: *Bilten* ŽOŽ 46-47/1996, 6.

_____."Njemački desant na otok Rab-operacija "Illusion", Bilten ŽOŽ, 39-40/1996, 10-11.

Indig-Ithai, Josef. "Children of Villa Emma", Herzer Ivo, ed. *The Italian Refuge: Rescue of Jews During the Holocaust*, Washington: D.C., Catholic University Press, 1989.

_____."Djeca bježe,"Beograd: JA 1963-1964, 1965,) 129-136.

Jakovljević, B. "Putevi stradanja, borbe i spašavanja Jevreja Jugoslavije," 1941–1945, JP 1-2/1982, 27-34.

Janković, Milovoj. *Rat špijuna u Kraljevini Jugoslavije*, Zagreb: 1982.

Jareb, Jare. *Zlato i novac Nezavisne Države Hrvatske izneseni u inozemstvo*, Zagreb: Hrvatski Institut za Povijest, Dom i Svjet, 1997.

Jelić-Butic, Fikreta. *Ustaše i Nesavisna Država Hrvatska, 1941–1945*, Zagreb: sveučilišna naklada Liber-Zagreb, 1977.

Jurak, R. "Uspomene iz logora u Kraljevici," *Bilten*, Zagreb: ŽOŽ 28-29/1993, 13-14.

Jun-Brpda. Ina. "Iz Moje 'Crne Bilježnice' Sjećanja iz partizanskih bolnica na dalmatinskim otocima," Beograd: JA 1965-1967, SJOJ 1967, 189-205.

Kamhi, Haim. "400-TA godišnjica Jevrejske opštine u Sarajevu."(400th anniversary of the Jewish Community in Sarajevo.) *Jevrejski Almanah*, SJOJ,1961-1962, 15-24.

Kaplan, Marion A. *Between Dignity and Despair: Jewish Life in Nazi Germany*, New York: Oxford University Press, 1998.

Kazimirović, V. *NDH u svetlu nemačkih dokumenata i dnevnika Gleza fon Horstenaua 1941-1944*, Beograd: 1987.

Kečkemet, Duško. "Židovski sabirni logori na području pod talijanskom okupacijom," Zagreb: AHA, 1996.

Kišić-Kolanović, Nada. "Hrvatski državni sabor NDH 1942," Zagreb: ÖSP 3/2000, 545-565.

_____. Podržavljenje imovine Židova u NDH, ÖSP 3/1998, 429-453.

Kolanović, Josip. "Holocaust in Croatia: Documentation and Research Perspectives," Zagreb:Arhivski vjesnik, 39/1996.

_____. Elektronska baza podataka zrtava drugog svjetskog rata s područja grada Zagreba (analiza projekta "Dotršćina"), HDA, neobjavljeno, unpublished,12 pages.

Kolar-Dimitrijević, Mira. "Akcija povjesničara dr. Rudolfa Horvata na spašavanju gradečkog Židova Arpada Sterna 1941 godine", *Novi omanut* Zagreb: ŽOZ 25, 997.

_____."The Material Losses of the Jewish Population of Croatia during World War II, *Voice*, # 4, Zagreb, winter 2002/2003, 43-46.

Konforti, Josef. "Doprinos ljekara jevreja zdravstvenoj zaštiti i kulturi Bosne i Herzegovine," Beograd: JA 1965-1967, SJOJ 1967, 105-121.

Kopsa, L. "O organizaciji ustaskog aparata vlasti na provotenju terora u tzv. NDH," in: *Zbronik: Zagrebu NOB –I socijalistickoj revoluciji*, Zagreb, 1971, 223-251.

Kovačić, D. "Zapovjednici i dužnosnici jasenovačke skupine logora 1941–1945 Godine," Zagreb: CSP 1/1999, 97-112.

Kovačić, Ivan. *Kampor 1942-1943 Hrvati, Slovenci i Židovi u Koncentracijskom Logoru Kampor na Rabu*, Rijeka: Printed Adamic, 1998.

Kraus, Ognjen. ed. *Anti-Semitism Holocaust, Anti-Fascism*, Zagreb: ŽOZ, 1997.

Krišto, Jure. *Katolička crkva i Nezavisna Država Hrvatska 1941–1945*,Vol. I, Zagreb: Hrvatski Institut za Povijest, Dom i Svijet, 1998.

_____. Katolička crkva i Židovi u vrijeme NDH, u: AHA, 139-147.

Kritić, Frano. *Dita*, Osijek: Komputerska odrada i tisak, Gradska tiskara Naklada, Primjeraka 21, 1997.

Krizman, Bogdan. *Ante Pavelić i Ustaše*, Zagreb: Globus 1983.

_____.NDH, izmedju Hitlera i Mussolinija, 3. izd., Zagreb 1986.

Krizman-Lengel, Narcisa. A Contribution to the Study of Terror in the So-Called Independent State of Croatia: Concentration Camps for Women in 1941-1942, Yad Vashem Vol. XX, Jerusalem, 1990.

_____. "Destiny of Jewish Survivors from the Rab, concentration camp 1943-1945", *Voice*, Zagreb: ŽOZ, Autumn 1998.

_____. A Contribution to the Study of Terror in the So-Called Independent State of Croatia: Concentration Camps for Women in 1941-1942. Printed from Yad Vashem Studies, Jerusalm: Vol.XX, 1990.

Lah, Ivo. Methods of Calculating the Future Population and Their Application to the Population of Prewar Yugoslavia" Statistilka revlija, Belgrade: I, no. 2, 1951.

Lebel, Jennie. ed., "Jevreji iz Jugoslavije ratni vojni zarobljenici u Nemačkoj", Spomen-album, pola veka od oslobodjenja, 1945-1995, Tel Aviv: 1995.

_____. *Haj Amin and Berlin*, Tel-Aviv: Technosdar Ltd., Davar, 1996.

Levental (Lowenthal), Zdenko. in Zločini *fašističkih okupatora i njihovih pomagača protiv Jevreja u Jugoslaviji*, Belgrade, JIM 1952.

_____. "Sećanje na medicinski rad u Jevrejskoj opštini u Zagrebu," *Bilten*, Zagreb:ŽOŽ 19-20/1991.

Levi Dale, David. "Savez Jevrejskih Opština Jugoslavije", *Spomenica, 1919-1969*, Belgrade: Savez jevrejskih opština jugoslavije, 1971.

Lichten, Joseph L. "Question of Judgment: Pius XII & the Jews," Jewish Virtual Library, A Division of the American Cooperative Enterprise.

Loker, Zvi. ed. Pinkas Hakehillot, *Encyclopedia of Jewish Communities, Yugoslavia*, Jerusalem: Yad Vashem. The Holocaust Martyrs' and Heroes' Rememberance Authority, 1988.

Maček, Andrej and Skrabe, Nino. Maček Izbliza, Zagreb: Disput 1999.

Magašić, M. "Iz logora na otoku Rabu I-II", *Bilten*, Zagreb: ŽOŽ 25/1992, 13; 26/1992, 10-11.

Magdić, Lj. "Prepoznala sam kolegice," Zagreb: Ha-Kol 61-62/1999.

Maričić, Zvonko. *Luka spasa, Židovi u Veloj Luci od 1937-1943*, Vela Luka: Matica Hrvatska, 2002.

Matković, Hrvoje. Povijest Nezavisne Države Hrvatske, Zagreb: Naklada P.I.P, 1994.

Meštrović, Ivan. "Stepinac, the Spiritual Hero," *Hrvatska revija*, (Buenos Aires: 6, no. 3, 1956: 201-6.

Mitrović, R. "The Fate of Jews in Areas Where German Minorities Groups (Volksdeutsche) Took Over the Power in April 1941," *Zbornik 2*, Belgrade: JIM, *Studije i gradja o učešću Jevreja u natodnooslobodilačkom ratu*, 1973, 265.

Morse, Chuck. *The Nazi Connection to Islamic Terrorism, Adolf Hitler and Haj Amin al Husseini*, New York: Universe, Inc., 2003.

Moore Bob. ed., "The Rescue of Jews in German Occupied Western Europe," New York: 2000.

Najfeld, Eta. "Sećanja na Židovsku menzu u Zagrebu", JP 5-6/1979, 29-33.

_____. " Sećanje iz vremena drugog svetskog rata,"JP 1-2/1975.

Nazor, Ante and Ladić, Zoran. *History of the Croatian, Illustrated Chronology*, Zagreb: Multigraf, 2003.

Novak-Steiner, *Zdenka. When Heaven's Vault Cracked*, Braunton: Devon 1995.

O'Brien of Thomond, Anthony Henry, Count. *Archbishop Stepinac: The Man and His Case*, Westminster: Md., 1947.

Paldiel, Mordecai. In his address at "Congregation B'nai Israel of Boca Raton," Boca Raton: FL, November 27, 1998.

Pattee, Richard. *The Case of Cardinal Aloysius Stepinac*, Milwaukee: The Bruce Publishing Company, 1953.

Perera, David. "Neki statistički podaci o Jevrejima u Jugoslaviji uperiodu od 1938 do 1965 Godine," *JA*, Beograd: 1968-1970, 132-147.

Perić, Marko. *Posebno demografsko istraživanje jevrejske zajednice u Jugoslaviji, Stanovništo,* Jerusalem: Institute for Contemporary Jewry, The Hebrew University of Jerusalem, Papers on Jewish Demography 1973.

Perić, Ivo. *A History of the Croats,* Zagreb: *Center of Technology* (ctt), 1998.

Petersen, N.H. *From Hitler's Doorstep: The Wartime Intelligence Reports of Allen Dulles,* 1942-1946, Philadelphia: 1996.

Phayer, Michael. *The Catholic Church and the Holocaust, 1930-1965*, Bloomington: Indiana University Press, 2000.

Poliakov, Léon and Sabille, Jacques. *Jews Under the Italian Occupation*, Paris, Editions Du Centre, 1955. (Published in English).

Polić, Branko. *Vjetrenjasta klepsidra, autobiografski Zapisi, Zagreb*: Durieux, 2004.

_____."Humanitarni doprmos Aleksandra Frelika», *Bilten*, Zagreb, ŽOŽ 14/1990, 8.

_____. "Logor Kraljevica i njegova dječija kuhinja," Bilten ŽOŽ 28-29/1993.
Radej, S. "Hinko Gottlieb", *JA,* Beograd: JIM, 1954, 127-131.

Redžić, Enver. *Bosna iI Hercegovina u drugom svjetskom ratu*, Sarajevo: Sarajevo, Ex Libris, Zlatko Hasanbegović, 1998.

Reitlinger, Gerald. *The Final Solution.* London: Valentine Mitchell, 1953.

Roatta, Mario. *Otto milioni di bainonette.* Milan, 1946.

Romano, Jaša. *Jevreji Jugoslavije 1941–1945, Zrtve genocida i učesnici narodno-oslobodilačkog rata,* Belgrade: JIM, Published by the Federation of Jewish Communities in Yugoslavia, 1980.

_____. "Jevreji u logoru na Rabu i njihovo uključivanje u narodnooslobodilački rat," *Zbornik* JIM 2, Beograd, 1997.

_____. "Jevreji zdravstveni radnici Jugoslavije 1941–1945. Žrtve fasističkog terora i učesnici u NOR," *Zbornik* JIM 2, Beograd 1973, 73-258.

Rotschild, Joseph. *East Central Europe between Two World Wars*, Seattle: University of Washington Press, 1988.

Rosenzweig, Viktor. *Nas Život*, Zagreb: Published by Cultural Society Miroslav Shalom Freiberger and Jewish Community, 2001.

Rubinstein, William D., The *Myth of Rescue: Why the Democracies Could Not Have Saved More Jews from the Nazis,* London: Rutledge, 1999.

Samokovlija. Danko. *Dolar Dnevno*, Sarajevo: Biblioteka Specijalnih izdanja, Džepna Knjiga, 1956.

Schwarz, Gavro. *Povijest zagrebačke židovske općine od osnutka do 50-tih godina 19. vijeka*, Jews and Minorities Rights, Zagreb: Stamparija Gaj, 1939.

Shelah, Menahem. *The Yugoslav Connection-Alyah B, 1938-1948*, Hebrew University, Tel-Aviv, Am Oved Publisher, Israel, 1994.

_____. *Holocaust in Yugoslavia,* Yad Vashem Jerusalem, 1999.

_____. "Kako su Talijani spasavali Židove," *Novi omanut* 24, Zagreb 1997.

_____. "Sudbina jevrejskih izbeglica na otoku Rabu," *Zbornik* JIM 7, Beograd 1997, 190-197.

_____. *Blood Account. Rescue of Croatian Jews by the Italians 1941-1943*, Tel-Aviv: Sifriat Poalim Publishing House Ltd. 1986, (in Hebrew).

_____. *History of the Holocaust in Yugoslavia,* Jerusalem: Yad Vashem, 1990.

Shomrony, Amiel. "Kako su prodani certifikati," Ha-kol 51-52/1997.

_____. Svjedočenja, gdje je Freibergerova biblioteka, Bilten ŽOŽ 30/1993, 10-11.

_____. Prenosimo, Glas koncila, 21 travnja 1996. Razgovor s dr. Amielom Shomronyjem, promicateljem istine of Kardinalu Stepincu, "Kardinal Stepinac je svetac i mučenik," Bilten ŽOŽ 40-45/1996, 19.

Sobolevski, M. "Pakao u kamenoj pustinji. Ustaški koncentracioni Logor Slana na Pagu," Novi list, Rijeka 26.VH-18.K.1985.

_____. Hapšenje 165 židovskih omladinaca u Zagrebu u svibnju 1941 godine, Novi omanut 31, Zagreb 1998, 6-9.

Steinberg, Jonathan. *All or Nothing: the Axis and the Holocaust 1941-1943*, New York: Routledge Taylor and Francis Group, 2002.

Steckel, Charles, W. *Destruction and Survival,* Delmar Publishing Company, Inc. (Los Angeles, CA: 1973.

Steiner, Stjepan. "Sjećanje na Židove liječnike u NOB," Bilten ŽOŽ 11, 12/1989.

Stillman, Norman. *Jews in Arab Lands, History and Source Book*, Philadelphia: The Jewish Publication Society of America, 1979.

Šišić, Fredo. *Dokumenti of postanku Kraljevine Srba, Hrvata i Slovenaca, 1914-1918*, Zagreb: Matica Hrvatska, 1920.

Strčić, P. "Pljačka zlata zagrebačkih Židova u NDH," Ha-Kol 48/1997.

Štambuk-Skalić, M., Kolanvić, J., Razum, S. ed., *Proces Alojziju Stepincu, Dokumenti*, Zagreb: Krščanska Sadašnjost, 1997.

Štefan, Ljubica. "From Fairy Tale to Holocaust: Serbia – Quisling Collaboration with The Occupier during the Third Reich with Reference to Genocide against the Jewish People," Zagreb, 1993.

Švarc, Božo. "Kako sam preživio," Ha-Kol 69-70/2001.

_____. "Put do slobode, Sećanje na bekstvo iz koncentracionih logora," Beograd: JA, 1965-1967, SJOJ, 1967.

Švob, Melita. *Židovi u Hrvatskoj*, Zagreb: Židovskih Opčina, 1997.

Thompson, Mark. *A Paperhouse: The Ending of Yugoslavia*, New York: Pantheon Books, 1992.

Tolentino, Emilio. "Fašistička okupacija Dubrovnika 1941–1945 godine i rješavanje jevrejskog pitanja," Zornik JIM 1, Beograd 1971.

Teveth, Shabtai. *Ben-Gurion and the Palestinian Arabs, From Peace to War,* (New York: Oxford University Press, 1985.

Tomasevich, Jozo. *War and Revolution in Yugoslavia, 1941–1945: Ocupation and Collaboration*, Stanford University Press, California, 2001.

Vajs, Albert. "O antisemintizmu pre i za vreme Nacisma," *JA 1963-1964*, Beograd: SJOJ, 1965.

Von Hassel, Ulrich. Von Andem Deutschsland, trans. Allen W. Dulles, intro. to *Von Hassel Diaries*, New York: Doubleday, 1974.

Wasserstein, Bernard. *Britain and the Jews of Europe, 1939-1945*, Clarmond: Oxford, 1979.

Wyman, David, S. *The Abandonment of the Jews; America and the Holocaust, 1941–1945*, New York: Pantheon Books, 1984.

Zanić-Nardini Jasna. "Sveznici nisu upozorili talijanske židove da im prijeti holokaust, Zagreb" *Vjesnik* (Politika) 20.08.2000.

Zemljar, A. "Relativnost poznavanja koncentracionog logora Slana na Pagu," *Novi Omunut*, Zagreb 1999.

Žerjavić, Vladimir, "Yugoslavia--Manipulations with the Number of Second World War Victims," Zagreb: Croatian Information Center, 1993.

_____. Demographic Indicators of the Jewish Ordeal in the Independent State of Croatia; in Kraus, Ognjen, ed. *Antisemitism, Holocaust, Anti Fascism*, Zagreb: Jewish Community, 1993.

_____. *Population Losses in Yugslavia 1941–1945,* Zagreb: Dom and Svjet, 1997.

Zimmels, H.J. *Ashkenazim and Sephardim,* London: Oxford, University Press, 1958.

Znidaričić, Lav, Alojzije Stepinac. *O stotoj godišnjici rodjenja,* Zagreb: Matica Hrvatska, 1998.

Index